Ethnicity and Equality

*The Shiv Sena Party and
Preferential Policies in Bombay*

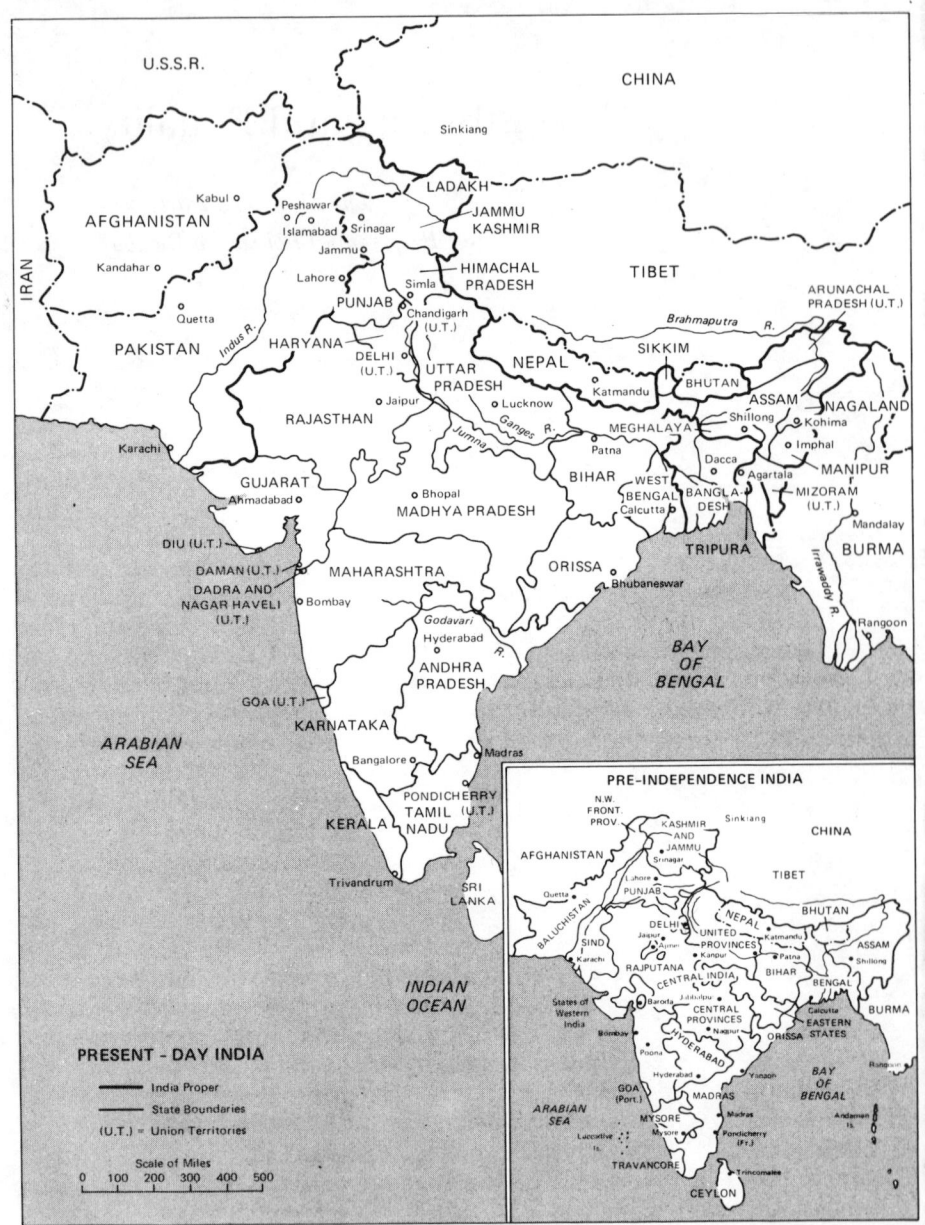

India's political boundaries. (From Richard L. Park and Bruce Bueno de Mesquita, *India's Political System*, 2d ed., © 1979, p. 3. Reprinted by permission of Prentice-Hall, Inc., Englewood Cliffs, N.J.)

Ethnicity and Equality

*The Shiv Sena Party and
Preferential Policies in Bombay*

Mary Fainsod Katzenstein

Cornell University Press
Ithaca and London

THIS BOOK HAS BEEN PUBLISHED WITH THE AID OF A GRANT
FROM THE HULL MEMORIAL PUBLICATION FUND OF CORNELL UNIVERSITY.

Copyright © 1979 by Cornell University

All rights reserved. Except for brief quotations in a review, this book, or parts thereof, must not be reproduced in any form without permission in writing from the publisher. For information address Cornell University Press, 124 Roberts Place, Ithaca, New York 14850.

First published 1979 by Cornell University Press.
Published in the United Kingdom by Cornell University Press Ltd.,
2–4 Brook Street, London W1Y 1AA.

International Standard Book Number 0-8014-1205-6
Library of Congress Catalog Card Number 79-4163
Printed in the United States of America
Librarians: Library of Congress cataloging information appears on the last page of the book.

To Peter

Contents

Preface	11
1. India's New Ethnicity	17
2. Shiv Sena and the Bombay Setting	40
3. Demographic Causes of Nativism	53
4. Economic Origins of Shiv Sena: Middle-Class Job Competition	63
5. Shiv Sena's Working-Class Support	82
6. The Recruitment of Party Activists	97
7. Shiv Sena's Front Ranks: Political Stability and Interethnic Relations	116
8. Preferential Policies and Their Impact: The Bombay Case	141
9. Preferential Policies and Judicial Response: The National View	160
10. Modernization and Meritocracy	191

APPENDIXES

I. Indexes of Class Background, Voter Survey, 1971	215
II. Designation of Criteria for Sample Design	216
III. Purposive Sampling Scheme, Voter Survey, 1971	217
IV. Ethnic Character and Shiv Sena Strength in Surveyed Neighborhoods	218
V. Questionnaire, Voter Survey, 1971	219
VI. Constitution of India, Articles 14–16, 19 (as Amended up to November 1, 1969)	220
VII. Summary of Replies Received from State Governments regarding Admission of Students from Other States	222
VIII. Implementation of National Integration Committee Recommendations	224
IX. Education and Employment in Bombay	227
Index	231

Tables

1. Outcome of 1961 and 1968 municipal elections   35
2. Outcome of 1973 municipal elections   36
3. Population of Bombay by mother tongue, 1881   43
4. Literate percentage of Bombay's population, 1872–1961   48
5. Distribution of major language groups in Bombay   56
6. Proportion of "locals" to "outsiders" in India's nativist localities   59
7. Levels of outmigration from Indian states, 1961   59
8. Bombay families by income and mother tongue   66
9. Percentage of Maharashtrians employed in selected Bombay industries by salary level, 1970   68
10. Relationship between class factors and party vote   70
11. Age and party vote among middle-class Maharashtrians   73
12. Educational mobility and party vote among middle-class Maharashtrians   73
13. Interethnic relations, governmental authority, and party vote among middle-class Maharashtrians   74
14. Relationship between class character of neighborhood and party vote   86
15. Interethnic relations, governmental authority, and party vote among working-class Maharashtrians   91
16. Maharashtrian estimates of Bombay's South Indian population and the ethnic composition of neighborhoods   93
17. Maharashtrian estimates of South Indian population and party preference   93
18. Age and party vote among working-class Maharashtrians   94

19. Migration history and party vote among working-class Maharashtrians — 94
20. Educational background of Shiv Sena party workers — 99
21. Educational background of Bombay municipal councilors — 120
22. Travel experience of Bombay municipal councilors — 123
23. Mother tongue of Bombay municipal councilors, 1961 and 1968 — 124
24. Marathi component of political parties in Bombay Municipal Corporation — 124
25. Background profile of Maharashtrian councilors in Bombay Municipal Corporation — 125
26. Attitudes toward the use of force among Bombay municipal councilors — 130
27. Attitudes of Congress and Sena voters toward South Indians — 135
28. Recruitment of managers in twenty-five Bombay companies — 152
29. Maharashtrians in higher-level positions in Bombay establishments — 153
A1. Organized sector employment, Greater Bombay — 227
A2. Applicants on the live register of employment exchanges — 228
A3. Educational enrollment in Greater Bombay in Marathi-medium schools — 228

Figures

1. Shiv Sena party structure — 98
A1. Employment growth in Bombay's organized sector — 229

Preface

If the concept of modernization embodies any single idea, it is the idea of mobility. Modernity implies movement—the shifting of residences and the reordering of societal hierarchies. With modernization comes an upheaval of both status and domicile.

In the West it has long been believed that the "rules" governing such mobility are individualistic. The choice to change residences, to seek work outside the region of one's birth, is thought to be a personal one. Similarly, opportunities for occupational advancement are presumed to result from one's diligence and merit. It is indeed widely believed that Europe's Industrial Revolution was founded upon a shift in societal norms from ascription and corporatism to meritocracy and individualism.

In modern society, rules of individualism have been both heeded and ignored. While some have sought advancement, like Horatio Alger's heroes, through the application of discipline and talent, others have elected a different route. It is striking that in the United States, patronage, machine politics, and even family networks operating illegal economic dynasties have been vehicles for the mobility of some members of ethnic groups. Such digressions from the rules of meritocracy and individualism are not limited to the erstwhile disadvantaged. Established elites in the United States have at times endeavored to preserve their dominance by constructing racial, sexual, and ethnic barriers to avenues for advancement. But whatever have been the actual routes to success, individualism and merit have long been considered the norms of Western society.

Increasingly, however, both in the West and in the developing states, these norms have come under attack. Minorities in the United States and majorities in many developing countries seek the protection of group interests rather than the assurance of individual opportunities. Group interests, by this view, are to be secured through the establishment of policies that give preference in university admissions, jobs, housing, government loans, land, and so forth on the basis less of individual qualification than of ethnic or racial status.

This book is about one such challenge to the meritocratic rules of modernity. The setting for this study is Bombay, one of the most modern cities of South Asia. There, in 1966, a local political party with the name of Shiv Sena rose to citywide power by mobilizing opposition to "outsiders" who had gained a predominant share of the desirable jobs in the modern sector of the city's economy. Claiming to represent the interests of "native" Maharashtrians, Shiv Sena demanded that job recruitment in the public and private sectors favor native over outsider.

This study explores the relationship between ethnicity and equality in Bombay. It attempts to identify the forces that gave rise to the demand for preferential policies, to account for the governmental response to such demands, and to analyze the consequences of the preferential policies pursued.

Shiv Sena's name evokes strong feelings in India. Some view Shiv Sena from a classically liberal perspective, arguing that the party's demands impair meritocratic recruitment and thus weaken the cornerstone on which a modern society must be built. Others, most prominently Marxists, argue that Shiv Sena's demands pose no threat either to meritocracy or to the other modern values that a capitalist society espouses. Rather, they argue, demands for preferential treatment help the already privileged middle class, coopt the discontented, and protect the status quo. Many others, Maharashtrians and non-Maharashtrians alike, believe that special reservations in jobs or university admissions may be desirable but question policies of ethnic or caste preferences that fail to distinguish between the economically advantaged and the poor. Even those who feel there is legitimacy in Shiv Sena's claims, however, decry the violence and xenophobia for which Shiv Sena is known.

This book neither condemns nor justifies Shiv Sena's claims, nor does it offer a normative assessment of the more general issue of preferential treatment. Its argument is more limited:

Whatever the merits of the case, preferential policies are here, it seems, to stay. The forces that generate such demands are not remnants of traditional society but are powerful components of the present drive for equality. Meritocracy is not the only basis by which mobility can or will be achieved. To believe otherwise would be to ignore the evidence that Shiv Sena and other vociferous claimants to preferential treatment lay before us.

In writing this book I have become indebted to numerous institutions and individuals. The Ford Foreign Area Fellowship Program provided financial support for a year of research in Bombay (1970–1971). During my stay I was affiliated with the International Institute for Population Studies. Later, a Ford-Rockefeller grant to the Center for International Studies at M.I.T. for a project on migration directed by Myron Weiner enabled me to spend an additional month in India in 1974.

This study includes small portions of material previously published in the following journals: "Origins of Nativism," *Asian Survey*, 13:4 (April 1973); "Politics of Population Movements," *Economic and Political Weekly*, 10:51 (December 20, 1975); and "Mobilization of Indian Youth in the Shiv Sena," *Pacific Affairs*, 50:2 (Summer 1977); and a larger portion of "Preferential Treatment and Ethnic Conflict in Bombay," *Public Policy*, 25:3 (Summer 1977), copyright © 1977 by the President and Fellows of Harvard College, reprinted by permission of John Wiley and Sons, Inc. I am grateful to the publishers of these journals for permission to use this material.

My reliance on the language and research skills of several assistants in Bombay and in Ithaca cannot be adequately attested to in the study's footnotes. Mrs. S. R. Sawe, Mrs. Neelam Kanodia, Mrs. T. C. Daswani, and Diane Sousa were helpful at various stages of research. Rhonda Wasserman provided invaluable research and editorial assistance. Ritu Anand, who interviewed businessmen, Pratibha Joshi, who translated *Marmik*, and, in particular, Vijay Vaidya, who accompanied me during limitless hours of interviewing in Bombay, deserve my gratitude. The same is due Michael Busch and Mayerlene Frow, who typed many versions of the manuscript, Jane Dieckmann, who prepared the index, Miriam Hurewitz, who edited the manuscript, Dan Snodderly, of Cornell University Press, and Ved Kayastha, South Asian librarian at Cornell.

The family of the late Dr. Vasant Ranadive generously shared with me their home in Bombay. After my husband and I moved to Ithaca, Yen Troung and the Bui family took over our household and adopted our two young children as their own. Without their kindness, there would have been no book.

This book had the help of family as well as friends. Johnny Fainsod improved an earlier version of the manuscript with her practiced editorial pen. My father-in-law, Gerhard Katzenstein, responded to the manuscript with manuscript-length comments. Although my debt must now be recorded to his memory, it is no less profound.

A number of other colleagues were generous with their time and ideas: Frank F. Conlon, Wayne A. Cornelius, John O. Field, Pauline Kolenda, David Laitin, and Lucian W. Pye commented on early versions of the manuscript. Several colleagues at Cornell, Milton J. Esman, T. J. Pempel, Myron Rush, Martin Shefter, and Sidney G. Tarrow, made useful suggestions. Bertram F. Willcox read Chapter 9 with a lawyer's eye for detail and with his own unique patience and good humor. Richard L. Park's suggestions sent me back to the drawing board and led to a much improved manuscript. I owe him a special thanks. Kartikeya Sarabhai, with whom I jointly conducted a survey of Bombay voters, was a wonderful colleague who constantly saw the lighter side of even the most difficult situations. I am particularly indebted to Myron Weiner for his encouragement, his consistently positive outlook, and the intellectual direction he provided.

Above all, to Peter, my thanks.

The topic of preferential treatment, irrespective of its national setting, is one that evokes strong reactions. A number of the persons and institutions mentioned above do not share the book's conclusions. For those, I alone am responsible.

M.F.K.

Ithaca, New York

Ethnicity and Equality

*The Shiv Sena Party and
Preferential Policies in Bombay*

1 | India's New Ethnicity

In a crowded party office in the Girgaum section of Bombay, a number of boys are seated on benches talking animatedly in Marathi. Above them is a garlanded picture of the seventeenth-century warrior-hero Shivaji. Campaign posters with the familiar swords-and-shield emblem line the wall. The party's name, Shiv Sena ("Army of Shivaji"), is printed in bold orange letters on the posters. A saffron flag on a long stick juts out above the portrait of Shivaji. Two boys walk into the office. There are cheerful shouts from across the room. The boys go and join the others on the benches and clasp hands. Attentions turn back to the matter under discussion, the election campaigns of the upcoming week.

In a modern Bombay business establishment, two municipal councilors, about forty years old, and two younger men are escorted toward an elevator. The two councilors are dressed in white *khadi* (hand-spun, rough-woven cloth). The two younger men wear Western-style pants and shirts. One of the younger men appears uneasy. His mustache adds some years to his otherwise boyish face. The shirt he wears, made from a shiny, synthetic material, hangs loosely over his slight body frame. As the elevator stops at the fourth floor, the four are led into an air-conditioned foyer, seated, and asked to wait. A few minutes later an office door opens and a peon (office servant) motions them in. An older man in suit and tie sits behind the desk in the spacious room. The greetings exchanged are courteous but not warm. Tea is brought. "Gentlemen," the executive begins in English, "I do not understand the purpose of your visit. We have so many Maharashtrians here. Whenever there is a vacancy, you can be assured, we look first for a local man. Just last month we

17

had an opening in our sales department. We tried to find a Maharashtrian. Unfortunately, no qualified person came forward."

In a New York conference attended by leading executives of several multinational corporations, the seminar discussion turns to employment problems. One American businessman recounts the dilemma he faced in recruiting local employees in his company's Bombay subsidiary. "We were told repeatedly we had to hire Maharashtrians," he says. "Who are Maharashtrians?" the man seated to his right asks.

So run three fragments of a story that takes place in Bombay. But these are also pieces of a larger subject, the development in India of a new form of ethnic politics. This new ethnicity, exemplified in Bombay by the political party Shiv Sena, has as its objective ethnic equality. It is a quest that expresses itself as a demand for preferential treatment. Known in India by the phrase "sons-of-the-soil," these newly organized groups have sought preferences for "local" persons as against "outsiders" in jobs, housing and college admissions. Why such a movement as Shiv Sena arose and what consequences it has had are the questions this book will address.

The Shiv Sena party was formed in 1966 to safeguard the interests of Maharashtrians, the Marathi-speaking inhabitants of Maharashtra, a western Indian state on the Arabian Sea, of which Bombay is the capital. Maharashtrians, the Sena claimed, were being robbed of opportunities for economic advancement by outsiders said to be flooding into Bombay from elsewhere in India. Bombay was part of Maharashtra, but Maharashtra, the Sena protested, was not part of Bombay. "Maharashtra for Maharashtrians," the Sena rallying cry proclaimed. The solution, Shiv Sena asserted, was to reserve for Maharashtrians "80 percent of the jobs, skilled or otherwise, in governmental, semigovernmental, private, and public undertakings."[1]

The story of Shiv Sena is only in part about Bombay and

---

1. Kapilacharya (pseudonym), *Shiv Sena Speaks: Official Statement* (Bombay: Bal K. Thackeray, editor, Marmik Cartoon Weekly Office, 1967), p. 47.

Maharashtra. It is also, more generally, about the demand for preferential treatment which has reverberated in recent years within and outside India, in developing and industrialized nations alike. Claims to preferential treatment such as that advanced by Shiv Sena reflect two crucial developments: the evolution in the last decades of a new form of ethnicity and the germination of a new view of equality. In the forefront of the "old" form of ethnicity has been the demand for regional autonomy. The subnationalist movements of Austria-Hungary and the Ottoman Empire in the nineteenth century, Scottish and Basque nationalism of contemporary Europe, and the linguistic states movement in India in the 1950s have been associated above all with territorial aspirations. The "new" ethnicity has as its objective not territory but quotas. Minority demands in the United States, Malay claims to jobs and political representation, Sinhalese claims in Sri Lanka, and scheduled caste politics in India have revolved not around territorial demands but around preferential treatment.

The distinction between "old" and "new" forms of ethnicity is not one of motivation. Both "instrumental" economic motivations and "primordial" ties of *Blut und Boden* ("blood and soil") have to varying degrees played a role in all ethnic movements. Nor is the distinction entirely chronological. As the already cited examples of Scottish and Basque nationalism indicate, the "old" ethnicity is found very much in the present. The "new" ethnicity, however, is almost entirely modern.[2] Its emergence ensues directly from the development of the modern welfare state.[3] As the state has taken over an increasingly prominent role in the mobilization and allocation of goods and services, it is not sur-

2. The demand for preferential treatment was on occasion voiced in the nineteenth century by such nativist groups as the American Party. At their opening convention in 1886, they demanded the use of government patronage for the assistance of native Americans. John Higham, "The American Party: 1886–1891," *Pacific Historical Review*, 19 (February 1950), 39–40.

3. A similar argument is made by Nathan Glazer and Daniel P. Moynihan, eds., *Ethnicity: Theory and Experience* (Cambridge: Harvard University Press, 1975), p. 8. They discuss the welfare state in the context of the rise of interest-based ethnicity, which they see succeeding earlier conflicts revolving around cultural, linguistic, and religious differences.

prising that the political strategy of ethnic groups accommodates itself to this change. Although ethnic groups may still see it to their advantage to seek economic advancement indirectly through demands for regional autonomy, the option of seeking direct guarantees in the form of a certain percentage of jobs, university places, etc., becomes increasingly compelling.

A new view of equality has emerged parallel to this new form of ethnicity. Nineteenth-century liberalism envisioned a society in which equality was to mean equal opportunity. The liberal view assumed that with the removal of discriminatory legal barriers, success would depend merely on talent and hard work. Over the last decades, this view has come under increasing attack. Critics of liberalism have argued that legal guarantees of equal opportunity are ineffective in the presence of rigid economic and social stratification. As long as structural imparities obtain, meritocratic principles in recruitment and university admissions merely aggravate existing inequalities. A truly egalitarian society, this view suggests, can be realized only through differential access to resources, through policies of preferential treatment. This view of equality embracing preferential treatment is not, its advocates maintain, an Orwellian sleight of hand. A distinction is to be made between preferential treatment of a group long subordinated and preferential policies intended to safeguard the position of an already dominant stratum. This "new" equality and ethnicity converge in the story of Shiv Sena.

The Old Ethnicity in India: Challenge to Nationhood

In India the waning of the older form of ethnic politics is mirrored in the changing themes that have dominated Indian politics. In the 1950s and early 1960s, warnings of India's potential disintegration were repeatedly sounded. With Partition a recent memory, with linguistic reorganization and language disturbances the dominant events of the 1950s and 1960s respectively, India's ethnic diversity appeared a profound threat to its national unity. Selig Harrison, writing in 1960, cautioned against the potential hazards posed by India's regional elites and caste lobbies: "The prospect that anarchy, fascism, and totalitarian small nationalities will each torture this body politic in the decades ahead is a measure . . . of the challenge built into Indian nationalism."⁴ Throughout the decade of the 1960s, other mostly journalistic reports continued to echo warnings against the "centrifugal" and "fissiparous" pressures militating against a unified India.

By the end of the decade, a number of studies had appeared which stressed the success of India's integrative efforts. The emergence of subnational organizations, it was argued, was not necessarily inconsistent with the establishment of a strong, integrated nation-state. In their study of caste associations, the Rudolphs proposed that "by providing a structure for the pursuit of political power, social status, and economic interest, the paracommunity based on caste sentiment and interest makes secular concerns and representative democracy comprehensible and manageable to ordinary Indians."⁵ Following a similar theme, Jyotirinda Das Gupta's study of language associations denied that the organization of subnational sentiment boded ill for political stability. Das Gupta concluded: "Both in respect of building the national community and furthering the representative institutions, language politics in general and language associations in particular have provided crucial support. . . . The more important point is that language politics has proved to be one of the most important political channels for pursuing political integration as well as political development."⁶

4. Selig Harrison, *India: The Most Dangerous Decades* (Princeton: Princeton University Press, 1960), p. 4. Ainslie Embree points out that although for many Indian intellectuals the Harrison book was a prophecy of national disintegration, "for most Western readers [at the time], the book was a cautiously optimistic statement, given the background of Indian politics against which it was written." Ainslie Embree, "Pluralism and National Integration: The Indian Experience," *Journal of International Affairs*, 27:1 (1973), 43.
5. Lloyd and Susanne Rudolph, *The Modernity of Tradition: Political Development in India* (Princeton: Princeton University Press, 1967), p. 36.
6. Jyotirindra Das Gupta, *Language Conflict and National Development: Group Politics and National Language Policy in India* (Berkeley: University of California Press, 1970), p. 270. Similar arguments are made by Iqbal Narain in "Cultural Pluralism, National Integration, and Democracy in India," *Asian Survey*, 16 (October 1976), 903–17; and by Marguerite Ross Barnett in *The Politics of Cultural Nationalism in South India* (Princeton: Princeton University Press, 1976). This debate on Indian politics parallels a dialogue in studies of ethnicity and nation-building. One school pictures the development of nationhood and the

National Integration and the Politics of Compromise

The shift away from the admonitions of the early 1960s accords with the actual waning of linguistic conflict in India. The 1953 fast to death of Potti Sriramulu in Andhra, the early and strident Tamil demands for an independent state, and the successive language demonstrations and riots did appear two decades earlier to raise the specter of a fragmented Indian nation. But the threat of secession movements which loomed large in the 1950s and early 1960s has clearly receded. Linguistic riots have diminished in number and intensity. Since the DMK [7] separatist demand, subsequently abandoned, there has been virtually no threat to India's territorial integrity. There are large numbers of minority linguistic communities contained within states dominated by other linguistic groups which have pressured, and will probably continue to pressure, for greater autonomy for their region or even for the redrawing of state boundaries. But the issue of India's nationhood, of national integrity, is now muted.

How has this once troubling issue been dissipated? The an-

---

presumed waning of ethnic identities as a linear movement. Clifford Geertz, in "The Integrative Revolution," in C. E. Welch, ed., *Political Modernization* (Belmont, Calif.: Wadsworth, 1971), pp. 199-200) writes: "It is the crystallization of primordial and civil sentiments that gives to the problems variously called tribalism, parochialism, communalism . . . a more ominous and deeply threatening quality than most of the other also very serious and intractable problems the new states face." In modern states, Geertz suggests, while ethnocentrism cannot be destroyed, it must be modernized; primordial attachments cannot be wished out of existence but can be "domesticated." A different perspective is offered by studies seeing the relationship between ethnic feeling and national identity as less inherently conflictual. The formation of ethnic associations may hinder, but also help to strengthen the institutions of the nation-state. Caste and tribal association may inculcate the necessary political skills and the needed channels of expression upon which stable political institutions depend. See, for instance, Joseph R. Gusfield, "Misplaced Polarities in the Study of Social Change," in Welch, ed., *Political Modernization*, pp. 47-63, and Immanuel Wallerstein, "Ethnicity and National Integration in West Africa," in Harry Eckstein and David Apter, eds., *Comparative Politics: A Reader* (New York: Free Press, 1963), pp. 665-70.

7. Initials of Dravida Munnetra Kazhagam, a Madras-based regional party that has controlled the state of Tamil Nadu for most of the period since 1967.

swer lies in the politics of compromise. Compromise explains both India's success in building an overarching national polity as well as its difficulties in other areas, particularly in surmounting the obstacles to economic growth.

The theme of compromise, of the incorporation of diversity, permeates Indian society and politics. Gandhi, for instance, was fond of remarking that his spiritual strength derived from a religious faith that had absorbed the best from diverse traditions: "My Hinduism is not sectarian. It includes all that I know to be best in Islam, Christianity, Buddhism, Zoroastrianism. . . ."[8] The caste system, it is said, enveloped diverse elements to the point of embracing bandit groups as special groups called *"thuggee."*[9]

Indian politics has been marked by much of the same syncretism and compromise. These are apparent both in language policy, where it has "worked," as well as in economic policy, where it has not. Economic policy in India prior to the June 1975 Emergency, Myron Weiner has remarked, was conditioned by the fusion of a right-of-center political structure and a left-of-center ideology.[10] On the one hand, antimonopoly acts,[11] licenses, and permits constrained business to the extent that a new or growing enterprise encountered severe difficulties maximizing efficiency of production. On the other hand, major redistributive reforms —land reform, for instance—faltered for lack of a political structure prepared or able to undertake their implementation.

But while the politics of compromise has diluted the potential for economic change, it has afforded an extremely effective vehicle for arriving at the goals of national integration. The first compromise policy in the history of linguistic conflict was

8. William Theodore deBary, ed., *Sources of Indian Tradition*, II (New York: Columbia University Press, 1958), p. 272.
9. See Barrington Moore, *Social Origins of Democracy and Dictatorship: Lord and Peasant in the Making of the Modern World* (Boston: Beacon Press, 1966), p. 339.
10. Myron Weiner, "India's New Political Institutions," *Asian Survey*, 16 (September 1976), 901.
11. The antimonopoly act prevents a firm from holding more than a given share of the market for a particular product, irrespective of the size of the market. This inhibits the development of new products since a firm entering a new market area will have a large share of the market and be disallowed from expanding to take advantage of necessary economies of scale.

adopted over the states reorganization in the mid-1950s. In a move that some at the time termed capitulation, the Nehru government reacted to the disturbances in the Andhra region by creating separate Tamil and Telugu states out of the old state of Madras and by later redrawing many state boundaries to accord with linguistic lines. Rather than immersing India in crisis as some predicted it would, this policy decision opened the way to the incorporation of a new level of elites and the buttressing of a stable polity. The reorganization of states meant that knowledge of English, the link language common to political debate and discourse in the old multilingual states, was no longer as necessary as before. With the redrawing of boundaries, those proficient in the regional languages rather than in English assumed an advantage. The urban, foreign-educated lawyers who earlier dominated parliament were replaced in large numbers by *khadi*-wearing rural landowners, whose mother tongue was that of the region. Through this means, those who had enjoyed power in the rural areas but lacked representation were brought into the state and national governments and given experience, a voice, and a stake in the political affairs of the nation.

The reorganization of states was followed in the 1960s by further compromises with respect to the language of education and governmental affairs. The tension between the Dravidian South (more proficient in English) and the Hindi-speaking North intensified through the 1950s and early 1960s, in part because of the constitutional provision which set 1965 as the date by which Hindi was to replace English as the official language. In response to riots and demonstrations, primarily in South India, this deadline was extended.[12] A short time later, another compromise measure, known as the Three Language Formula, was issued. Designed to assuage both the pro-Hindi and pro-English factions, it called for educational instruction to be carried out in the regional language. In addition, children were to be taught English and a second Indian language in South India and English and a second Indian language in North India. Other directives

---

12. See comprehensive discussion in Das Gupta, *Language Conflict*, chs. 6 and 8.

prescribed that government communiqués, if issued in the regional language, were to be accompanied by a Hindi translation. Examinations for the prestigious civil service were to be offered in any of the regional languages, Hindi, or English. In sum, language policy was directed at assuaging linguistic antagonism; largely because of its compromise nature, it succeeded.

The New Ethnicity: Sons-of-the-Soil and the Demand for Equality

Although the likelihood of secession from or fragmentation of the Indian nation has receded, a new form of ethnic politics has emerged which presents a different type of challenge to the Indian government. This new form of ethnicity is embodied in the "sons-of-the-soil" movements, as they are termed in India. These movements are distinguished from other varieties of ethnic organizations by their objectives. The sons-of-the-soil movements are not secessionist. Nor are they, for the most part, regional movements seeking greater autonomy for the area in which their ethnic constituency predominates.[13] Rather, they are movements whose principal aim is social and economic equality for their ethnic group, an equality which is to be gained by seeking preferences or quotas in jobs and educational institutions.

Sons-of-the-soil sentiment is pervasive. It can be found, for instance, in the tiny North Indian town of Khajuraho, where a successful small eating establishment has changed its conspicuously South Indian name to one ethnically nondescript. Where this sentiment has become politicized, it has taken the form largely of organized pressuring for jobs. In Gauhati, Assam, where the largest number of jobs lies in the central government public sector, the "native" Assamese have sought preferential treatment over the economically more advantaged Bengali. In Bangalore, the Kannada Chaluvalagars ("agitators") have contested municipal elections on a platform protesting the alleged Tamil and Telugu usurpation of public sector jobs. In Telengana, conflict has fulminated between "natives" of the Telengana region and people from the eastern districts of the state over

---

13. The leading exception is the nativist movement in Telengana, which sought greater regional autonomy and at one point a separate state.

jobs in the state and local administrative services. In Chota Nagpur, the local tribal population has endeavored to secure jobs in the central government undertakings and in secondary school teaching posts. In Bombay, the focus of this study, sons-of-the-soil sentiment has found expression in a political party, the Shiv Sena, formed in 1966 to safeguard local Maharashtrian interests. The Shiv Sena has sought preferences largely in middle-class clerical jobs and in upper-class administrative posts which, the Sena has charged, are monopolized by South Indians.

Nativist or sons-of-the-soil organizations appear to be distinguishable from the broader category of ethnic movements by the seemingly antimigrant component of their protestations. The sons-of-the-soil organizations make frequent use of terms such as "outsiders" and often encase their demand for preferences in reference to the protection due "local people."

But this language is more rhetoric than reality. When the leaders of Shiv Sena demand jobs for local persons, they have in mind more "race" than residence. A Maharashtrian, for Shiv Sena, is one who is born a Maharashtrian, who by mother tongue is raised a Maharashtrian. A South Indian who has lived in Maharashtra (as the Bombay expression has it) "for generations" and who may speak fluent Marathi is not in the Sena's understanding Maharashtrian. On occasion, Shiv Sena has avowed that a Maharashtrian is anyone who has lived in the state for a given period of years or (more lyrically) anyone who "shares the joys and sorrows" of Maharashtrians. But many of the speeches of Sena leaders, and more importantly their actions, indicate that such professions are only casual declarations.[14] Because the terms "local" and "outsider" refer, at least in the Bombay case, to linguistic descent rather than to residence, no distinction between nativism and ethnicity can profitably be made. In this

---

14. The Shiv Sena official publication explicitly denies that the party considers a Maharashtrian to be a "Marathi-speaking Maratha" (*Shiv Sena Speaks*, p. 7), but see the report of Sena speeches in the *Times of India* (Bombay), July 31, 1973, and the Sena's Glaxo encounter, cited in Chapter 8, note 4. The only non-Maharashtrian high in the ranks of Shiv Sena leadership was Arun Mehta, formerly the head of the Sena's trade union branch and a Gujarati by lineage. (*Note*: All references to the *Times of India* in this book are to the Bombay edition).

book, nativism, ethnicity, and sons-of-the-soil will be employed interchangeably.

The nativist demand for preferences has touched off a debate over the nature of equality and how it should be achieved. The "liberal" position against preferences argued by probably a minority in Indian political circles is twofold. First, the argument is made—particularly in business circles—that a system of preferences for local persons undermines the principle of meritocracy (in hiring), valued either for its own sake or as a requisite of economic efficiency. Second, some charge that a system of preferences is unworkable and undesirable because there is neither a practical nor a just way of determining which of the many groups in India's plural society should be eligible for special benefits. Proponents of this argument point to, as they term it, the "excesses" of efforts to institute quotas for low-caste groups, citing such situations as Karnataka state, where many non-Brahmin castes came to be defined as backward and where reservations in medical and engineering colleges reached three-quarters of all seats.[15]

The argument in favor of preferences or quotas is made by many state and central government leaders as well as by "sons-of-the-soil." Although the reasoning varies, the arguments offered are also basically twofold. First, some contend, there has never been a real system of meritocratic recruitment.[16] Employment, nativists particularly charge, is decided even now on the basis of influence wielded through ties of kinship, caste, or ethnic group. Secondly, some claim, equal opportunity in employment is not possible in the light of the different levels of educa-

---

15. Figures, although not the argument, from Marc Galanter, ed., "Legal Materials for the Study of Modern India" (Chicago, 1965, mimeograph), pt. III, pp. 30–40, as cited in Glynn Wood, "Planning and Public Demand in Indian Higher Education," *Minerva*, 10 (January 1972), 88.

16. Daniel Bell reviews a similar argument which suggests that equality of opportunity could *never* exist: "The principle of equality of opportunity, even if fully realized on the basis of talent, simply re-created inequality anew in each generation.... This is the argument employed in New York City, for example, where it is charged that in the school system Jews 'used' the merit system to dispossess the Catholics...." See Daniel Bell, "On Meritocracy and Equality," in *Public Interest*, 29 (Fall 1972), p. 43.

tion and other disabilities or advantages which attend different ethnic groups by the time their youth enters the job market. As one Maharashtrian government leader expressed this idea:

> If you have two plants, one with hardy roots and broad leaves and the other with only weak roots and small leaves, they can not drink the water, the soil nutrients, or absorb the sun's energy with the same efficiency. The weak plant needs more attention so that it can catch up and one day produce beautiful fruit.

Policies of preferential treatment are not new to the subcontinent. The system of reservations originated in colonial times. In fact, India's experience with quotas or preferences as a tool to eliminate group disparity (caste, religious, as well as ethnic) is perhaps longer than that of any country in the world.

As early as the nineteenth century special benefits were extended to lower-caste groups in several of the states, Madras, Travancore, and Baroda among others. In Travancore, the maharajah maintained a list of depressed classes which was used for educational land grants and nominations to the legislative council. Lower-caste groups were also later included in the system of political preferences by the Montagu-Chelmsford reforms of 1919.[17]

The first *widely* recognized system of preferences, however, was instituted with the Morley-Minto reforms of 1909. These reforms created separate electorates for the Muslim community in India in order to assure Muslims adequate political representation. As the British devolved power further, other communities came to make similar claims for political preferences.[18]

A system of regional preferences in employment was practiced in other areas as well. Several of the state administrative services, prior to Independence, extended preferences to those who were locally "domiciled." In Bihar, Das Gupta notes, the sons-of-the-soil supporters became particularly strident over the issue of Bengali employment in the Bihar state services. "What

17. See short account of development of protective discrimination in Lelah Dushkin, "Scheduled Caste Politics," in J. Michael Mahar, ed., *The Untouchables in Contemporary India* (Tucson: University of Arizona Press, 1972), pp. 170–75.
18. Ibid.

was proposed in Bihar in an open declaration," Das Gupta comments, "was pretty close to what was only suggested whether loudly or in organized whispers in almost all regions of India."[19]

India's constitution gives legitimacy to the concept of special preferences, requiring for scheduled castes and tribes the reservation of legislative seats (Article 330) and permitting for scheduled castes, tribes, and other "backward classes" the special reservation of government jobs (Article 16 (4)) or any further special provisions for their advancement (Article 15 (4)). Under the "right to equality," the constitution also stipulates that the state may make special provision for women and children (Article 15 (3)). In addition, reservations (now terminated) were extended to Anglo-Indians in the legislature and in the railways, customs, and postal services (Articles 333, 336). The only constitutional clause that approximates a comparable provision for sons-of-the-soil is Article 16 (3), which reads:

Nothing in this article [providing for equality of opportunity] shall prevent Parliament from making any law prescribing, in regard to a class or classes of employment or appointment to an office under the Government of, or any local or other authority within, a State or Union territory, any requirement as to residence within that State....[20]

Other articles expressly prohibit discrimination based on place of birth, and bar any law that would obstruct freedom of movement to citizens of India.

It is thus far from clear whether there are firm constitutional grounds for sons-of-the-soil claims. If nativist movements were merely transient phenomena, this issue would be one of little consequence. But if sons-of-the-soil movements should prove to be an enduring feature of Indian politics, the legitimacy of their claims and the range of possible governmental responses will need to be carefully weighed.

19. Jyotirindra Das Gupta, "Ethnicity in India," in Glazer and Moynihan, eds., *Ethnicity: Theory and Experience*, p. 474. See also Myron Weiner, "Changing Conceptions of Citizenship in a Multi-Ethnic Society: Migration, Protected Labor Markets, Law, and Citizenship in India," Migration and Development Study Group Working Paper MDG/75-4C/75-6, pp. 18–20.
20. *The Constitution of India* (as modified up to April 1, 1958) (Delhi: Government of India Press, 1958), p. 10.

The Bombay Experience

Bombay has been the setting for one of the most powerfully organized and electorally successful of the nativist movements in India. In Bangalore, the nativist political party made few inroads into municipal politics, capturing only a few of the seats on the city corporation. In Assam, the nativist element was incorporated into, but did not dominate, any single political party. Perhaps only in the Telengana Praja Samiti did nativist demands find a vehicle comparable in organization and purposiveness to the Shiv Sena.

The value of studying the Bombay case at close range lies in the interesting cross-pressures that have attended the determination of government policy. On the one hand, there is strong pressure from nativist forces organized within the tightly structured nativist political party, the Shiv Sena. This pressure is intensified by the ethnic bond which links the Maharashtrians of Shiv Sena to the Maharashtrians who dominate the state government. On the other hand, the object of their demands, middle-class jobs, lies to a large extent within the powerful private sector, dominated by non-Maharashtrians hitherto relatively immune from intervention by government in employment decisions. In many regions of India where public-sector employment forms a substantial portion of the total job market, this issue is not of much importance. In Bangalore, in Assam, in Telengana, and in Chota Nagpur, the jobs to which the sons-of-the-soil aspire are predominantly in the public sector. In Bombay, however, the case is quite different. Bombay, with its huge and growing industrial economy, boasts a very large private sector. The realization of nativist aspirations in this city depends to a large extent on the government's interest in and willingness to intervene in the hiring practices of private business. The government's policy choices in this situation afford rich material for a study of the political quest for ethnic equality.

In what sort of setting does nativism set roots? One bus ride through Bombay is all that is needed to sense the city's rich blend of ethnic cultures and the range of class circumstances. At the southern tip of Bombay, modern housing developments with names like "Oyster Apartments" loom above the vast expanse of sea beyond. Maharashtrian women, wearing nine-yard sarees drawn through their legs and wrapped tightly around their bodies, sometimes sit at the base of the apartment buildings with baskets of fish. The bus starts off through surprisingly open land, a green expanse of garden well tended, with a sign indicating that a naval enclave with hospital, residences, and harbor lie beyond. A little farther north, the housing becomes suddenly dense; several churches suggest that this is a neighborhood with a large Christian population. A South Indian coffee shop with an open front advertises *idlee* and *dosa* (a South Indian rice-based specialty). The journey continues down the main thoroughfare, the Causeway, past shops, restaurants, movie houses, and a museum, into the fort area with its large stone buildings, fountains, and banks. The bus veers out toward Marine Drive along the ocean lined with apartments, hotels, a stadium, up into the posh residential area of Malabar Hill where winding streets pass high-rise apartments and huge single dwellings. The apartments are inhabited by people of mixed ethnic origins. Many of the single dwellings are owned by Gujarati families.

The bus continues down one side of Malabar Hill, past the famous Parsee Towers of Silence, Parsee residences, a bakery with delicate biscuits and cakes, run by a Parsee woman. A change of buses continuing north goes over a bridge past a rectangle of slum dwellings into Parel. Here the textile mills, some still with British names, are barely visible beyond the high fences with huge, swinging wooden gates. Long rows of tenements, three or four stories high, with rickety wooden balconies, line the streets. Parel, like the crowded but middle-class area of Dadar just beyond, is predominantly Maharashtrian. Past Dadar the bus continues into the middle-class neighborhoods of Sion and Matunga. On the side streets, the signs on the shops and a clothing stall with tables piled high with lungi (a skirtlike garment worn by men) indicate the presence of large numbers of South Indians. Slowly the bus leaves the dense crowds of the city again over a bridge past another slum colony. This area is inhabited by a mixture of ethnic groups, but the different streets and paths within the slum are occupied by people of a single state, district, and even village. The bus continues toward the suburbs, where middle-class housing colonies alternate with makeshift temporary dwellings. Neighborhoods of Sindhi, Gujarati, North Indian, and Maharashtrian populations follow one upon another.

In the world of work, only some of this ethnic variety is muted. In Bombay offices, shirts and pants and the six-yard saree replace the distinctive regional dress of dhoti, lungi, and nine-yard saree. Company cafeterias or office canteens in some establishments have eliminated the ethnic distinctions in dietary customs; and in some offices English or Hindi supplants the regional tongues spoken in Bombay's neighborhoods.

But the office does not homogenize all distinctions. Regional dietary customs are not entirely erased in Bombay's offices since many workers still receive lunch containers from home. This is made possible by a remarkably efficient transport network whereby a small cylindrical metal lunch container, called a tiffin carrier, is picked up in the morning from the worker's home, sometimes a suburb miles outside the city, and carried along with hundreds of virtually identical-looking containers on wooden carriers. They are then carried on foot or train to a junction where the thousands of containers are then sorted, transferred to other wooden carriers, re-sorted, and finally delivered, sometimes still warm, to the worker's office.

Many trades, skills, and occupations are dominated by one particular ethnic group. Gujaratis are considered commercial people; Andhras or Kamathis are found in large numbers in construction; South Indians are associated with clerical and white-collar jobs. It is less easy to pinpoint a characteristic occupation of Maharashtrians, although they serve in large numbers as laborers and domestics, as workers in the textile factories, and as typists in government offices.

Even in those offices or factories where there is a mixture of ethnic backgrounds, distinctions often persist. Skin color still broadly differentiates a South Indian from a North Indian. The accent of the English or Hindi spoken is often traceable to a specific state or region of India. Hand gestures, hair style, and subtle mannerisms enable those attuned to Bombay's ethnic variety to identify more specifically the locality from which a person comes.

The Shiv Sena

Out of this combination of ethnic populations, Shiv Sena emerged in 1966. The Sena's principal charge was that Maharashtrians, who then accounted for somewhat over 40 percent of the city's population, were being excluded from jobs by the incursions of South Indians, who made up less than 10 percent (see Chapter 3, Table 5). The Sena directed their complaints against the South Indians—rather than, for instance, the Gujarati population, which was numerically twice as large—principally because the South Indians held jobs that the Maharashtrians coveted. Maharashtrians, it is readily acknowledged, have shied away from commercial occupations, lacking the capital, perhaps the skills, and the cultural traditions that characterize the middle-class Gujarati community in Bombay. There is, however, a tradition among Maharashtrians in the city of looking to a "secure" office job; and it is in these white-collar office jobs that South Indians are to be found in some number.

It was over the issue of safeguarding the jobs of Maharashtrians that Shiv Sena achieved a notoriety that developed seemingly overnight. Bal Thackeray, the Sena's founder, was then a political unknown. He was, and continues to be, a cartoonist and editor of the Marathi weekly, *Marmik*. His father, Keshav Sitaram Thackeray, had been himself the editor of a journal and gained a reputation in Maharashtra for his spicy and outspoken articles which advanced the cause of anti-Brahminism. Bal Thackeray's family is from a high, largely urban caste, the Chandraseniya Kayastha Prabhus. Although Thackeray never completed his matriculation examination, his fluency in English and his trenchant wit, especially pointed on contemporary political events, make any characterization of him as "uneducated" inaccurate.

His formal education having ended at age sixteen, Thackeray was taken on as a cartoonist by the *Free Press Journal* and somewhat later joined the soon-to-be-defunct *Newsday*. A quarrel with his South Indian co-workers reputedly contributed to his bitterness; but colleagues at the time report that in the quiet worker who kept mostly to himself there was scarcely any indication of the political personality he would later become.

Although Thackeray was unknown, his "cause" had won considerable attention. In the several years prior to 1966, *Marmik* had published weekly lists of the top officers in Bombay businesses and bureaucracies which, augmented with editorials and cartoons, poignantly documented the low proportion of Maharashtrians in top positions. These lists soon became the talk of young Maharashtrians living in Bombay. In June 1966, Thackeray called a rally in Bombay's Shivaji Park. A huge crowd gathered, and during the course of the rally thousands of young Maharashtrians reportedly came forward to sign the membership roster—and the party was born.

Although by its leader's declaration the Shiv Sena was a movement without political intent, it soon became involved in political campaigning. In 1967 the Sena participated in the general election supporting the Congress candidate against the well-known former defense minister V. K. Krishna Menon, whom the Sena attacked as an "outsider." Six months later the party contested the municipal elections in Thana, a suburb of Bombay and, winning seventeen out of forty seats, became the largest party on the municipal corporation.

In the spring of 1968 the party, then only two years old, contested the Bombay municipal elections and won an impressive 42 out of 140 seats. The Sena's seats, as Table 1 illustrates, were won mostly at the expense of the parties that had earlier joined in the Samiti, a leftist coalition.

Encouraged by the results of the 1968 municipal elections, Shiv Sena tried to enlarge its political base. With an eye both to improving its political fortunes in Bombay and to establishing itself as a political force elsewhere in Maharashtra, the Sena endeavored to broaden its ideology. Specifically, it attempted to downplay its image as a parochial or nativist party. In order to gain the support of non-Maharashtrians in Bombay and of Maharashtrians in other cities where economic competition with

Table 1. Outcome of 1961 and 1968 municipal elections

	Seats won				
	1961			1968	
	#	%		#	%
			Shiv Sena	42	30
Congress	59	45	Congress	65	46
Samiti	34	26	—		
Republican party	3	2	Republican	2	1
Communist	18	14	—		
Peasants and Workers party	8	6	—		
Revolutionary Communist Party of India	2	2	Communist (CPI- and CPI-M)	3	2
Lal Nishan	1	1	—		
Janata Agadhi	1	1	—		
Hindu Mahasabha	1	1	—		
Praja Socialist Party	14	11	Praja Socialist party	11	8
Jan Sangh	4	3	Jan Sangh	6	4
Socialist party	3	2	Samyukta Socialist party	2	1
Muslim League	4	3	Muslim League	2	1
Republican party (Kamble group)	3	2	—		
Independents	10	8	Independents and others	6	4
—			Swatantra	1	1
Total	131	100	Total Seats	140	98*

*Column does not add up to 100% because of rounding.
Sources: B. A. V. Sharma and R. T. Jangam, *The Bombay Municipal Corporation* (Bombay: Popular Book Depot, 1962), p. 102; and G. S. Badhe and M. U. Rao, *The Bombay Civic Election of 1968* (Bombay: All India Institute of Local Self-Government, 1968), p. 124.

"outsiders" had not been an issue, it recognized the need to divest itself of its xenophobic reputation. After 1968, therefore, its attacks on migrants subsided. Instead, it became a fierce critic of antinationalism, decrying both Muslims and Communists, many of whom, it claimed, owed primary allegiance to foreign governments.

This strategy did not succeed in boosting the Sena's political strength. In Nasik, Poona, Colaba, and other places outside Bombay and Thana where it contested elections, the party failed in its bid for seats. Even in state and national elections in Bom-

Table 2. Outcome of 1973 municipal elections

	Seats secured #	%
Shiv Sena	39	28
Congress (R)	45	32
Congress (O)	4	3
Samyukta Socialist Party / Praja Socialist Party	8	6
Jan Sangh	15	11
Swatantra	—	—
Communist Party of India	3	2
Communist Party of India (Marxist)	1	1
Republican party	—	—
Independents (Muslim League, etc.)	25	18
Total	140	101*

*Column does not add up to 100% because of rounding.
Source: Shri R. M. Oza, "Municipal General Ward Elections 1973," *Bombay Civil Journal*, XX (March 1973), 13–14.

bay, its record was poor. Its two candidates, and a third Sena-supported candidate in the 1971 parliamentary elections in Bombay, were defeated. Only one of its candidates for the state assembly proved successful in the 1972 elections.

For a number of years, however, the Sena managed to maintain its strength in the Bombay municipality. In the 1973 city elections, as shown in Table 2, almost the same number of Sena candidates were returned as in the 1968 contests.

Since 1972 Bombay has had four Shiv Sena mayors,[21] and many of the important municipal committees have been chaired by Shiv Sena councilors. Nativist politics, in sum, established a firm footing in cosmopolitan Bombay. We now turn to its causes and consequences.

The Causes and Consequences of Nativism

Although nativism may be distinguished from other ethnic movements by the nature of its goals, its genesis is similar to theirs. At the root of nativism is a perceived inequality of situations. As Paul Brass writes in his study of language and religion

21. Hemechandra Gupte, Manohar Joshi, Sudhir Joshi and Wamanrao Mahadik.

in North India, "The basic condition for group conflict based on ethnic differences is the perception of the existence of unevenness in development between two or more groups."[22]

These perceptions of inequality accompany all outbreaks of ethnic conflict, nativist and otherwise, and help to explain the present pervasiveness of ethnic tensions. They are not, however, sufficiently specific, as Brass argues, to explain why some movements reach the level of highly politicized, articulate, and effective protest, while others remain sporadic and unorganized. For example, what are the reasons, as Brass asks, for the widely recognized struggle of the Sikhs and the mostly unacknowledged grievances of the Maithili-speakers of Bihar? Why has there been a highly volatile agitation in Telengana while the organization for separatism in Vidharbha is still immature? Why has a well-organized nativist political party emerged in Bombay while in Calcutta, a socially heterogeneous city where ethnic inequalities clearly also obtain, there is no analogous sons-of-the-soil movement? To answer such questions demands a consideration of the particular pattern of ethnic inequalities which gives rise to political conflict.

First, it is important to consider the nature of the demography of interethnic group relations. Do sons-of-the-soil movements arise when the proportion of "outsiders" to the "local" ethnic group reaches a certain numerical level? Do such movements ensue from a sudden immigration of ethnically distinct populations? Following an account in Chapter 2 of the background to Bombay nativism, these are the questions discussed in Chapter 3.

Ethnically heterogeneous regions and cities in India are not uncommon. Close to one-third of India's population is migrant. Of this fraction, slightly under two-thirds have simply moved within the same district of the state in which they were born. An additional 20 percent have moved outside the district but within the same state. The remaining approximately 15 percent have migrated either across state borders or from outside India.[23]

22. Paul Brass, *Language, Religion, and Politics in North India* (Cambridge: Cambridge University Press, 1974), p. 419.
23. Census of India, *Migration Tables*, 1961, vol. 1, pt. II-C (iii) (New Delhi: Government of India Press, 1961). The 1971 census data, at least the 1% sample,

Since state boundaries generally coincide with linguistic and cultural divisions, the percentage of interstate migration serves as an approximate indicator of interethnic migration and suggests that (discounting foreign migrants) over 5 percent of India's population has at least temporarily changed cultural milieu. But because sons-of-the-soil movements exist in only some of these multiethnic regions, it is worth considering whether there is a particular set of demographic conditions that precipitates the outbreak of nativist conflict.

What kinds of economic inequity are to be found in regions where sons-of-the-soil movements arise? Do nativist movements ensue from situations where the native population, the sons-of-the-soil, are better or worse off than the "outsider"? Does conflict result from a change in the actual economic status of local and outsider populations or from a change in the perceptions of those conditions? Do the changes or perceptions of changes which give rise to nativism occur among the middle class, working class, or both? These questions are the subject of Chapters 4 and 5.

What kind of organization is able to politicize nativist economic grievances? As Chapter 6 asks, do "successful" (well-organized) nativist movements recruit party workers through ideological appeals, through patronage, or through other incentives?

All of these questions are important to an explanation of existing sons-of-the-soil movements and to estimating the future potential of still nascent nativist sentiment. But a complete analysis must assess the consequences as well as the causes of the nativism of India.

The emergence of Shiv Sena is itself a consequence of nativist tensions. In Chapter 7, we will examine the attitudes of Shiv Sena leaders and the impact of the Sena leadership on interethnic relations and political stability in Bombay. To what extent do Shiv Sena leaders feel that non-Maharashtrians must con-

---

indicate that the percentages are approximately the same. A comprehensive analysis of migration patterns is presented in Myron Weiner, *Sons of the Soil: Migration and Ethnic Conflict in India* (Princeton: Princeton University Press, 1978). Many of the articles by Myron Weiner referred to in subsequent pages have been elaborated upon in this recently published book.

form to Maharashtrian culture? Has the leadership encouraged a change in Maharashtrian attitudes and aspirations? The chapter further considers attitudes of Sena leaders toward the political process. Has the extremist and violent rhetoric for which the Sena is known affected party behavior and the conduct of politics in Bombay?

Sons-of-the-soil movements also pose fundamental questions about the means by which the problem of economic inequality between ethnic groups is to be resolved. In Chapter 8, we explore state government policy and its impact on the economic status of Maharashtrians in Bombay. In Chapter 9, central government measures and court decisions are examined with a view to identifying the nature of national policy on the preferential treatment of sons-of-the-soil. Finally, in Chapter 10, we consider the causes and consequences of Shiv Sena's claims to preferential treatment in the light of similar claims made elsewhere, within and beyond India's borders.

In India and elsewhere in the world, one consequence of egalitarian ideology and of the welfare state has been the political mobilization of disadvantaged groups around demands for preferential treatment. In expressing this new ethnicity and equality, Bombay's Shiv Sena raises a question central to our understanding of contemporary politics: How important is meritocracy to modernity?

2 | Shiv Sena and the Bombay Setting

Bombay, its inhabitants claim, is one of India's most cosmopolitan cities. By Bombay usage, the epithet denotes less the "bright lights" of the city than its rich ethnic diversity. Calcutta, by contrast, despite its enormous size and burgeoning industrial growth, is a distinctly Bengali city.[1] Similarly, the Tamil character of Madras is announced unmistakably by the road and shop signs, the restaurants, the language spoken in the marketplace, and the dress of those who move about the streets. But Bombay is not a Maharashtrian city and to its Maharashtrian residents, "cosmopolitan" is an ambiguous accolade. Indeed, the heterogeneous ethnic identity of Bombay has been at the core of Shiv Sena's genesis.

In the course of the last century, the ethnic character of Bombay has changed. Although Shiv Sena appeared to arise overnight with its maiden Shivaji Park rally of June 1966, the party is in fact an outgrowth of a long-standing historical process: the gradual strengthening of the Maharashtrian political position in Bombay. Until recently, Maharashtrians in Bombay had been relegated to subordinate economic and political roles. Independence in 1947, however, and the division of the old Bombay State into the separate states of Gujarat and Maharashtra in 1960 boosted the political status of Maharashtrians. Although Maharashtrians did not succeed to positions of economic dominance, they did gain instant control of the state government. This new political status released expectations about the prospective position of the Maharashtrian community in Bombay to which Shiv Sena's emergence can be traced.

1. Bengali-speakers form two-thirds of Calcutta's population, and, as Surajit Sinha states, "dominate the cultural profile of the city." Surajit Sinha, ed., *Cultural Profile of Calcutta* (Calcutta: Indian Anthropology Society, 1972) p. 3.

The relatively lackluster historical role of Maharashtrians in the city of Bombay contrasts with the drama of Maharashtra's past. A rich literary tradition and the martial conquests of the Mahratta Empire distinguish Maharashtrian history. The feats of the seventeenth-century hero, Shivaji Maharaj, prefaced the extension of Mahratta power throughout a sizable portion of the subcontinent and won recognition throughout India. The center of Maharashtrian culture and politics, however, was in the interior, around Poona. It is no accident that Shiv Sena, "the Army of Shivaji," with its orange replica of Shivaji's own flag, the *bhagwa zenda*, has now sought to secure Bombay for Maharashtrians.

Bombay and the Changing Status of Maharashtrians

Bombay's "cosmopolitan" past dates well back into ancient times. As a leading port of Western India, the city attracted Arab, Abyssinian, Persian, Israelite, Portuguese, and British traders. In the year 1534, Sultan Bahadur of Gujarat ceded Bombay (then a cluster of islands) to the Portuguese. In 1661, the Portuguese presented Bombay Island to England as part of the dowry which attended the marriage of Charles II to the Infanta of Portugal. Seven years later, Charles transferred his possession to the East India Company for an annual rent of ten pounds. The next century saw the British, eager to protect their commercial interests, engaged in diplomatic and military maneuvers against the naval forces of the Mughals and the military might of the Mahrattas. With the decline of the ruling house of the Peshwas and the conclusion of the Treaty of Bassein in 1802, Mahratta sovereignty came to an end.[2]

2. For an overview of Maratha history, see Government of Maharashtra, *Maharashtra State Gazetteers* (Bombay: Directorate of Government Printing, 1967); S. R. Sharma, *The Founding of Maratha Freedom* (Bombay: Orient Longmans, 1964); W. S. Desai, *Bombay and the Marathas* (New Delhi, Munshiram Manoharlal, 1970); C. A. Kincaid and D. B. Parasnis, *A History of the Maratha People* (Bombay: Oxford University Press, 1925). For a general history of Bombay, see S. M. Edwardes, *The Gazateer of Bombay City and Island* (Bombay: Times of India Press, 1909) 3 vols.; Samuel T. Sheppard, *Bombay* (Bombay: Times of India Press, 1932); M. D. David, *History of Bombay* (Bombay: University of Bombay Press, 1973); Christine Dobbin, *Urban Leadership in Western India: Politics and Communities in Bombay City 1840–1885* (London: Oxford University Press, 1972).

The nineteenth century saw the city of Bombay flourish. Small handicraft industries producing silks, cottons, and brass and copper vessels were replaced gradually by large factories. The first textile mill in Bombay was established in 1851. By the end of the century, somewhat over 100 factories had been established and Bombay became the center of textile production in India.

Immigration to Bombay, however, began well before the late-nineteenth-century industrialization. Records from the early 1800s note the presence of significant numbers of Gujaratis, Parsees, Banias (both Hindu and Jain), and Muslim Bohras. Koli fishermen (thought to be the original natives of Bombay), Sonars (goldsmiths), Kesars (coppersmiths), Bhandares,[3] Pathare Prabhus, and Chitpavan, Saraswat, and Deshasth Brahmins are also mentioned frequently in accounts of the period.[4]

Although these groups were drawn from the neighboring areas of the present Gujarat and Maharashtra, further records show that there were also populations in the city that had migrated from quite distant areas of India. Kamathis (from the region of Andhra Pradesh) are known to have been employed as laborers in construction as early as 1757.[5] A large group of Kamathis was also thought to have formed a settlement (from which the present Kamathipura dates) in Bombay in the 1830s.[6]

By the mid-nineteenth century, then, before the emergence of Bombay's industries, the population was ethnically diverse and heavily migrant. Some estimates suggest that as much as 80 percent of the city's residents were born outside the Islands of Bombay. The first comprehensive statistics on the linguistic character of Bombay's population were recorded in the latter part of the

---

3. Bhandares were once tappers of toddy palms and later were employed in military and police service. See S. M. Edwardes, *The Rise of Bombay* (Bombay: Times of India Press, 1902), p. 335.

4. Dobbin, *Urban Leadership in Western India*, chs. 1 and 2. Dobbin also remarks on the presence of Bene-Israel Jews (*Urban Leadership*, p. 7); and Edwardes observes that a significant number of Chinese resided in Bombay (*The Rise of Bombay*, p. 255).

5. Edwardes, *Rise of Bombay*, p. 186.

6. Ibid., p. 253.

Table 3. Population of Bombay by mother tongue, 1881 (language groups numbering over 1,000 in population)

Language group	Population	Percentage of city population
Marathi	387,939	50.2
Gujarati	207,209	26.8
Hindustani (including Urdu)	89,369	11.6
Konkani (Portuguese or Goanese)	38,260	4.9
Telugu	13,611	1.8
English	10,878	1.4
Marwari	8,227	1.1
Arabic	4,393	.6
Persian	3,164	.4
Tamil	2,112	.3
Sindhi	1,421	.2
Kanarese	1,146	.1
Total	773,196	

Source: *Bombay*, Census of India, 1881, vol. II, pp. 38–41.

nineteenth century. These statistics confirm the presence of a heterogeneous population. The census of 1881 records those born in Bombay as numbering slightly under 30 percent of the city's population. Ten percent of Bombay's population was noted as coming from regions of India outside Bombay province.[7] The figures in Table 3 reveal a fairly wide ethnic mixture and indicate that Maharashtrians constituted only a very slim majority of the city inhabitants. Although the percentage of Marathi-speakers in the Bombay population has dropped somewhat since the late nineteenth century, the decline, as shown in similar tables in appropriate census volumes, has been both gradual and slight. After increasing from 50.2 percent in 1881 to 50.9 percent in 1911, it decreased to 47.6 percent in 1931 and to 42.8 percent in 1961.

The economic preeminence of non-Maharashtrians in Bombay dates back at least as far as the mid-nineteenth century. Several studies remark on the displacement of Marathi-speaking elites, the Pathare Prabhus, by "the more enterprising Bhatias

7. Census of India, *Bombay*, vol. I (1881), pp. 104–5.

and Banias."[8] Edwardes in *The Gazetteer of Bombay* notes that although up to about 1870, the dress of the Prabhus was considered model attire, the once wealthy Prabhu families soon began to desert their large Bombay residences for more simple, economical flats.[9] At the end of the nineteenth century, large numbers of Maharashtrian laborers came from the Deccan and Konkan to work in the textile mills, contributing to the image of Maharashtrians as predominantly from the laboring classes. With the growth of Bombay's importance as a port under the British, non-Maharashtrian trading communities moved into the city and established a central position in Bombay's commercial life. According to Christine Dobbin's excellent account of the period, it was primarily sections of the Parsee population, a Zoroastrian community originally from Persia, which "rose to prominence and wealth as agents for European houses, contractors to government for the supply of troops, importers of English provisions and wines, and finally shipowners and traders on their own account."[10] Hindu and Jain Banias and Muslim Bohras also figured in the banking and trading of the period. With the growth of the textile and other industries in the latter half of the nineteenth and early twentieth century, many of these same communities, along with Marwaris from Rajasthan, carried their capital and entrepreneurial skills from commercial to industrial pursuits.

By contrast, the Maharashtrians in Bombay by and large followed occupations outside the commercial and industrial sector. The Kolis, whose presence in Bombay predates most other communities, are still seen among the city's fishermen. Late in the nineteenth century, the industrial houses began to recruit labor from the Maratha castes of Ratnagiri and the Deccan. The Pathare Prabhus and subsequently several Maharashtrian Brahmin castes came to occupy key administrative and clerical

8. Edwardes, *The Gazetteer of Bombay*, vol. I. p. 168. See also Sheppard, *Bombay*, p. 119. Edwardes suggests that the Marathi-speaking Pathare Prabhus originally migrated from Gujarat (I, 241).
9. Edwardes, *Gazetteer of Bombay*, I, 168–73.
10. Dobbin, *Urban Leadership*, p. 3.

positions in Bombay under the British. But the only Maharashtrians who approached the wealth and economic status of the Gujarati merchants were individuals from the Sonar[11] and Kesar castes who through their hereditary occupations had come to trade in jewels and ornaments.[12] The absence of major trading communities among Maharashtrian castes is important in explaining the historical dominance by other communities of Bombay's economy and politics.

The nineteenth-century commercial preeminence of non-Maharashtrians in Bombay deprived Maharashtrians of a dominant role in Bombay politics. In British India, when suffrage was limited to taxpayers, wealth rather than numbers was the overriding determinant of political strength. Although Maharashtrians outnumbered other communities in Bombay, in municipal politics they played a relatively subordinate role.

Dobbin's account of the 1873 election gives evidence of the political advantage that non-Maharashtrians gained from their superior economic position. Under the Municipal Act of 1872, ratepayers (taxpayers) were enfranchised and permitted to elect, with the Fellows of Bombay University, thirty-two members to the municipal council. As Dobbin writes:

A list of ratepayers paying Rs. [rupees] 50 per annum and upwards in house, police and lighting rates were then drawn up, which produced an electoral roll of 3,918. Of the 0.6 percent of the city's inhabitants who were thus enfranchised, 1,621 were Hindus, 1,040 Parsis, 896 Muslims, 167 Europeans, 113 Goans, 29 Jews and 52 Companies. The Parsis' affluence is particularly noticeable. Forming 6.8 percent of the city's population, they accounted for 26 percent of the electoral roll. Muslims achieved a very fair share of the roll, providing as they did 21.4 percent of the city's population, and 23 percent of the voters. Hindus, with such a large laboring and menial population, were of course grossly underrepresented on the roll: they formed only 41 percent of those enfranchised, although they were 63.4 percent of the total population. It is impossible to state the proportion of Gujarati to Marathi-speakers enfranchised, although it is natural to assume

11. One prominent Sonar Shetia of the period was Jagannath Shankarshet.
12. See Dobbin's account, *Urban Leadership*, p. 173.

that the former comprised the majority of Hindu property-owning classes.[13]

In the 1873 elections, ten Parsees, eight Maharashtrian Hindus, five Gujarati Hindus, three Muslims, four Europeans, one Goan, and one other were returned. Two years later, in the next election, fourteen Parsees, six Gujarati Hindus, five Muslims, four Maharashtrians, and three Europeans were elected.[14]

By Independence, the complexion of Bombay politics had begun to change. The prominence of the Parsee community in municipal affairs was waning. The post-Independence movement for linguistic states and the uncertain future of Bombay aroused the political energies of Maharashtrians in the city. In the mid-1950s, with a decision on the reorganization of Bombay State pending, the arguments for and against the inclusion of Bombay in a prospective state of Maharashtra grew vocal. The arguments against the city's incorporation into Maharashtra, G. S. Singh has noted, included the claims that:

1. Marathi-speaking people are not in a majority in the City of Bombay and their proportion has been falling.
2. Bombay is the trade centre of the entire country and not exclusively of Maharashtra. . . .
3. Bombay was never a part of Maharashtra.
4. It is mostly the non-Maharashtrians that developed the city by their capital and managerial skill.[15]

Supporters of Bombay's inclusion in a prospective Maharashtra state argued that Maharashtrian castes had been the true natives of Bombay, that Bombay's wealth had been built on the backs of Maharashtrian labor, and that Maharashtrians, if not a majority,

13. Ibid., p. 173.
14. Ibid., pp. 174–76. Members of other (English, Christian, etc.) communities were also elected.
15. G. S. Singh, *Maratha Geopolitics and the Indian Nation* (Bombay: Manaktalas, 1966), p. 51. For a detailed account of the period, see Robert W. Stern, *The Process of Opposition in India: Two Case Studies of How Policy Shapes Politics* (Chicago: University of Chicago Press, 1970). See also Marshall Windmiller, "The Politics of States Reorganization in India: The Case of Bombay," *Far Eastern Survey*, 25 (September 1956), 129–144; and Henry Hart, "Urban Politics in Bombay," *Economic Weekly*, 11 (June 1960), 983.

were the largest linguistic community in the city. Although the 1960 reorganization of Bombay State resolved the issue in favor of the incorporation of Bombay into the newly created state of Maharashtra, the controversy had been all too indicative of the equivocal position of Maharashtrians in the city of Bombay.

By the early 1960s, the political status of Maharashtrians in the city had significantly improved. Compared to the Maharashtrian representation of 12 percent in the municipal council of 1875, 43 percent of the 1961 municipal council was Maharashtrian. And at the state level, Maharashtrians monopolized the ministerial posts and legislative assembly seats. Still, within the city, many Maharashtrians felt that the community did not receive its share of power. In 1965, for instance, one year prior to the Sena's founding, twenty-five Maharashtrian members of the Congress party signed a memorandum drawing attention to their reputed underrepresentation on the important committees of the civic body.[16]

Nevertheless, the introduction of universal suffrage just prior to the 1948 municipal election and the creation of Maharashtra State had clearly helped to raise the numbers of Maharashtrians in political office in Bombay. The enhancement of Maharashtrian political status paved the way for the inevitable questioning of the community's continued economic difficulties. Shiv Sena's exploitation of this discontent rested on one very important additional change in Bombay society: the growth of Maharashtrian literacy.

Literacy, Marmik, and Shiv Sena Appeal

The significance of widespread literacy for the success of Shiv Sena is readily apparent. Shiv Sena did not emerge as a splinter group or offshoot of an already existing party. At the time of its founding in 1966, its leaders were unknown politically and its organization nonexistent.[17] For a nativist or for any political

---

16. See *Times of India*, Apr. 25, 1965.
17. Although a fairly high percentage of Shiv Sena leaders were mobilized during the Samyukta Maharashtra movement, only one or two had acquired any political recognition. See Ram Joshi, "The Shiv Sena: A Movement in Search of Legitimacy," *Asian Survey*, 10 (November 1970), 973.

Table 4. Literate percentage of Bombay's population, 1872–1961

Census year	Literate population
1872	16.3
1881	23.2
1891	24.0
1901	19.1
1921	23.3
1931	23.8
1941	40.8
1951	49.3
1961	58.6

Source: D. T. Lakdawala et al., *Work, Wages and Well-Being in an Indian Metropolis: Economic Survey of Bombay City* (Bombay: University of Bombay, 1963), p. 32. 1961 data from *Maharashtra at a Glance* (Bombay: Directorate of Publicity, Maharashtra State, 1969), pp. 62–63.

group to counter established parties possessing extensive political organization, a means of reaching and organizing the voter was mandatory. In Bombay, as distinct from many other rural or even urban localities, widespread literacy opened the possibilities of using the media to elicit public interest and support.

By the mid-1960s, Bombay had achieved a high level of literacy. Census figures record the growth of literacy over earlier decades, as shown in Table 4. By 1961, the level of literacy in Bombay was twice as high as the average for Maharashtra State.

Shiv Sena's emergence owes much to its effective use of the printed word. The party's genesis, in fact, can be traced directly to the popularity of the Marathi weekly, *Marmik*, edited by the Sena leader, Bal Thackeray. *Marmik* played a crucial part in drawing the attention of Bombay's Maharashtrian community to the proclaimed injustices inflicted on local people and thus in laying the foundation for Shiv Sena. In 1965, when the magazine was five years old, Thackeray began to include in *Marmik* lists of the top officers of important Bombay firms, "exposing" the "discrimination" against Maharashtrians. Many of these lists, compiled ingeniously by surveying names of Bombay industrial houses and their officers listed in the Bombay telephone directory, showed a predominance of non-Maharashtrian names.[18]

18. The names of themselves do not indicate the actual place of birth or length of residence of those designated as non-Maharashtrians.

The survey reported that out of 1,500 executives, only 75 were "Maharashtrian."[19] The first set of lists was accompanied by a caption which stated, "Read and keep quiet."[20] Subsequently the lists appeared with the exhortation, "Read this and think." With the publication each week of these lists and additional polemical articles and cartoons highlighting the implication none too subtly suggested by the lists themselves, the circulation of *Marmik* skyrocketed, nearly doubling in one year until in 1966 it reached an estimated 40,000.[21]

Marmik's popularity can be accounted for in large part by these attention-winning "exposés" of 1965–66; but there are other reasons as well. The fact that it is a Marathi weekly makes it available to a far more extensive readership in the Maharashtrian community than if it were in English. At least as important, the style of humor of the cartoons and articles is one that appeals to a broad range of the population. The use of language in *Marmik* ranges from crude and juvenile to sophisticated plays on words, offering "something for everyone." There are references to the Communist "monkeys"[22] and to the "rhinoceros"[23] skin of Krishna Menon; cartoons show politicians as food items;[24] the leftist Peasants and Workers Party is referred to as the "red daughter-in-law who has come to the *ukirada* (a crude word denoting the place in the back of the house where one washes or throws garbage for scavenger animals)."[25] There are con-

---

19. Kapilacharya (pseudonym), *Shiv Sena Speaks* (Bombay: V. D. Limaye Printing Works, 1967), p. 13.
20. See reference in Dr. Vasant D. Rao, "Shiv Sena—A Case Study in Regionalism in India," *Quarterly Review of Historical Studies* (Calcutta), 13:1 (1973–74), 135.
21. Estimate is based on *Marmik* office's own figures. A slightly lower figure of 31,336 appears in Ministry of Information and Broadcasting Office of Registrar for Newspapers; *Press in India*, Pt. I (Delhi: Government Central Press. Annual report consulted 1965–70).
22. *Marmik*, Jan. 12, 1969.
23. Ibid., Mar. 12, 1961.
24. Ibid., October 1970. The Muslim politician, Fakruddin, is pictured as a "nonvegetarian kebab."
25. Ibid., July 6, 1969. Crude language is not the monopoly of Shiv Sena. A Communist party cartoon refers to Bal Thackeray as the "*shenapati*," meaning cow dung, rather than "*senapati*," leader. See report in *Indian Express*, Feb. 16, 1971.

tinual references to the South Indians, using the term "*Yandug-unduwala*"—a play on the rolled-tongue sound of South Indian languages. For those with an appreciation of a more refined humor, there are numerous puns and plays on words: Gulab*mao* instead of Gulabrao Acharya;[26] Dange of the CPI written as Comrade "Donge," meaning, in Marathi, one who deceives.[27] There are the usual attacks on governmental corruption. Charging Congress with nepotism, Thackeray warns lest Indira Gandhi's son assume the "throne"—using a word in Marathi that also denotes the stool on which the *panwalla* (person who sells *pan-supari*, betel leaf in which spices, lime, and betel nut are wrapped) sits.[28]

The articles, too, range from simple to sophisticated. The excerpt that follows is from one of the satirical pieces, a tongue-in-cheek portrayal of what Bombay will be like when South Indians have taken over the state. In A.D. 2065, in Madramatungam a special day is celebrated and the writer is assigned the job of interviewing the guest of honor:

> In the calm and quiet of night, I went to the house of Ganapati Maratham, and greeted him with Namaskar, informing him that I had come to take his interview. Ganapati looked at me with surprise and said: "Oh, after so many years the old Marathi language is again spoken today. How do you know this language?" "I took the subject 'Old Marathi langugage' for my Ph.D.,"—I replied. He said, smiling, "Nowadays this language is never heard. In my childhood, Marathi was spoken in pure form; now that pure language is heard only in a small habitation of Chambal valley. A hundred years ago in Bombay, Madrasi governors, mayors and sheriffs were appointed. The Marathi people of that time used to call these people outsiders. Then, the Madrasi lungi was a topic for fun. Today everyone wears a lungi." "Yes," I said, "Recently in a fancy dress competition, one man wearing a dhoti received a prize from the Governor. . . . What a strange garment."[29]

26. *Marmik*, July 12, 1970.
27. Ibid., Mar. 12, 1961 (an uncommon expression).
28. This reference was made by Thackeray on March 12, 1971, at a rally in Shivaji Park. It is noteworthy that the Sena leadership, which had on many occasions freely ridiculed Mrs. Gandhi and her son, became under the Emergency their staunch supporters.
29. "The Interview of Purnashambu for Marmikam," by T. Balkeshavan, *Marmik*, Aug. 15, 1965.

While occasionally the articles treat historical subjects (one noting that in the seventeenth century the British made a case for giving preferences to local people),[30] the essays and articles are scarcely intended to be intellectual analyses. Mostly they are short, humorous denunciations or parodies, sketches, or accounts of some current social or political issue or event.

It seems plausible that a deliberate effort is made to include cartoons and articles with a range of humor that will appeal to educated and noneducated alike. As one of the Sena organizers commented, speaking about the rhetoric and propaganda used at rallies: "We try to talk in a way that the common people, too, will understand. We speak of 'monkeys' rather than using a more complicated term. That has more meaning to them; it excites people."[31]

Marmik's success in reaching a cross-section of the Maharashtrian population is evident from its readership figures. According to a Bombay research organization, the readership includes a substantial group from the low-, middle-, and upper-income groups.[32] The bulk (77 percent) of *Marmik*'s readership, however, is concentrated in the lower-middle class, claiming in 1972 a monthly income of less than 500 rupees. The specialized character of *Marmik*'s appeal is further seen in the age classification of its readers, with over half falling in the fifteen to twenty-four age bracket.

Whether it is the content or style of humor that explains the large circulation, it would be impossible to dispute the magazine's popularity. By 1966, *Marmik* had achieved an estimated readership between 200,000 and 300,000, thereby reaching between 40 and 50 percent of the literate Marathi-speaking adult population (fifteen years and over).[33] In June of the same year, the Sena was founded. It is unlikely that the Sena could have

---

30. See, for instance, Jan. 12, 1969, "There Is Historical Support for the Demand for Local People"; and July 7, 1968, "The Disease in the Abdomen, Treatment in the Leg," which notes that even in Britain the Scottish and Welsh experience indicates that regionalism has not been overcome.
31. Interview with Datta Pradhan, January 1971.
32. Figures made available privately.
33. Readership figures arrived at by multiplying circulation by 5—the figure used by marketing research analyses in Bombay.

been organized in the absence of *Marmik*. Established by men who several years earlier were political unknowns, the Sena needed not only a cause but a means of broadcasting that cause before the party could hope to register, as it proved later able to do, thousands of names on their membership rosters.

Shiv Sena grew out of a changing Bombay. The city, which had historically rested at the edge of Maharashtrian society, was in 1960 incorporated within a Maharashtrian state. Having played a political and economic role in Bombay secondary to that of other communities, Maharashtrians became the purveyors of power in state politics and attained a prominent political position within the municipality. This new political voice afforded Maharashtrians an opportunity to question their economic position in Bombay. The high level of literacy in Bombay, and Thackeray's clever exploitation of the Marathi news medium, ensured that such questioning would gain a hearing.

3 | Demographic Causes of Nativism

> Every day 300 families come to Bombay. On a conservative estimate, a lakh [100,000] of people are added [yearly] to the City's population.
>
> —*Shiv Sena Speaks*

Migration to Indian cities has been relatively slow-paced compared to that of urban areas in Africa or Latin America. Latin American migration, for instance, has rapidly altered the ratio of rural to urban dwellers; but the percentage of India's population living in urban areas has remained at a practically constant 20 percent between 1950 and 1970.[1] Except for a few of India's larger cities, migration accounts for a rather small proportion of the population increase in urban India.[2]

Nevertheless, the influx of migrants into cities such as Bombay or Bangalore is visually dramatic. A train pulling into a station unloads in a few minutes' time hundreds of newcomers, often differently dressed, speaking the language of a distant region. This drama has not been lost on resident city dwellers nor on resident (or nonresident) social scientists, who have on occasion attributed the eruption of urban violence to the influx of migrants. These once popular theories have in time been largely

---

1. See Ashish Bose, *Studies in India's Urbanization 1901–1971* (Bombay: Tata McGraw-Hill, 1973); figures on urban-rural population percentages in ch. 2. Between 1950 and 1970 the urban population in Brazil grew from 36 to 55 percent; in Chile, from 60 to 76 percent; in Venezuela, from 54 to 78 percent. See *America en Cifras* 1974 (Washington, D.C.: Secretaria General de la Organizacio de Los Estados Americanos, 1974), pp. 43–45. No definition of "urban" is given, but generally an urban area in Latin America is considered to be a locality with a population of over 2,000.

2. Myron Weiner notes that a larger proportion of the urban growth of African than of Indian cities is the result of migration than natural population increase. In only five of India's twenty largest cities is more than half of the growth due to migration. "Sons of the Soil: Migration, Ethnicity and Nativism in India" (Center for International Studies, M.I.T. Working Paper MDG/75-3C/75-5, February 1975), p. 17.

discredited.³ Yet even if it can now be demonstrated that the individual migrant is not, any more than anyone else, the perpetrator of riots and protest, it is conceivable that the influx of migrants into a city creates a systemic impact on urban life which feeds the growth of political conflict. This chapter questions whether it is possible to trace ethnic conflict in Bombay to a particular pattern of migration.

In exploring the demographic foundations of Shiv Sena's emergence, three hypotheses warrant examination: (1) that nativism in Bombay is in part a reaction to a sudden change in the rate of in-migration; (2) that nativism arises with large numbers of migrants from other ethnic regions.⁴ These high levels of in-migration may be of particular importance in combination with conditions specified in a third hypothesis: (3) that nativism in Bombay results from low levels of out-migration of Maharashtrians—a proposition that derives from the assumption that out-migration siphons off potential discontent.⁵

Rate of Migration

Sudden flows of people cityward was not a factor in Shiv Sena's emergence. Shiv Sena's organization was not precipitated

---

3. Shiv Sena has charged that much of the crime, bootlegging, and violence in Bombay is traceable to migrants who move into Bombay slums. A critique of these sorts of assumptions is made by Joan Nelson in *Migrants, Urban Poverty, and Instability in Developing Nations* (Cambridge, Mass.: Center for International Affairs, Occasional Papers in International Affairs, Harvard University, November 22, 1969).

4. This and the preceding hypothesis are suggested in several studies, among which is Robin M. Williams, Jr., *The Reduction of Intergroup Tensions* (New York: Social Science Research Council, 1947). The proposition as cited in R. A. Schermerhorn, *Comparative Ethnic Relations: A Framework for Theory and Research* (New York: Random House, 1970), p. 241 is: "Migration of a visibly different group into a given area increases the likelihood of conflict; (a) the larger the ratio of the incoming minority to the resident population, and (b) the more rapid the influx."

5. Marcus Lee Hansen in his study of nineteenth-century migration notes that one motivation for the simplification of emigration procedures in Germany in the 1850s was the belief that emigration abroad would avoid political conflict at home. "The governments reversed their attitude of a decade before when they had looked upon every emigrant as a national loss and had hindered departure by a multitude of regulations. A strong motive was doubtless the belief that 'bloodletting' would preclude a revival of social disorders." *The Atlantic Migration* (Cambridge: Harvard University Press, 1941), pp. 288–99.

by any rapid surge of in-migration to Bombay. In fact there had been a more rapid influx of migrants in the decade 1941–51 than in the 1951–61 decade preceding Shiv Sena's founding. Between 1941 and 1951, the city of Bombay experienced a net increase of 950,000 migrants, a figure which dropped to 600,000 in the subsequent decade.[6] The percentage of the population that was migrant also dropped prior to the emergence of Shiv Sena. In 1951, migrants were 72.1 percent of the city's population;[7] in 1961, they were 64.5 percent.[8] In the decade 1951–61, migration accounted for only 49.5 percent of Bombay's growth, whereas in the previous decade (1941–51), migrants made up 73.3 percent of the city's population increase.[9] Shiv Sena's appearance, then, was not due to a sudden influx of migrants.

The percentage of *all* people born outside Bombay is clearly not the only relevant statistic in a consideration of how the rate of migration might have contributed to Shiv Sena's emergence. If either the percentage of Maharashtrians (Marathi-speakers) had suddenly declined or the percentage of South Indians, the original targets of Sena animosity, had rapidly increased prior to Shiv Sena's founding, then the rate of migration might serve as a plausible explanation. Neither phenomenon in fact occurred. In 1961, Marathi-speakers constituted 43 percent of the city's population, only 1 percent less than in 1951.[10] South Indians, moreover, did not migrate to Bombay in suddenly increased numbers. Between 1951 and 1961, the percentage of South Indians living in Bombay rose by less than 1 percent.

As Table 5 demonstrates, the rate of in-migration scarcely helps to explain either the growth in the 1960s of antimigrant

6. K. C. Zachariah, *Migrants in Greater Bombay* (New Delhi: Asia Publishing House, 1968), p. 47.
7. Ibid., p. 45.
8. Census of India, *Maharashtra*, vol. X, pt. X (1-B), 1961 (Bombay: Government Central Press, 1964), p. 202.
9. N. Baskara Rao, "Estimate of Migration in the Four Major Cities of India 1941–51 to 1951–61," *The Asian Economic Review*, 9 (November 1966), 63. In the course of the decade the absolute number of migrants grew from approximately 2.1 million to 2.7 million.
10. Census of India, *Bombay*, vol. IV, pt. II A, 1951 (Bombay: Government Central Press, 1953), p. 135; Census of India, *Maharashtra*, vol. IX, pt. X (1-B), p. 185.

Table 5. Distribution of major language groups in Bombay

	Bombay population	Marathi-speakers	Hindi-speakers	Gujarati-speakers	South Indians
1951	2,839,270	1,236,874 (43.6%)	211,323 (7.4%)	523,127 (18.4%)	220,819 (7.8%)
1961	4,152,056	1,775,114 (42.8%)	330,529 (8.0%)	792,771 (19.1%)	350,885 (8.4%)

Sources: Census of India, *Maharashtra*, 1961, vol. X, pt. X (1-B) (Bombay: Government Central Press, 1964), p. 185; and Census of India, *Bombay*, 1951, vol. IV, pt. II A (Bombay: Government Central Press, 1953), pp. 135-38.

feeling or the nature of the antagonism against South Indians in particular.[11] In the years leading up to 1966, the demographic "balance" between migrants and nonmigrants and between Maharashtrians and South Indians remained essentially unchanged. Shiv Sena did not owe its existence to any sudden change in the total number of migrants in Bombay or in any particular subgroup.

High In-migration and Low Out-migration

Although the rate of in-migration does not account for the growth of nativism in Bombay, it is important to consider the role other demographic variables might play. As suggested at the outset of the chapter, in particular instances nativism may be an outgrowth of two demographic factors working in combination, the high level of in-migration from other ethnic regions and low out-migration from the nativist locality.

The importance of high in-migration from other ethnic regions lies in the weak numerical position in which the local, native group is placed—a factor that may carry implications for their political and economic position. The role of low out-migration as a force contributing to nativism lies, as several studies

11. In 1951 the South Indian population in Bombay included speakers of Telugu (78,000), Tamils (59,295), Malayalam (31, 513), and Kannada (52,011). As 1961 census figures show, their population growth rates over the decade 1951–61 were faster for Tamil and Malayalam speakers (76% and 108% respectively) than for Telugu and Kannada speakers (25.6% and 59.3%). The numbers of Marathi-speakers in Bombay rose by 43.5% over the decade. In 1961, despite their fast growth rates, Tamils and Malayalees were only 2.51% and 1.58% of the city's total population.

have suggested, in the possibility that out-migration serves as an alternative to political protest.[12] As long as improved economic opportunities can be sought through out-migration, discontent and political activism can be contained. But as the possibility of out-migration and thus an avenue for advancement is cut off, the more ambitious groups that would have left the native village remain home and form a ready source for political mobilization. As outlined below, such a pattern of low out-migration as well as high in-migration from other regions, contributing to a situation of great social pressures, proves to be a recurring although not universal prelude to nativism.

Demographic Pressure in Bombay

A demographic profile of Bombay clearly reveals a pattern of high in-migration and low out-migration. Bombay ranks third highest (with 33.8 percent) among India's largest cities with populations over 100,000 in terms of its population born outside the state.[13] Because state boundaries in India coincide closely with linguistic divisions, this 33.8 percent figure suggests that fully one-third of Bombay's population has migrated to the city from other ethnic regions. The nonnative population of Bombay appears even larger if mother-tongue, rather than place-of-birth, figures are considered. As shown in Table 5, only 42.8 percent of Bombay's population speaks the local language, Marathi, as its mother tongue.

Not only, then, is a majority of Bombay's population non-Marathi speaking, indicating that Bombay draws people from a wide area throughout India, but also as further migration data demonstrate, Bombay is, not surprisingly, the preferred destination for vast numbers of Marathi-speaking migrants. The extremely low incidence of Maharashtrians living elsewhere in India provides considerable evidence that economic and educa-

12. See J. S. MacDonald, "Agricultural Organization, Migration and Labour Militancy in Rural Italy," Economic History Review, vol. 16, ser. 2 (1963–64), pp. 61–75. See also Hansen, Atlantic Migration, and Weiner, "Sons of the Soil."
13. This figure does not include the segment of Bombay's population born outside India. Census of India, Migration Tables, 1961, vol. I, pt. II-C (iii), pp. 586–93. The cities with still higher out-of-state populations are Bally (34.9%) and Bhatpara (39.9%), both located in West Bengal.

58 | *Ethnicity and Equality*

tional opportunities in Bombay have diverted Maharashtrians from seeking jobs and schooling outside the state. With slightly over 2 percent of its population residing in other states, Maharashtra ranks lowest next to West Bengal and Assam in the percentage of out-migrants (see Table 7). It is significant, moreover, that Bombay City attracts more Maharashtrian migrants than all of Maharashtra's other largest cities (over 100,000) combined.[14] A high incidence of in-migration from other ethnic regions, a similarly high influx from Maharashtrian areas, and a low out-migration of Maharashtrians to other destinations in India provide a powerful stimulus to interethnic tensions and nativist conflict.

Demographic Pressure in Other Indian Cities

Like Bombay, most of the other localities where nativist agitation has arisen have been characterized by a similar combination of low out-migration and high in-migration. The size of in-migration from other ethnic regions has been extremely large not only in Bombay (Maharashtra) but also in Gauhati (Assam), Bangalore (Mysore), and Chota Nagpur (Bihar)—all areas where antimigrant movements are prevalent (see Table 6).[15] By comparison with India's other cities of over 100,000 population, these areas have an extremely high proportion of interstate (interethnic) migrants in their populations. The percentage of interstate (interethnic) migration to India's 103 largest cities ranges between a low of 1 to 2 percent to a high of around 35 percent—the mean being 10.4 percent.[16] The four cities men-

14. In 1961 there were a total of 848,510 migrants living in Maharashtra's eleven largest cities exclusive of Bombay, compared to 1,110,553 in Bombay. Figures computed from Census of India, *Cities of Maharashtra*, vol. X, pt. X (2-12) (Bombay: Government Central Press, 1961).
15. The Telengana area was not included in the table since nativist agitations in that area do not involve interstate migrations. Census data on the Andhra population living in Telengana or in Hyderabad (other than interdistrict migration data) is not available. That population is, probably, considerably lower than the "outsider" population in the cities listed in the table.
16. See Mary F. Katzenstein, "Migration and Electoral Participation in India," in Myron Weiner and John Osgood Field, eds., *Electoral Politics in the Indian States*, vol. III (Delhi: Manohar Press, 1977), pp. 126–27.

Table 6. Proportion of "locals" to "outsiders" in India's nativist localities

City	Language	Percentage of population claiming mother tongue to be local language	Percentage of population born outside state
Bombay	Marathi	42.8	33.8
Gauhati	Assamese	45.2	19.2
Bangalore	Kannada	50.9	20.2
Chota Nagpur	Tribal languages including Munda, Ho, Oraon, Santali	5.8–39.6*	(not applicable)
Mean percentage of India's 103 largest cities:			10.4

*Figure indicates range of tribal population in districts of Santal Parganas, Palamau, Hazaribagh, Ranchi, Dhanbad, and Singhbum.

Sources: Place-of-birth data from Census of India, *Migration Tables*, 1961, vol. 1, pt. II-C (iii), Table D-V; excludes population born outside of India. Mother-tongue data from 1961 handbooks for districts in which city is located. Gauhati figure represents non-Assamese-speakers in urban area of Gauhati subdivision. Bangalore and Bombay city figures coincide closely with district figures. Chota Nagpur data from Myron Weiner, "Socio-Political Consequences of Inter-State Migration in India," in W. Howard Wriggins and James F. Guyot, eds., *Population, Politics, and the Future of Southern Asia* (New York: Columbia University Press, 1973), p. 210.

Table 7. Levels of out-migration from Indian states, 1961

State	Nativist locality	Rate (%)*
Punjab		6.7
Rajasthan		5.8
Bihar	Chota Nagpur	4.5
Kerala		3.7
Gujarat		3.6
Uttar Pradesh		3.6
Mysore	Bangalore	3.5
Madras		3.3
Madhya Pradesh		2.7
Andhra Pradesh	Telengana	2.5
Maharashtra	Bombay, Thana	2.3
West Bengal		1.8
Assam	Gauhati	1.0

*Rate computed by calculating the number of people born in a given state but living outside the state, divided by the number of people born in that state and still living there.

Source: Census of India, *Migration Tables*, 1961, vol. I, pt. II-C (iii).

tioned above rank in the highest quartile. If mother-tongue rather than place-of-birth data is examined, nativist localities appear to have a much higher proportion of "migrant" or "outsider" populations. In Bombay and Chota Nagpur, more than half the population are "outsiders"; in Gauhati and Bangalore, just under one-half the urban population claim to speak a language other than the local mother tongue.

Bombay, Chota Nagpur, Bangalore, and Gauhati are regions, then, with very high levels of in-migration. They are also regions with low levels of out-migration. This is particularly true of Gauhati and Bombay, which are located in states with among the lowest levels of out-migration in India (see Table 7). Bangalore is located in the state of Karnataka (formerly Mysore), which has an out-migration rate of 3.5 percent, the all-India mean. Although located in a state (Bihar) with a high out-migration pattern, Chota Nagpur appears in recent years to have had rather low levels of out-migration.[17]

The pressure-filled situation bred by high levels of in-migration and low levels of out-migration, thus, obtains in most of the localities in India where nativism has emerged.[18]

---

17. The rate of out-migration of tribals from the Chota Nagpur region is low compared with that of Bihar as a whole, a fact which would be easier to demonstrate if out-migration rates for smaller units (cities and districts) were available. See Myron Weiner, "Socio-Political Consequences of Inter-State Migration in India," in W. Howard Wriggins and James F. Guyot, eds., *Population, Politics, and the Future of Southern Asia* (New York: Columbia University Press, 1973), pp. 210–11.

18. For a careful discussion of the relationship between different measures of migration flows (linguistic dispersal, out-migration and nativist protest, etc.) see Myron Weiner, *Sons of the Soil: Migration and Ethnic Conflict in India* (Princeton: Princeton University Press, 1978), pp. 278–80.

It is instructive that the same combination of demographic factors that play an important role in Indian nativism also figures in the antimigrant reaction of nineteenth-century America. Nativism in the United States appeared periodically throughout the middle and late nineteenth century in the form of spontaneous demonstrations as well as organized political movements. The emergence of nativism as a political force was most pronounced in the East. In Massachusetts, for instance, in the mid-1850s, the nativist party captured the entire state senate, most of the house, and the governorship in several consecutive years. All along the Atlantic seaboard, heavy migration of rural Yankee Protestant groups into the cities and mill towns as well as a large influx of foreigners into such cities as New Orleans, Providence, Boston, New York, and Philadelphia increased interethnic tensions. As one study suggests, moreover, it was not only the in-

Inadequacies of a Demographic Explanation

Although a large influx of migrants from other ethnic areas combined with low levels of outward migration characterize many nativist movements, these demographic factors by themselves do not explain the emergence of nativism in India. Several problems are apparent: In some instances, nativism exists in the absence of at least one of the two specified demographic conditions. In several cases, high in-migration and low out-migration occur without stimulating the rise of nativism. Even in those instances where all three occur, the demographic factors fail to account for either the targets or the timing of nativist movements.

As discussed above, the incidence of nativism in most localities is accompanied by low rates of out-migration of the native community to other regions or very high rates of in-migration into the area from outside. There are exceptions, however. The state of Karnataka, in which Bangalore is located, has higher rates of outward migration than many Indian states (see Table 7). In the Telengana case, the level of migration of Andhras into the region is substantially lower than in the other nativist localities.

The fact that nativism has not emerged in many regions characterized by high rates of in-migration and low rates of out-migration also points to the inadequacy of the demographic explanation. Many examples can be cited of cities with out-of-state populations substantially higher than those with active nativist movements. Calcutta, with an out-of-state population of 28.5 percent and situated in a state with a low rate of out-migration, has never experienced an organized nativist movement. Nor can demographic factors explain why nativism in Chota Nagpur has been more active in Ranchi than in Jamshedpur, with its very high rates of in-migration (32.4 percent of the pop-

---

migration of different groups which contributed to antimigrant reactions, but also the lack of a ready means of out-migration: "As such, they [the foreign immigrants] were in visible competition with native stock groups which had migrated internally to the cities. In this respect, it cannot be stressed too strongly that in the pre-Civil War era, prior to the invention of the electric streetcar, practically no 'suburban escape' from close urban compaction was available for either middle-class or upper-class people" (Walter Dean Burnham, "A Note on Political Nativism in the United States," Unpublished Working Paper, p. 8).

ulation was born outside Bihar),[19] or why nativist movements have not erupted in Kolar (Karnataka) or Bhopal (Madhya Pradesh), which also have high levels of in-migration.

Even in the many localities where nativism has been accompanied by high in-migration and low out-migration, demographic variables do little to explain the timing of the antimigrant mobilization. In Bombay, for example, there had been a large inflow of migrants from other regions and low rates of migration away from Maharashtra for decades prior to the emergence of Shiv Sena. To explain why Shiv Sena was organized in the mid-1960s rather than at an earlier (or later) period clearly requires a consideration of factors other than migration.

Although a very rapid influx of immigrants might seem to be the demographic factor most likely to stimulate nativist reaction, the Shiv Sena experience demonstrates the possible occurrence of nativism in the absence of any sudden alteration in the percentages or ratios of migrant vs. native populations. Other demographic factors—large in-migrations from other ethnic regions combined with low out-migrations from among the local community—can be seen to contribute to the emergence of nativism. Yet while these demographic conditions are enabling forces in particular instances, they are neither sufficient nor even necessary prerequisites of nativism in general. Even where the demographic conditions obtain, they fail to provide an adequate explanation of nativist agitation. What is there about the numbers of "outsiders" that incites reaction? Why exactly does the confrontation between native and migrant, wrought by a high level of in-migration and low out-migration, prove conducive to political protest? Is it because the migrants are a social threat or because they endanger the political or economic position of the local community? To answer these questions requires pressing beyond the boundaries of demographic explanation.

19. Calcutta and Jamshedpur figures from Census of India, *Migration Tables*, 1961, vol. I, pt. II-C (iii), pp. 586–93.

4 | Economic Origins of Shiv Sena: Middle-Class Job Competition

Jobs, not numbers, explain the emergence of nativism in Bombay. Although the presence of a large population of "outsiders" contributed to the formation of Shiv Sena, the critical force giving rise to a sons-of-the-soil movement in Bombay has been the competition over jobs between middle-class Maharashtrians and non-Maharashtrians.

At the time of the reorganization of Bombay State, supporters of a separate Maharashtra protested what they described as the relegation of Maharashtrians to jobs as "clerks and coolies." It is the cause of the clerks, not of the coolies, that Shiv Sena has taken up. The desired occupation of Maharashtrian youth, Bombay wisdom has it, is an office job. Many young Maharashtrians whose fathers are laborers and who are the first in their family to get a secondary education set their sights on clerical and office work. Their ambitions are stymied, according to Shiv Sena, by "outsiders" who have moved to Bombay and usurped the desirable white-collar jobs. Shiv Sena's emergence is encapsulated in the story of one party worker, Mr. Jayakar.

Mr. Jayakar lives, with his father, mother, and two sisters, in two rooms on the third floor of a mill-owned *chawl* (tenement) on Ambedkar Road, Parel.[1] The kitchen, visible through the doorway, is small and dark with one high barred window to the outside. An iron cot stands in one corner of the sparsely furnished room next to the kitchen. Beside the cot are a table with a large radio, a locked trunk, and a bookcase with about twenty books. On the wall over the table is the room's single light. Sev-

---

1. The interview on which this profile is based was conducted in 1971. Jayakar is a pseudonym. In keeping with the individual's desire to remain unidentified, several other minor facts have been changed.

eral calendars with brightly colored pictures (two of Krishna playing the flute, one of a girl's face) are the only decorations on the wall.

Jayakar is a Maharashtrian Hindu of the Pathare Prabhu caste. Unlike most of the other families in the *chawl*, who have come from Ratnagiri or from other districts of the Konkan, his family has always lived in Bombay. Some relatives own land in Colaba district just south of Bombay. He has visited them but never stayed there.

Jayakar is twenty-one. His father, educated up to the seventh standard (several years past primary education), worked for many years as a mill laborer and is now a supervisor in one of the nearby mills. Jayakar's mother had several years in a Marathi-medium school, enough to write and read a little. Jayakar, himself, spent a few years in a municipality-run English-language school and then completed his schooling in Marathi-medium. He had several years of college, up to interarts (two years of college), but decided not to continue, he says, because he needed to earn money. Jayakar worked for a while in one of the mills, but he left his job after his supervisor got angry with him for irregular attendance. By then, Jayakar explained, he had already begun to work for Shiv Sena. A few months later he tried for a job in Voltas (a very large Bombay firm). At the interview he was asked his mother tongue and knew then, he insists, that he would not get the job. Now he is a full-time social worker[2] and the Sena's *shakha pramukh* (branch leader) for his area. He will look for another job before too long.

Jayakar explains that Shiv Sena is a social movement without political ambitions. It has gained much popularity in Bombay because it has pointed out many injustices, most important the practices of outsiders who come mainly from South India and who get jobs in the city, occupy government housing, and then bring relatives from their villages. These relatives do the same, and so the cycle continues. Jayakar says he does not know any South Indians personally (except one or two casual acquaintances who were in his college); in any case, he avows, his Voltas

2. The term "social worker" in India is a catchall phrase which describes someone engaged in community service, some of which may be highly political.

interview is an example of the problems Maharashtrians face.

Jayakar came to work for Shiv Sena through a friend of his, now a municipal corporator, who knew Bal Thackeray, the Sena's founder. He volunteered for work because he felt that there was a lot that could be done to improve conditions in his *chawl* and neighborhood. Jayakar and his co-workers have organized a small reading room; they have planned "functions" on special religious and national days; and they have organized help when someone had a problem (when there was a serious roof leak, they went to see the man in charge of the *chawl* and asked him to make repairs).

Jayakar is not sure where his life will take him over the next years. He may try to start a small business with a friend of his. Right now, he is happy spending his time in social work.[3]

Middle-Class Competition and the Rise of Shiv Sena

Whether Jayakar will realize his hopes of starting a small business remains to be seen. Both critics and sympathizers of Shiv Sena are quick to observe that the usual aim of an educated Maharashtrian is to find a good, secure office job. Maharashtrians, it is argued, do not have the ambition, guile, sense of gain, or capital to take up business; far better to find a safe, if low-salaried, office job than to enter into the risks of commercial pursuits. In the competition for office jobs, however, non-Maharashtrians, particularly South Indians, often fare better. Maharashtrians have difficulty competing, according to Bombay lore, either because South Indians will hire only from their own community or because South Indians speak better English, try harder to please their employers, and are better typists and stenographers than their Maharashtrian counterparts. Because Shiv Sena drew attention to the difficulties Maharashtrians had faced, the party won widespread sympathy among the Maharashtrian community.

Data on the relative occupational status of different linguistic

3. See also profile of a Shiv Sena worker, Mr. More, reported by Bryan Sharpe. "Bombay Teachers and the Cultural Role of Cities," Research Monograph No. 10, Center for South and Southeast Asia Studies, University of Berkeley, Berkeley, Calif., April 1973, pp. 63–83.

Table 8. Bombay families by income and mother tongue

Monthly family income (in rupees)	Mother tongue					
	Marathi		Gujarati		South Indian	
	#	%	#	%	#	%
Less than 50	175	2.9	64	2.1	14	1.9
50–74	349	5.7	117	3.9	22	3.0
75–99	915	14.9	176	5.9	72	9.8
100–149	1,759	28.7	449	15.0	177	24.0
150–249	1,583	25.8	806	27.0	196	26.6
250–499	978	16.0	796	26.6	176	23.9
500–999	244	4.0	304	10.2	58	7.9
1,000+	54	0.9	213	7.1	16	2.2
No or inadequate information	73	1.2	64	2.1	5	0.7

Source: D. T. Lakdawala et al., *Work, Wages and Well-Being in an Indian Metropolis* (Bombay: Bombay University Press, 1963), p. 281. © Bombay University. Reprinted by permission of Bombay University.

communities in Bombay demonstrate overwhelmingly that Maharashtrian perceptions of the competition from "outsiders" are realistically based. A large survey conducted in the early 1950s by a Bombay University professor, D. T. Lakdawala, revealed that in occupational status and in education, Maharashtrians lagged behind other communities living in Bombay.[4] The income figures shown in Table 8 indicate the relative economic backwardness of the Marathi-speaking communities. In Lakdawala's sample, for instance, the percentage of Maharashtrians earning a middle- to upper-middle-class salary (500–1,000 rupees per month) is distinctly lower (4.0 percent) than for the Gujarati (10.2 percent) or South Indian (7.9 percent) communities. Later studies have also concluded that Maharashtrians are underrepresented in higher-status jobs (administrative, professional, and clerical).[5]

---

4. D. T. Lakdawala, et al., *Work, Wages and Well-Being in an Indian Metropolis* (Bombay: Bombay University Press, 1963), chs. 5 and 6.

5. See analysis of CIDCO 1971 survey presented in S. P. Mohanty, "Sons of the Soil and their Socio-Economic Problems in Greater Bombay," *Journal of the Gujarat Research Society*, 36 (July 1974), p. 70. See also Mary F. Katzenstein, "Origins of Nativism: The Emergence of Shiv Sena in Bombay," *Asian Survey*, 13 (April 1973), p. 391.

Economic Origins of Shiv Sena | 67

The extent of Maharashtrian underrepresentation is revealed by Bombay-wide occupational figures; but the picture of economic competition confronting middle-class Maharashtrians is even more striking when a distinction is made between the newer and older industries of the city. A survey of employment rolls, conducted by the author in 1970, focused on selected industries, including relatively older ones, such as textiles, tobacco, and printing, and relatively new ones, such as chemicals, pharmaceuticals, insurance, and other service industries. As Table 9 demonstrates, it is in the newer industries that Maharashtrians are most poorly represented. In several of the older companies whose records were inspected, Maharashtrians at all salary levels were present in large numbers—well above the Maharashtrian percentage in the population (although, interestingly, even in the very large textile company #2, the percentage of Maharashtrians decreased with an increase in the salary level).

In the new companies, with rare exceptions Maharashtrians are employed in proportion to their population percentage of 43 percent only in the lower-income brackets designating manual labor. This underrepresentation of Maharashtrians in the better-paid jobs of the new industries is shown in the table. The areas where the percentage of Maharashtrian workers is at least equal to the population mean fall along a nearly perfect diagonal, showing how Maharashtrians share in the better-paid jobs in the older industries but are excluded from those jobs in the newer industries.[6]

6. In this study of job competition, names of company employees were used as indicators of ethnic background. A purposeful sample of twelve Bombay companies was selected which included large companies with more than 800 employees belonging to the traditional and modern sectors of the Bombay economy. All high-salaried employees earning above 500 rupees per month were counted. For the lower four salary brackets (0–199, 200–299, 300–399, 400–499) a sampling procedure was adopted. A random sample of 36 percent (n = 339), stratified by the four lower salary brackets, was drawn from the employment register of one of the companies, and it was assumed that the different proportions of ethnic communities in this sample approximated the ethnic population mixture of the company work force as a whole. Two subsamples of 18 percent (n = 173) and 3 percent (n = 36) were then drawn for that sample. For each of the four salary brackets a chi-square test was performed, testing for significant differences between the ethnic proportion of the assumed population values and the two subsamples. Since none of the eight tests indicated a statis-

Table 9. Percentage of Maharashtrians employed in selected Bombay industries by salary level (in rupees), 1970

	Semiskilled to white-collar							Laborer—Unskilled	
	1,500–1,000	999–800	799–600	599–600	499–400	399–300	299–200	0–199
Textile								
Company 1 (3,000 workers)	75*	43*	44*	66*	68*	65*	70*	52*
Company 2 (1,000 workers)	50*	44*	53*	80*	68*	80*	95*	82*
Tobacco								
Company 1 (1,500 workers)	13	39	13	4	32	44*	41*	27
Printing								
Company 1 (3,000 workers)	—	—	—	45*	66*	33	83*	66*
Heavy Machinery								
Company 1 (3,500 workers)	26	25	47*	58*	64*	61*	70*	77*
Chemicals								
Company 1 (800 workers)	18	20	15	44*	33	20	25	68*
Company 2 (1,000 workers)	31	21	31	32	55*	33	46*	75*
Company 3 (700 workers)	—	36	32	33	28	36	63*	50*
Company 4 (400 workers)	55*	—	20	33	60*	60*	100*	80*
Insurance								
Company 1 (400 workers)	—	—	—	—	25	14	—	—
Company 2 (300 workers)	6	—	12	14	20	40	44*	20
Company 3 (80 workers)	—	—	18	—	—	25	20	—

*Percentage of Maharashtrian workers is equal to or above population mean.
Source: Employment rosters of selected companies. "Maharashtrian" origin identified by surname of employee.

The economic competition between Maharashtrians and "outsiders" in Bombay is not a canard set afloat by Sena propaganda to delude Maharashtrian voters. Maharashtrians *are* economically behind several other communities in Bombay. As evidenced by the recruitment patterns of newer industries in the city, this situation substantially intensified prior to the Sena's emergence.

Shiv Sena Voting Strength and the Middle Class

The underrepresentation of Maharashtrians in middle-class jobs explains Shiv Sena's success in mobilizing Maharashtrian middle-class support. This success is vividly illustrated by the Bombay-wide results of the 1968 and 1973 municipal elections. In the solidly Maharashtrian middle-class constituencies of Girgaum and Dadar, Shiv Sena polled between 54 and 67 percent of the 1968 vote—higher than in any other Sena-contested constituency. In the predominantly Maharashtrian working-class areas, however, even where Shiv Sena candidates were elected, the margin of victory was considerably smaller.[7]

The 1973 municipal elections revealed much the same pattern. Although Sena candidates were elected by slighter margins in almost all constituencies, Sena candidates again fared better in middle-class neighborhoods. In several of the middle-class Dadar constituencies, Sena candidates won about 56 percent of the vote, 10 percent higher on the whole than in the labor areas of Parel.[8]

---

tically significant difference, a sample of 3 percent of each company work force was deemed sufficient for inferring the ethnic distribution in the lower salary brackets. This procedure was then applied to all twelve companies.

7. G. S. Badhe and M. U. Rao report in *The Bombay Civic Election of 1968* (Bombay: All-India Institute of Local Self-Government, n.d.), pp. 110ff. that Shiv Sena voting support was very high in Thakurdwar and Gymkhanas (54.3%), Opera House and Chowpati (49.1%), Dadar and M. Gandhi Swimming Pool (66.4%), Shivaji Park (63.7%), and Ruparel College and Kohinoor Mills (58.9%), but in working-class constituencies, even the successful Sena candidates won just over 50 percent of the vote.

8. See *Bombay Civic Journal*, 20 (March 1973), pp. 17–36. This middle-class/working-class differential exists irrespective of incumbency. See for example the more successful returns in Manohar Joshi's and Sudhir Joshi's contests in the solid middle-class area of Dadar as compared to the less impressive margins of Vijay Parvatkar and Vijay Gaonkar in the working class/lower-middle class area of Parel. All four were incumbents in the 1973 election.

Table 10. Relationship between class factors and party vote[10]

		Shiv Sena #	Shiv Sena %	Congress #	Congress %
Education	(n = 360)				
Low	(n = 203)	78	38.4	125	61.6
	(n = 82)	38	46.3	44	53.7
	(n = 50)	28	56.0	22	44.0
High	(n = 25)	16	64.0	9	36.0
Property	(n = 363)				
Low	(n = 195)	81	41.5	114	58.5
	(n = 78)	36	46.2	42	53.8
	(n = 73)	34	46.6	39	53.4
High	(n = 17)	11	64.7	6	35.3
Occupation	(n = 229)				
Low	(n = 102)	42	41.2	60	58.8
	(n = 55)	26	47.3	29	52.7
	(n = 58)	30	51.7	28	48.3
High	(n = 14)	7	50.0	7	50.0

The middle-class appeal of Shiv Sena is revealed not only in the electoral results of working- and middle-class constituencies but also in a survey of individual Bombay voters. In a 1971 study conducted by the author and a colleague, several different measures of class background pointed to the greater success of Shiv Sena among middle-class Maharashtrian voters. Table 10 shows the findings; the sampling procedure, questionnaire development, and indices are explained in Chapter 5.[9]

Shiv Sena's strength among the Maharashtrian middle class[10] in Bombay is impressive but not total. As the 1971 survey revealed, there are still large numbers of middle-class Maharashtrians who do not support Shiv Sena. Of the middle-class Maha-

---

9. Although class categories are scaled in the table from low to high, the "high" categories do not include the upper class of Bombay. The survey was conducted in slum, working-class, and middle-class neighborhoods and therefore excludes the extremely wealthy families living in neighborhoods of South Bombay. The n used in computing the occupational categories is low as female respondents were excluded.
10. Throughout the rest of this chapter the middle class will be defined as the educated elite: those who have matriculated, secured a diploma, or had any college or professional education. (Matriculation is equivalent to the completion of secondary education.)

rashtrians polled, 41 percent reported voting for Congress.[11] What explains why some middle-class Maharashtrians support Shiv Sena while others do not? The answer to this question is interesting not because it helps us to learn why Shiv Sena has been unable to increase its municipal representation: Shiv Sena's success in most of the Maharashtrian middle-class constituencies means that further inroads into Maharashtrian middle-class support would not change the Sena's position in the municipal corporation. Yet an answer to this question provides useful insights into the nature of Shiv Sena's special appeal.

Two casual impressions prevail in Bombay about the Maharashtrian middle-class voter who supports Shiv Sena and the middle-class supporter of Congress. One commonly held view suggests that no difference really exists. Examples are cited of members of the same families who are divided in their loyalties: former municipal corporators R. and D. Salvi are two of five brothers; three were active in Shiv Sena, two in Congress. What this view in fact suggests is that in terms of social or economic background, there is no discernible difference between the middle-class Maharashtrian who casts his vote for Congress or the one who casts his for Shiv Sena. A second opinion suggests that although there may not be a difference in social or economic attributes of Shiv Sena and Congress supporters, there are clear differences in attitudes. This view suggests that, at the very least, Congress voters are not explicit in their Maharashtrian "patriotism" or in their condemnation of "outsiders." Congress supporters, according to this view, sympathize with Sena objectives but take exception to the Sena's aggressive declarations and activities. As one Congress worker declared:

The Sena and Congress are no different in their concern for Maharashtrians. But the Congress as a national party cannot be so open. Take this election [the 1971 Parliamentary election]: the Sena claims to be the party of Maharashtrians. It has stood two Maharashtrians and supports a South Indian. Congress has nominated five Maharashtrians for five

11. Of the middle-class respondents who voted, all but 2 percent voted either for Shiv Sena or for Congress.

Bombay seats. We do not broadcast this from the public rostrum. As Congress, we cannot. But in campaigning from door to door, this is pointed out.[12]

This line of argument is extended to the Maharashtrian Sena and the Maharashtrian Congress voter. Both, it is contended, believe the demand for preferential treatment championed by Shiv Sena to be just. Their divergence occurs over the means and the openness with which the Maharashtrian cause is to be pursued.

A profile of the middle-class respondents from the 1971 survey suggests that neither view is entirely correct. There are important socioeconomic differences between the middle-class Maharashtrian who sympathizes with Shiv Sena and his Congress counterpart: the Shiv Sena middle-class supporter is younger and more socially mobile. In addition, as the second view correctly asserts, there are distinct attitudinal differences between Shiv Sena and Congress followers: although both Congress and Sena voters are strong advocates of quotas and preferences espoused by Shiv Sena, there is a clear divergence in their views of other aspects of interethnic relations and governmental authority.

Although the absolute numbers are small, Table 11 illustrates a greater tendency among the young, middle-class Maharashtrian than among older voters to support Shiv Sena. Of the youngest age group, twenty-one to thirty, the respondent was three times as likely to support Shiv Sena as to vote for Congress.

Shiv Sena's appeal appears strongest not only among the young but also among the most upwardly mobile. It is widely believed in Bombay that Shiv Sena finds particular sympathy among young Maharashtrians who are first in their families to be educated and who are pressured by the desire to improve on the father's blue-collar status and by the stark realities of the job market. This assessment is supported by the results of the 1971 survey. As illustrated in Table 12, Shiv Sena's voting strength

12. The Congress party worker quoted here requested not to be cited by name.

Table 11. Age and party vote among middle-class Maharashtrians (n = 75)

Age	Shiv Sena #	%	Congress #	%
21–30	19	76.0	6	24.0
31–50	21	52.5	19	47.5
51+	4	40.0	6	60.0

Table 12. Educational mobility and party vote among middle-class Maharashtrians (n = 54)

Educational mobility	Shiv Sena #	%	Congress #	%
Low	8	53.3	7	46.7
Medium	10	41.7	14	58.3
High	11	73.3	4	26.7

improves with increased social mobility from one generation to the next.[13]

Almost as interesting are the factors which *fail* to differentiate the Marathi-speaking middle-class supporter of Shiv Sena from his Congress counterpart. Among middle-class Shiv Sena voters there are no particular pockets of strength in certain castes;[14] nor, as might have been anticipated, are native Bombay voters more likely to support Shiv Sena than middle-class Maharashtrian migrants.[15]

In their normative views of interethnic relations, the supporters of Shiv Sena and Congress are also alike in several important respects. Shiv Sena and Congress voters both subscribed

13. The n of 54 for Table 12 is smaller than the number of respondents in the previous table since it was necessary to include only males in the analysis of educational changes over a generation. See Appendix 1 for measure of educational mobility.

14. When controls for education are introduced, caste does not appear to influence voter choice. Eighty-five percent of the Brahmin, 14% of the Maratha, and 92% of CKP/SKP caste groups fall in the middle-class category. Sixty percent of the Brahmin, 55% of the Maratha, and 57% of the CKP/SKP respondents favored Shiv Sena.

15. 59% of Shiv Sena supporters were migrants compared to 61% of Congress supporters.

Table 13. Interethnic relations, governmental authority, and party vote among middle-class Maharashtrians

	Shiv Sena		Congress	
	#	%	#	%
Gujarati identification with Maharashtra (n = 73)				
Yes	20	51.1	17	48.9
No	20	64.5	11	35.5
Don't know or refuse	2	40.0	3	60.0
South Indian identification with Maharashtra (n = 72)				
Yes	8	57.1	6	42.9
No	31	60.8	20	39.2
Don't know or refuse	4	57.1	3	42.9
Muslim loyalty toward India (n = 72)				
Yes	30	56.6	23	43.4
No	10	71.4	4	28.6
Don't know or refuse	3	60.0	2	40.0
Assimilation: who should change (n = 75)				
Migrants	32	72.7	12	27.3
Migrants and natives (neither or both)	12	38.7	19	61.3
Don't know or refuse	0	—	0	—
Migration controls (n = 75)				
Desirable	28	62.2	17	37.8
Undesirable	14	51.9	13	48.1
Don't know or refuse	1	33.3	2	66.7
Dictatorship for India (n = 75)				
Desirable	23	71.9	9	28.1
Undesirable	20	50.0	20	50.0
Don't know or refuse	1	33.3	2	66.7

almost unanimously to the extension of quotas for local residents in universities, government housing, and both skilled and unskilled jobs.[16]

Shiv Sena supporters, however, differed from Congress voters with respect to their views on migration policy and interethnic assimilation. As Table 13 illustrates, middle-class advocates of migration controls voted in relatively large numbers for Shiv Sena. Those who felt it was the responsibility of migrants rather

16. As is indicated in Appendix 2D, the question was phrased to provide a definition of "local" as meaning "of the state." In the overall poll, 25 of 479 distributed evenly among parties disagreed with the desirability of introducing quotas. This 5 percent negative response held for middle class and non-middle class alike.

than of migrants and natives together to adjust to the exigencies of Bombay's interethnic society voted in similarly disproportionate numbers for Shiv Sena. Shiv Sena voters are also somewhat more skeptical about the likelihood that "outsider" communities will identify with either Maharashtra or India.[17]

Unlike the background distinctions identified earlier, the differences in attitudes expressed by Shiv Sena and Congress voters could be as much the result as the determinant of their political preferences. By the time of the 1971 survey, Shiv Sena had been in existence for five years and the views of the Sena leadership on such issues as dictatorship and Muslim loyalty to India were widely known. It is possible that Sena voters had adopted, and were echoing, the opinions of the Sena leadership rather than expressing core or fundamental views of their own which had earlier drawn them into the Sena fold. Although these differences in attitudes between the middle-class Sena and Congress voter may not help specify the motivating factors that elicited electoral support, they do suggest that as of 1971, Sena and Congress middle-class voters held distinct outlooks toward important social and political matters. Younger, more educationally mobile Sena voters were also more impatient with social diversity and with the limited role that democratic values assign to government.

The Timing and Targets of Shiv Sena
  Timing

The difficulty that middle-class Maharashtrians have faced in the Bombay job market is long-standing. Why, then, did Shiv Sena arise only in 1966 and not earlier? The answer to this question lies partly in economic, partly in psychological factors.

First, it should be emphasized that Shiv Sena did not emerge from a situation of economic stagnation. Bombay has been one of India's most rapidly growing industrial centers. The city has

---

17. This skepticism appears less strong among Shiv Sena supporters in the case of attitudes toward South Indians. It may be explained by Thackeray's attempt prior to the 1971 elections to amend the Sena's xenophobic image and to court South Indians. The Sena's support of General Cariappa, a South Indian, for one of the parliamentary seats in Bombay was part of this campaign.

enjoyed an unrivaled position as a capital of textiles in India, and has in recent decades become a center of metal and chemical industries. The city's port accounts for slightly under one-half of the total customs revenue from shipping for all of India; perhaps the most striking measure of Bombay's commercial and industrial preeminence is the fact that Bombay alone accounts for 30 percent of all income tax collected in the country.[18]

In the years leading up to Shiv Sena's founding, the Bombay economy fared well. One estimate suggests that between 1962 and 1967 the number of office jobs increased by 28 percent in contrast to an 8 percent increase in industrial blue-collar employment.[19] In the organized sector, where most middle-class jobs lie, employment grew steadily in the first half of the sixties.[20] It was in this period of relatively strong growth that *Marmik*'s comments on the "injustice" to Maharashtrians (which appeared regularly in the 1965–66 issues) won wide appeal. And it was in this period, in 1966, that Shiv Sena was founded.

In the next several years after 1966, Bombay like the rest of India suffered an economic recession. The accompanying decline in employment probably enhanced Shiv Sena's prospects at the polls in 1968. But even this correlation may be spurious. In nearby Thana, where Shiv Sena captured the municipality in 1967, employment in the organized sector in fact grew between 1966 and 1967.[21]

Shiv Sena's founding in 1966, and the party's success in Thana in 1967, thus followed periods of economic growth, not stagnation. Nevertheless there is good reason to think that the relatively bright employment picture in Bombay did not correspond to Maharashtrian perceptions of job prospects. There are two reasons why this may be so. The first is that along with the growth in job opportunities, there was an explosion of qualified (educated) job applicants. In the fifteen years before Shiv Sena's

18. B. A. V. Sharma and R. T. Jangam, *The Bombay Municipal Corporation: An Election Study* (Bombay: Popular Book Depot, 1962), pp. 2–3.
19. Shanti Patel, "Twin City Bombay," lectures given at Vasantvyakhanmala, Poona, May 17, 1971, p. 5.
20. See Table A1 in Appendix IX.
21. Heather and Vijay Joshi, *Surplus Labour and the City: A Study of Bombay* (Bombay: Oxford University Press, 1976), p. 58.

founding, the growth in educational enrollment in the Bombay area was phenomenal. Between 1960 and 1966, primary enrollment doubled from 2 million to 4 million students in western Maharashtra. Secondary enrollment rose from slightly under 2 million to 6½ million students.[22] At the University of Bombay alone, enrollment rose by about 300 percent, from 24,000 in the early 1950s to a total of nearly 90,000 students in the early 1970s.[23]

The key educational development, however, was the rise in the number of matriculates (graduates from secondary school).[24] In 1950, in western Maharashtra, 22 percent of the male population age thirteen to fifteen was enrolled in school. By 1965, this figure had risen to 43 percent. From this fact, it can be safely assumed that the number of matriculating males doubled in fifteen years. A sudden rise in the number of matriculates meant a

22. Government of Maharashtra Education Department, *Educational Development in Maharashtra State, 1950–51 to 1965–66* (Bombay: Government Central Press, 1968), fol. p. 90.

23. Statistics taken from annual reports of appropriate years. See *University of Bombay Annual Report* (Bombay: Bombay University Press).

24. It is improbable that Maharashtrian educational levels have risen at a faster rate than those of other communities. Although there is little data on this topic, it is generally believed that if any group has advanced in education at a disproportionately rapid pace, it is the Gujaratis. The assertion is commonly made that Gujaratis as a commercial community traditionally brought their sons into the family business and thus saw little need for education. Now, as Gujaratis seek other occupations and as education becomes more generally valued, Gujaratis are eager—and have the funds—to see their children educated. A sketchy look at the numbers and nature of the newer constituent colleges in Bombay bears this observation out. For the most part, the older colleges, built in the 1950s, have a cosmopolitan or predominantly Maharashtrian enrollment. The new constituent colleges, however, founded after 1960, seem to cater chiefly to the Gujarati community. Of the colleges established in the 1950s, Ruparel, Parle, Kirti, and Siddharth are predominantly Maharashtrian. Kishinchand Chelleram is predominantly Gujarati and Sindhi; Siddharth College of Law and Nair Dental College are cosmopolitan. Of those established in the 1960s, Dayanand College is Maharashtrian and SIES is cosmopolitan. Semaiya, Kelavi Mandal in Vile Parle, Jhaveri, Jhunjhunwala, Patkar, Semavi, Dahunukar College of Commerce, Kunhani, Chinai, Narsee Mongee, Sidhana College of Education, and Sardar Patel College of Engineering are predominantly Gujarati. (Identification of colleges based on an estimate by an employee in the University Registrar's Office, Bombay.)

While Maharashtrians have entered educational establishments in rapidly growing numbers, it seems unlikely that their educational mobility exceeds that of non-Maharashtrian groups in Bombay.

sudden growth of job seekers, unequipped with technical or professional skills but unwilling to accept manual labor. Many of these matriculates were the first in their families to be educated. With fathers often employed in factory labor, the pressure on the son to find nonmanual employment was extreme. For this pool of job seekers, clerical and office jobs were positions of first priority. In Bombay's tight job market, Shiv Sena's nativist appeals likely found particular sympathy among this large group of newly educated young males.[25]

The second reason the Maharashtrians may have been more distressed about job prospects than growth figures might have warranted is not economic but psychological. In 1960 the efforts of the Samyukta (independent) Maharashtra movement were rewarded, after nearly five years of heated struggles, with the formation of a unilingual state, the capital of which was Bombay. With this change in political status, Maharashtrians expected a change in their economic prospect within the city. As one Maharashtrian social scientist observed, "the frustrating feeling . . . of being nobody, though felt earlier too, was more poignant now because Bombay was no longer just another metropolis but a capital of their own state."[26] Shiv Sena was quick to remind its followers of the unfulfilled promises of Samyukta Maharashtra: speaking in particular to the lot of government employees, an article in *Marmik*, appearing in 1966, began, "After Independence, and especially after Samyukta Maharashtra came into existence, it was the expectation of Government employees that their condition would improve in this state. . . ."[27] When such expectations seemed to carry little hope of fulfillment, the Sena was able to find fertile soil for the organization of nativist protests. The combination of the raised hopes of the early 1960s, the explosion of educated job-seekers, and the economic set-

25. Several school and college principals whom I interviewed in the labor area of Parel (H. R. Karnik, Dayanand College; H. D. Gaokar, KEMS High School) observed that Shiv Sena's attraction was probably strongest for students in their institutions who were the first in those students' families to matriculate but were unable to find "suitable" (white-collar) jobs.
26. Sudha Gogate, *Rise of Regionalism in Bombay City* (New Delhi: Sampradayikta Virodhi Committee, 1970), p. 16.
27. "Maharashtra State Government Employees—This Is Your Story," Feb. 6, 1966.

backs of the mid-sixties contributed to stimulating the rise of the Sena in 1966 and to winning the party the support of a large section of the Maharashtrian middle class.

Targets

Several questions remain to be answered about Shiv Sena's targets. Why should the party have singled out South Indians among Bombay's many non-Maharashtrian communities? And why should the Sena have leveled responsibility for Maharashtrian economic difficulties on an *ethnic* target rather than on a *class* of industrialists or "capitalists"?

The Sena's pinpointing of South Indians as targets for nativist animosity can be explained by middle-class economic competition far more satisfactorily than by demographic factors. South Indians in Bombay, constituting 8.5 percent of the city's population, are scarcely greater in number than Hindi-speakers and constitute well under one-half of the Gujarati-speaking population. As mentioned in Chapter 3, moreover, South Indians did not move to Bombay in sudden large numbers prior to the Sena's emergence.

The Sena's focus on South Indians rather than the as numerous Hindi-speakers derives principally from the fact that the bulk of Hindi-speakers in Bombay are laborers and present no competition for the Maharashtrian middle class.[28] The explanation, however, for the Sena's targeting of South Indians rather than Gujaratis—a relatively prosperous community in Bombay—is only partially economic. It is true that, as the Sena claims, South Indians are concentrated in middle-class, clerical, and office positions. Contrary to common beliefs, however, their numbers in these white-collar occupations are somewhat less than that of the Gujarati community.[29] The Sena's preoccupation with South Indians, then, must be explained at least partially in cultural terms. In language, dress, food, and cultural traditions, South Indians are significantly more distant from Maharashtrians than are Gujaratis. This distance, rendering South Indians more conspicuous, contributes to the belief that they outnumber

28. Lakdawala et al., *Work, Wages and Well-Being*, p. 281.
29. See ibid., p. 468, and Mohanty, "Sons of the Soil," p. 70.

80 | *Ethnicity and Equality*

other communities in white-collar occupations and in turn makes South Indians likely targets for nativism. Finally, because they are fewer in number than Gujaratis in Bombay and are considerably less powerful politically, South Indians are *easier* targets.

Left-wing critics of Shiv Sena have charged the party with diverting Maharashtrian attention away from the fundamental economic problems of the city; class exploitation, not ethnic competition, bars Maharashtrians from economic equality, they say. But for middle-class Maharashtrians the Shiv Sena's position is closer to the mark: it is the non-Maharashtrian middle classes rather than the industrial and commercial magnates that stand between the jobs Maharashtrians have and those they want.[30]

The existence of middle-class competition in Bombay goes a long way toward explaining the emergence of Shiv Sena and, similarly, the absence of nativist movements in other cities. In Calcutta, where non-Bengalis constitute about 40 percent of the population, whatever nativist sentiment exists has never been organized into a political movement. This can be best explained by the absence of interethnic middle-class competition in the city.[31] As a West Bengal survey observed some years ago: "Amongst the total middle-class family units of Calcutta, the Bengali middle-class families constitute as much as 77.8 percent as against 50.7 percent for all classes combined."[32] While the

30. Even Samyukta Maharashtra leaders traded in nativist sentiment. As Robert Stern remarked, "The leftist leaders of the Samyukta Maharashtra Samiti found it more to their ideological taste to view the struggle for Bombay city as a class conflict rather than a sectarian struggle among 'communalists....'" Yet the anti-Gujarati sentiment of the period suggests that the Samiti's followers saw the movement as much in communal as in class terms. Robert W. Stern, *The Process of Opposition in India: Two Case Studies of How Policy Shapes Politics* (Chicago: University of Chicago Press, 1970), p. 47.

31. Middle-class competition for jobs is much higher in Calcutta than in Bombay, as indicated by figures on educated unemployment (see Appendix IX, Table A2). In Calcutta, however, the competition is among, rather than between, ethnic groups.

32. A Government of West Bengal survey, conducted in 1953, quoted in N. K. Bose, *Calcutta, Readings for Indian Civilization* (University of Chicago, 1961). Mimeographed, p. 12.

Bengali middle-class may dominate in Calcutta, the same can not be said of Maharashtrians in Bombay. The genesis of Shiv Sena lay principally in the competition for middle-class jobs between Maharashtrians and non-Maharashtrians in Bombay. Compared to their percentage in the population, Maharashtrians held fewer white-collar positions than did several other ethnic communities in Bombay. The protests voiced in *Marmik* and at the Sena rallies, pointing to the relative backwardness of the Maharashtrian community, were not political myths but economic realities.

Shiv Sena's great electoral success in 1968, however, would have been impossible had not large numbers of the Maharashtrian working class cast their lot with the new nativist organization. While job competition explains the wide appeal of Shiv Sena among the middle-class Maharashtrian community, it accounts less satisfactorily for the mobilization of the working-class vote. It is to the nature of working-class support that the next chapter is addressed.

5 | Shiv Sena's Working-Class Support

Middle-class job competition was a major factor in stimulating the rise of Shiv Sena. Yet the party's electoral success in the municipal contests of 1968 and 1973 owed as much to working-class as to middle-class support. In both municipal elections, Shiv Sena triumphed in virtually all of the predominantly Maharashtrian middle-class constituencies; but these middle-class pockets constituted no more than one-seventh of the total number of seats won by the party.[1] Clearly, Shiv Sena had mobilized working-class as well as middle-class voters.

But Shiv Sena's inroads into the working-class and poor constituencies were not strong enough.[2] Outflanked in 1968 by the (then undivided) Congress and in 1973 by Congress (R), the Sena has never controlled the corporation, acceding instead to the status of chief opposition. The party's inability to win more than 42 of the corporation's 140 seats was due only in part to the Sena's alienation of the non-Maharashtrian voter; it was also due to the Sena's failure to establish a firmer base among the Maharashtrian lower classes, many of whom cast their votes for the Congress party. The results of these elections pose the important question of the nature of Shiv Sena's working-class appeal and, particularly, of the difference between the Maharashtrian

---

1. In 1968, in the following eight constituencies, the losing Shiv Sena candidate came within 3 percent of the Congress victor (even a small increase in Maharashtrian working-class support would have meant the election of a Sena councilor): Wadi Bunder and Dongri Market (#26), Gloria Church and Narialwadi (#29), Nair Hospital and Arthur Rd. Hospital (#50), Ambedkar Nagar (#57), Hindu Colony (#87), Dharavi (N) and Sion (E) (#92), Sahar and Chakala (#109), and Mamlatdar Wadi (#118). See Badhe and Rao, *The Bombay Civic Election of 1968* (Bombay: All-India Institute of Local Self-Government, n.d.), pp. 109–21.

2. This is recognized by the Sena itself. See Pramod Nawalkar's analysis of the 1970 MLA bye-election: "We Fought, We Won," *Marmik*, Diwali issue, 1970.

who casts his vote for Shiv Sena and the Maharashtrian supporter of Congress in Bombay.

In this chapter, we explore three explanations which seek to account for this difference. The first suggests that the factors drawing the working-class Maharashtrian to Shiv Sena are much the same as for the middle-class voter: e.g., distress at the economic competition posed by "outsiders." The working-class Maharashtrian who fails to support Shiv Sena, then, would be one who does not perceive economic competition to be acute.

An alternative explanation is also primarily economic; it suggests that Shiv Sena is able to mobilize working-class votes more successfully by providing services and material amenities than by invoking alarm over job competition. If this is correct, working-class Shiv Sena voters should be found predominantly in localities where party infrastructure is strong and the delivery of goods and services effectively managed.

A third explanation suggests that the working-class support for Shiv Sena is based not on economic factors but on the "rightist" appeal of the party and the anti-Muslim, anticommunist, and authoritarian image that the party has assumed. By this argument, the working-class supporters of Shiv Sena and Congress can be differentiated by the extent to which they hold to what is commonly considered to be a "right-wing" ideology.

This analysis of the Sena's electoral support is based on 479 interviews with Maharashtrian voters and an approximately equal number of the South Indian electorate in Bombay. The survey was conducted immediately following the parliamentary elections of March 1971. The lists of respondents were compiled through a purposeful sample of neighborhoods and a random selection of names from the electoral rolls of those neighborhoods. The intent of this sampling procedure was to evaluate the effect of contextual and individual attributes on the political preferences of voters (see Appendix II). The neighborhood characteristics thought to be of greatest importance were the ethnic mixture, the previous strength of political parties, and the class character of the area. The scheme for the sample design is reproduced in Appendix III.

Economic Competition and the Maharashtrian Worker

Has Shiv Sena's claim about the economic threat posed by "outsiders" found a receptive hearing among the Maharashtrian working class? In answering this question, it is worth considering not only whether Maharashtrian laborers feel that they must compete for jobs with laborers from other ethnic groups but also whether such competition exists in reality. This latter, "objective" issue is not easily determined. The compartmentalized structure of the Bombay labor market suggests that the working-class job competition between ethnic groups is not very intense. There exists a high degree of occupational specialization by industry, with certain ethnic groups predominating in commerce, construction, etc. Furthermore, within an industry there has been and continues to be considerable job specialization. In textile labor, for example, Maharashtrians have traditionally predominated[3] but other ethnic groups are also represented. Within the mills, different ethnic groups are found concentrated in different departments. "Bhaiyas" from Uttar Pradesh are thought to be particularly suited to spinning (mixing to speed frame).[4] Weavers often include disproportionate numbers of South Indians. The same differentiation occurs in other industries. Traditionally, in the railway machine shops, Kamathis have predominated among the molders, Muslim Boris among the tinsmiths, and in the wheel shops the smiths have been mostly Lohars from Gujarat.[5]

Both between and within industries, then, there is a high level of ethnic specialization; but it is not total. At least several individuals from a wide cross section of linguistic groups can be found

---

3. In his study of the textile industry, Morris D. Morris writes that in 1943 the Bombay Millowners Association published an English-Gujarati-Marathi glossary of mill terminology to assist officers and supervisory staff who did not speak Marathi. *The Emergence of an Industrial Labor Force in India* (Berkeley: University of California Press, 1965), p. 131.

4. R. G. Gokhale, *The Bombay Cotton Mill Worker* (Bombay: Millowners' Association, n.d.), p. 19.

5. A. R. Burnett-Hurst, *Labour and Housing in Bombay* (London: P. S. King and Son, 1925), p. 98.

within the employ of most industries and departments in Bombay. It is possible, on the one hand, that job differentiation by ethnic group diminishes the sense of ethnic competition by isolating laborers of different linguistic groups from one another. On the other hand, because there is at least some ethnic heterogeneity both within industries and departments, and because of the chronic job shortage, there would seem to be potential for interethnic rivalry.

The results of the voter survey bear out the conclusion, however, that interethnic job competition did not figure heavily in the Maharashtrian laborers' support of Shiv Sena. Respondents were asked why they felt Maharashtrians experienced difficulty finding jobs. Several responses could be given. Of the 282 working-class (Maharashtrian) respondents who gave at least one answer, by far the largest number (135, or 47.9 percent) replied that it was because they had "no influence." Only 20 (7.1 percent) specifically mentioned that other groups made it difficult for Maharashtrians to find employment.

Respondents were also asked for what principles they felt Shiv Sena stood. Again, multiple responses were possible. Of the 380 middle- and working-class respondents who gave at least one answer, 19 percent of the working-class voters mentioned a job-related "principle," compared to 74 percent of the middle-class respondents who spoke specifically of Shiv Sena's protection of Maharashtrian economic interests. By far the largest number of working-class respondents (64 percent) included among the Sena's principles the idea of "Maharashtra for Maharashtrians." The 19 percent who mentioned job-related factors as preeminent were divided equally in their partisan preference, half of them supporting Shiv Sena and the other half supporting Congress.

One hypothesis around which the survey design was formulated postulated that the sense of economic competition might not be transmitted through the workplace but rather through the neighborhood environment. It was thought that the voter choice of working-class people in middle-class neighborhoods would, by this hypothesis, be more similar to the choices of mid-

Table 14. Relationship between class character of neighborhood and party vote

Neighborhood	Working-class vote for Shiv Sena (%)
Dharavi 7 (n = 30)	23
Parel 4 (n = 10)	37
Parel 1 (n = 21)	38
Matunga (n = 14)	39 (middle-class neighborhood)
Parel 2 (n = 22)	39
Kamathipura (n = 22)	42
Dadar (n = 8)	43 (middle-class neighborhood)
Dharavi 4 (n = 12)	45
Cumbala Hill (n = 17)	50
Wadala Springs 6 (n = 4)	90
Wadala Springs 4 (n = 0)	—

dle-class respondents in middle-class neighborhoods than to those of working-class voters in working-class neighborhoods. As Table 14 demonstrates, this turned out not to be the case.

Although Maharashtrian laborers have not felt the acute sense of economic competition experienced by the Maharashtrian middle class, economic factors were not irrelevant to Shiv Sena's initial ability to mobilize the working class.[6] Economic tensions between lower-income sectors of different ethnic groups are reported to have erupted in at least one instance over housing. A. R. Desai and S. D. Pillai recount the following about a Bombay slum where there are few South Indians:

It was reported that [Shiv Sena's] ire is therefore directed against another immigrant community, the Uttar Pradeshis or "Bhaiyas" and Muslims who, too, are largely immigrants from other regions. Some of these Hindi-speaking immigrants moreover are "landlords" of the area, and it appears that conflict was already there between Maharashtrian

---

6. There are certainly incidents of resentment of "outsiders" among Maharashtrian laborers. In one Shiv Sena *shakha* located in a slum area which the author visited, reference was made to Kamathi construction laborers taking jobs away from Maharashtrians. This observation was made, however, only when the author directly inquired whether non-Maharashtrians were moving into jobs that Maharashtrians could fill—not in response to earlier questioning about why Maharashtrians have difficulty finding jobs. The Shiv Sena union, Bharatiya Kamgar Sena, uses Maharashtrian-chauvinist slogans cautiously; its leaders concede that in the many unions which are composed of an ethnically mixed labor force, the use of such slogans will alienate support.

"tenants" and Hindi-speaking "landlords." . . . When some Maharashtrians wanted to pitch their shacks in a certain part of the slum they faced stiff opposition from the Uttar Pradeshi and Muslim "landlords" of that area.[7]

The economic pressures of the mid-1960s recession may have also created a climate favorable to a party of protest. The year 1965–66 was one of serious drought, influencing agricultural output and industrial production throughout the country. In Maharashtra, for instance, the production of food grains dropped from 6.75 million tons to 4.70 million tons.[8] In Bombay, employment declined, especially in labor-intensive industries. The demand for factory workers, which had been rising steadily through 1964, declined sharply. In 1965 and 1966 the absolute employment level in factories, not just the rate of growth, decreased.[9] The economic decline was particularly severe in the already troubled textile industries and therefore greatly affected Maharashtrian blue-collar employment. This economic setback may help to explain why many Maharashtrian laborers were drawn to Shiv Sena in the mid-1960s; but it does not provide an indication of why only some working-class Maharashtrians favored Shiv Sena.

Support for Shiv Sena in working-class and slum neighborhoods can be accounted for, to some extent, by the party's ability to provide needed services. V. S. Naipaul gives a vivid account of a visit he made to one slum where Shiv Sena's organization was strong. (Slums typically house white-collar workers, blue-collar workers, and the unemployed.)

---

7. A. R. Desai and S. D. Pillai, *A Profile of an Indian Slum* (Bombay: University of Bombay Press, 1972), p. 213.
8. Maharashtra Economic Development Council, *Maharashtra, An Economic Review* (Bombay: S. B. Sakhalkar, MEDC, 1971), p. 7. Also see Heather and Vijay Joshi, *Surplus Labour and the City: A Study of Bombay* (Bombay: Oxford University Press, 1976), Table III. 3.
9. According to the Statistical Abstract compiled by the Department of Economics and Statistics, Government of Maharashtra (unpublished), the total number of workers employed in Bombay factories, beginning with 1961, was as follows: 505,390; 522,862 in 1962; 552,389 in 1963; 572,738 in 1964; 572,447 in 1965; 552,672 in 1966; 556,357 in 1967; 539,005 in 1968, and 551,937 in 1969.

The most important discovery was the extent and nature of Shiv Sena's control. A squatters' settlement, a low huddle of mud and tin and tile and old boards, might suggest a random drift of human debris in a vacant city space; but the chances now were that it would be tightly organized. The settlement . . . was full of Sena "committees"; and these committees were dedicated as much to municipal self-regulation as to the Sena's politics: industrial workers beginning to apply something of the discipline of the factory floor to the areas where they lived. . . .

There were eight Shiv Sena committee rooms in the settlement. The one we went to was on the main lane. It was a stuffy little shed with a corrugated-iron roof; but the floor, which the engineer remembered as being of earth, was now of concrete; and the walls, formerly of plain brick, had been plastered and whitewashed. There was one portrait. And interestingly, it was not of the leader of the Shiv Sena or of Shivaji, the Sena's warrior-god, but of the long dead Dr. Ambedkar, the Maharashtrian untouchable leader. . . .[10]

In this colony, Naipaul was proudly shown the dustbins the committees had placed along the lanes for the disposal of refuse.

In the Cumballa Hill[11] slum area, where Shiv Sena received a high 50 percent of the vote, a large number of the respondents mentioned that the Shiv Sena men had put out a fire when some of the huts had been accidentally set ablaze, and that the Sena had been responsible for arranging the *zopadpatti* (slum) connection to the city's water main. A visit to a large slum colony in the suburbs (located in the constituency of a Shiv Sena coporator), gave the same impression. One of the leaders of the Shiv Sena organization in the colony, not a Maharashtrian but a Muslim from Andhra Pradesh, guided his visitors through Shiv Sena-paved lanes of one of the colony's sections—a stark contrast to the muddy paths and refuse-strewn alleys of the farther section of the slum. Elsewhere in the city, Shiv Sena *shakhas*, or committees, have organized other "civic improvements": an electric connection, permits to set up additional dwellings, etc. As Naipaul has written, "Lower down, in the *chawls* and the squatters' settle-

10. V. S. Naipaul, "Bombay: The Skyscrapers and the Chawls," *New York Review of Books*, June 10, 1976.
11. Cumballa Hill is a wealthy area of Bombay. The slum is located at the base of a hill on which rise the modern apartment complexes of Bombay's upper classes.

ments of the city, among the dispossessed, needs [are] more elemental: food, shelter, water, a latrine."[12] In the low-income areas of the city, Shiv Sena had not ignored these needs.

Right-Wing Extremism and the Maharashtrian Working Class

Yet does the inevitably pressing importance of economic concerns mean that other ideological issues among the working classes are unimportant? Are there no ideological differences between the Maharashtrian working-class supporter of Shiv Sena and his Congress counterpart? More specifically, how successful has Shiv Sena been in mobilizing working-class support through its "rightist" appeal?

The party has explicitly sought a rightist image. The Bharatiya Kamgar Sena, the Shiv Sena union, has declared itself the only organization capable of fighting communist unions "on their own terms" or, by implication, with violence. By virtue of its virulent anticommunism, Shiv Sena soon acquired a reputation for right-wing extremism. But that reputation had other foundations. The very name Sena (army), the highly disciplined public meetings, and the closely guarded style of the party organization all contributed to this image. It was not, in fact, until several years after the party's electoral debut in 1968 that it began to champion anti-Muslim and anticommunist causes. In 1971 a handbill passed out to voters by Manohar Joshi, a parliamentary candidate and right-hand man of Bal Thackeray, urged voters to "read this and think before it is too late. . . . Of the many violent tenets of communism, one is . . . godlessness. . . . Your valuable vote to Shiv Sena will put [a] hundred nails in the communist coffin."[13] After the state legislature bye-election of 1970, Bal Thackeray declared in *Marmik*, "I am not ashamed of calling myself Hindu. Our victory is a victory of Hindu-ness, the victory of true nationalism. What is shameful in it? Jan Sangh, Hindumahasabha, R.S.S., and Swantantra were with us. I thank them."[14]

12. "Bombay: Skyscrapers and Chawls," p. 29.
13. Manohar Joshi, "Read This and Think," political handbill of parliamentary candidate on Shiv Sena ticket, 1971.
14. *Senapati* (Bal Thackeray) editorial, *Marmik*, Diwali issue, 1970.

The responses of the Maharashtrian working-class voters interviewed in the survey indicate a general lack of sympathy with rightist or extremist principles. In their critical view of dictatorship and in their positive attitudes toward Muslim and non-Maharashtrian linguistic groups, the majority of working-class respondents express a tempered, moderate outlook. It is clear, however, that Shiv Sena working-class voters exhibit more extremist views than their Congress counterparts. Even this observation, however, bears qualification: Although on most questions those who express the more extremist views are more likely to support Shiv Sena than those who take a more moderate stand, on many questions a larger absolute number of persons exhibiting extremist or less tolerant opinions in fact support Congress.

On the issue of dictatorship, respondents were asked to give their reaction to the statement, "At least over the short run, what India needs is a dictatorship." Because the Shiv Sena leadership had publicly supported the idea of an "enlightened" dictatorship as a necessary short-term corrective to India's economic and social problems, one might expect a clear division of views between Sena and Congress supporters. As Table 15 indicates, however, the majority of working-class respondents did not concur with the statement, although a relatively high proportion of those who felt dictatorship was desirable, compared to those who felt it to be undesirable, claimed to support Shiv Sena.

Respondents were also asked to give their opinion on a statement about political violence: "These days to counter the violence of cèrtain groups, we must be prepared to use violence—you might say, 'sword for sword.'" Again, a relatively high percentage of those agreeing supported Shiv Sena, as compared to those who disagreed. But as is also the pattern for many of the other questions, in *absolute* figures, a higher number of those advocating the use of violence supported Congress than supported Shiv Sena (see table).

One of the questions that the survey attempted to probe was the success of Shiv Sena's anticommunist diatribes among the Maharashtrian working class. Until Shiv Sena's emergence, the parties of the Left, the Samyukta Maharashtra Samiti in particu-

Table 15. Interethnic relations, governmental authority, and party vote among working-class Maharashtrians

	Shiv Sena #	Shiv Sena %	Congress #	Congress %
Dictatorship for India (n = 279)				
Desirable	45	50.0	45	50.0
Undesirable	59	39.6	90	60.4
Don't know or refuse	12	30.0	28	70.0
"Necessary" use of violence (n = 276)				
Agree	67	43.2	88	56.8
Disagree	32	34.0	62	66.0
Don't know or refuse	14	51.9	13	48.1
Assimilation: who should change (n = 280)				
Migrants	80	44.7	99	55.3
Migrants and natives (neither or both)	23	34.8	43	65.2
Don't know or refuse	13	37.1	22	62.9
Migration controls (n = 279)				
Desirable	45	50.0	45	50.0
Undesirable	59	39.6	90	60.4
Don't know or refuse	12	30.0	28	70.0
Gujarati identification with Maharashtra (n = 283)				
Yes	62	40.3	92	59.7
No	41	45.1	50	54.9
Don't know or refuse	13	34.2	25	65.8
South Indian identification with Maharashtra (n = 279)				
Yes	16	29.1	39	70.9
No	72	48.6	76	51.4
Don't know or refuse	26	34.2	50	65.8
South Indian attributes (n = 285)				
Positive	71	35.5	129	64.5
Negative	45	52.9	40	47.1

lar, had been very popular among Maharashtrian workers. Although the survey did not attempt to question respondents directly about the communist parties, one question did reveal something of the voters' attitudes. When respondents were asked to identify the principles for which they thought Shiv Sena stood, up to five responses were recorded. Only thirty of the working-class respondents even mentioned that Shiv Sena was anticommunist and the majority of these remarks were the second, third, or fourth response given. Of these thirty, fourteen voted for Shiv Sena, sixteen for Congress. If anticommunist

92 | *Ethnicity and Equality*

feeling was present, it was certainly not a salient factor in the Shiv Sena's support among the Maharashtrian working class.

The questionnaire attempted also to discern the attitudes of the respondents on questions of interethnic relations (see Appendix V). Analysis of the responses reveals a strikingly similar pattern for almost all of the questions. Similar to the questions on dictatorship and violence, the responses on interethnic relations show that a relatively high percentage of the intolerant respondents support Shiv Sena; but with the exception of the question on South Indian attributes, the absolute number of extremist Congress supporters in fact equaled or exceeded their Shiv Sena counterparts.

The relatively higher number of Shiv Sena supporters expressing less tolerant attitudes toward other religious and linguistic communities, as was argued earlier, appears not to be based on economic competition. Contrary to one of the survey's initial hypotheses, it appears also not to be based on neighborhood envirionment. In the formulation of the sample design, it was hypothesized that the ethnic mixture of the neighborhood might influence voter choice. It was anticipated that in the ethnically heterogeneous neighborhoods, Shiv Sena would fare particularly well.

Interestingly, the survey showed that the ethnic character of the neighborhoods did color perceptions but that these perceptions did not influence the vote. As Table 16 indicates, respondent perceptions of the ethnic composition of the *city* were derived almost entirely from the ethnic composition of the respondent's *neighborhood*. Respondents from ethnically mixed neighborhoods estimated the percentage of South Indians in Bombay to be higher than did respondents from Maharashtrian-dominant neighborhoods.

There is, however, only a weak correlation between these estimates of South Indian populations and voter preference. Shiv Sena does not fare better among those individuals who believe that South Indians constitute a high percentage of the population than among those whose estimates are relatively low (see Table 17).

Table 16. Maharashtrian estimates of Bombay's South Indian population and the ethnic composition of neighborhoods (%)

	Mean numerical estimates of Bombay's South Indian population
Ethnically homogeneous neighborhoods (Maharashtrian dominant)	
Parel 1	12.2
Parel 2	9.0
Dadar 3	14.8
Cumballa Hill 5	9.6
Wadala Springs 5	10.5
Wadala Springs 6	15.6
Ethnically mixed neighborhoods	
Parel 4	18.1
Dharavi 4	21.8
Dharavi 7	18.9
Kamathipura 8	17.1
Matunga 9	22.3

Table 17. Maharashtrian estimates of South Indian population and party preference (actual citywide % = 8.5)

Percentage estimated	Shiv Sena #	Shiv Sena %	Congress #	Congress %
1–10	60	40.5	88	59.5
11–20	59	50.0	59	50.0
21–35	26	40.0	39	60.0
36–50	14	51.9	13	48.1

Socioeconomic Attributes

Working-class Shiv Sena and Congress supporters can then be differentiated by their attitudes on a number of issues: Shiv Sena supporters are inclined to support xenophobic and extremist positions. But it is also important to analyze the differential support of the Sena and Congress among certain age, caste, and other groups of Maharashtrian laborers.

Age, interestingly, does not correlate as highly with Shiv Sena working-class support as it does with the party's middle-class fol-

Table 18. Age and party vote among working-class Maharashtrians (n = 288)

Age	Shiv Sena #	Shiv Sena %	Congress #	Congress %
24–30	41	42.7	55	57.3
31–40	35	37.2	59	62.8
41–50	25	39.7	38	60.3
51+	14	40.0	21	60.0

Table 19. Migration history and party vote among working-class Maharashtrians

	Shiv Sena #	Shiv Sena %	Congress #	Congress %
Migrants (n = 221)	86	38.9	135	61.1
Nonmigrants (n = 64)	30	46.9	34	53.1
Generation migrating*				
Own (n = 150)	56	37.3	94	62.7
Father's (n = 124)	53	42.7	71	57.3
Grandfather's (n = 9)	5	55.6	4	44.4
Great-grandfather's (n = 1)	1	100.0	0	00.0

*Respondents were asked who in their immediate family was the first to migrate to Bombay.

lowing. As Table 18 indicates, Shiv Sena has no particular hold among the working-class youth.

Migrant history, however, does appear to influence the electoral choice of Maharashtrian laborers. As shown in Table 19, nonmigrants and those persons with relatively longer roots in Bombay are more likely to support Shiv Sena than are migrants or those with only recent ties to the city. Nevertheless, it should be noted that in absolute numbers, more working-class "natives" support Congress than support Shiv Sena.

Caste background is also a factor that distinguishes, although imperfectly, the Sena from the Congress working-class voter. Of the neo-Buddhist (or former Harijan) respondents, 76.9 percent supported Congress compared to 23.1 percent supporting Shiv Sena (n=26). Of the 104 working-class Marathas, nearly twice as many supported Congress as Shiv Sena. This may not, however, reflect the hold of caste affiliation as much as it indicates the strong position of Congress in rural Maharashtra, from where many Marathas have migrated. Apart from the pronounced pro-Congress leanings of neo-Buddhist and Maratha respondents, no other caste variation proved distinctive.

Economic competition between ethnic groups does not appear to be acute among Bombay's working class, nor does it seem to be a factor which, if it exists within some segments of the working class, drives many into the Sena camp. Shiv Sena's efforts to mobilize working-class support, however, were facilitated by other economic factors. The recession of the mid-1960s probably did aid the Sena's first efforts at mobilizing support; later, the Sena was able to build important pockets of support in low-income areas where its organizational infrastructure was strong. In slum areas, Shiv Sena mobilized votes largely through its efforts to address immediate material problems at hand, such as housing repairs, water problems, and sewage disposal.

Whether as a cause or consequence of Sena support, Shiv Sena working-class voters are distinguishable from their Congress counterparts in their attitudes on a range of social and political issues. As the 1971 voter survey suggested, a relatively larger number of those expressing extremist as opposed to moderate views on questions of dictatorship, violence, and interethnic relations support Shiv Sena; in absolute numbers, however, Congress extremists exceed their working-class Sena counterparts.

It is difficult to say whether the extremist views held by many Sena voters are the outcome or the origins of their support for the party. The wide publicity given to the statements of the Sena leadership—whose basic ideological predispositions have been distinctly rightist[15]—might indicate that the views expressed by

15. In the early years of *Marmik*, before the idea of Shiv Sena had been conceived and there was any mention of "outsiders" or "local" people, articles on the dangers of "Lalbhai" (Red brothers) and the alleged infiltrators from Pakistan were frequent. In an editorial in early 1961, Thackeray noted the "insult" to the national flag which had been allegedly hung upside-down next to the Pakistani flag in one section of Bombay: "Such incidents are serious and signify the would-be disaster and give inspiration to anti-nationalism . . . in the rule of the present government which is for communal unity, you should not have such a foolish desire that this insult will be compensated or the criminals punished" (*Marmik*, Feb. 5, 1961).

In 1963, this time admonishing the readers about the dangers of communism,

Sena supporters are mere echoes of the Sena's "party line" rather than core beliefs. Without knowing more about the attitudes of Sena supporters prior to the party's emergence, however, this must remain a matter of speculation.

An analysis of Shiv Sena's emergence cannot rest with a discussion of the party's electoral appeal. The mobilization of party activists was clearly also crucial to the party's formation. To account for the Sena's success in recruiting party activists, it is necessary to return to a discussion of the Maharashtrian middle class.

Thackeray wrote: "The Communists in India desired to bring to this country Communist rule by violent ways, to organize country-wide strikes, to bring about destruction, to create disorder... and to establish red dictatorship" (*Marmik*, Mar. 24, 1963). Anti-Muslim and anticommunist editorials such as these were among the dominant themes of Thackeray's writings from 1960 to 1964.

6 | The Recruitment of Party Activists

> Identity was what the young men of the Sena were reaching out to, with the simplicities of their politics and their hero-figures. . . . For the Sena men, and the people they led, the world was new; they saw themselves at the beginning of things: unaccommodated men making a claim on their land for the first time, and out of chaos evolving their own philosophy of community and self-help.
>
> —V. S. Naipaul

The Shiv Sainiks, as the Sena party activists are known, were identifiable above all by their youth. Like youthful cadres of other organizations, Shiv Sainiks were drawn into the party less because of ideological or material motivations than because of a phenomenon not easily described: the exhilaration of belonging, the excitement of being involved. As the Naipaul description so vividly captures, the Sena organization laid out for the young party worker a clearly marked road to self-definition.

By 1968, the party had mobilized a corps of youthful activists who outshone in number and discipline the organization of other, much longer established Bombay parties. These youthful cadres were vital to Shiv Sena's electoral success. They played a direct role in election campaigns, organizing campaign processions, plastering the city's walls with slogans and cartoons, sifting through constituency lists, and soliciting voter support. Indirectly too, through their neighborhood self-help projects, the young Shiv Sainiks carried Shiv Sena's name to the Bombay voter. The dedication of these young party workers can be credited less to a structured political ideology or to the hope for material self-advancement than to the desire for involvement and the search for purpose.

Sena Activists: A Profile

A small handful of party organizers has directed the Sena party machine.[1] Bal Thackeray, the Senapati or Sena father, was

1. Comprehensive accounts of Shiv Sena's organizational history are con-

98 | Ethnicity and Equality

Figure 1. Shiv Sena party structure

at the apex of the party structure (see Fig. 1). One party organizer and several close advisors consulted with Thackeray regularly. Beneath them was an army of Shiv Sainiks who staffed the branch offices and manned the election campaigns.

The characteristic that most clearly set the Sena worker off from his counterpart in other party organizations was youth. Even the top-ranking leaders of the Sena were young. When the Shiv Sena entered the municipal elections in 1968, Thackeray was forty-two. The chief organizers and middle-level *vibhag pramukhs* were either contemporaries of Thackeray or younger. Of the sample of thirty-seven *shakha pramukhs, upshakha pramukhs*,[2] and active Shiv Sainiks that this researcher together with assistants was able to interview, the average age was twenty-six.[3]

---

tained in Ram Joshi, "The Shiv Sena: A Movement in Search of Legitimacy," *Asian Survey*, 10 (November 1970), 967; and Dipankar Gupta, "The Shiv Sena Movement, 1966–1974: A Sociological Analysis," Ph.D. dissertation, Jawaharlal Nehru University, New Delhi, 1977.

2. *Vibhag pramukh* means division leader, *shakha pramukh* branch leader, and *upshakha pramukh* assistant branch leader.

3. Profile of *vibhag pramukhs* based on the description of a leading Sena party worker; slight differences from Ram Joshi, "The Shiv Sena," can be explained by the difference in the time of information collection. The description of the *shakha, upshakha*, and Shiv Sainik contingents is based on interviews of thirty-seven party workers, of whom fourteen are *shakhas*. Although this group seemed a good representation of the middle- and lower-level party worker, there was no

Table 20. Educational background of Shiv Sena party workers

	#	%
Attended but did not complete school	8	22
Matriculated	13	35
Matriculated and received additional diploma	6	16
Attended or completed college and/or advanced degree	10	27

While many of the active Sainiks who were "regulars" at the party office and who participated in election rallies were students or student age, this was not true of the Sena hierarchy (*shakha pramukh* up). This group was composed almost entirely of those, as the Bombay expression has it, "in service"—office or technical workers—employed in their first or second job.

The image of Shiv Sena as an organization of the lumpenproletariat, an image entertained by some of the educated elite in Bombay, is clearly misplaced. First, the Shiv Sena activist is not a youth just in from the countryside. Whereas two-thirds of the Bombay population as a whole are migrants, two-thirds of the thirty-seven Shiv Sainiks interviewed reported themselves to have been born in Bombay.[4] Second, the Sena workers had considerable education. As Table 20 indicates, only 20 percent of those interviewed had not matriculated. Third, most of the party workers were employed—in lower white-collar occupations.

The seven *vibhag pramukhs* included two skilled laborers in a textile and other factory, several clerks, and two self-employed small businessmen. The occupational list of the thirty-seven

---

way of establishing this impression statistically since the Sena organization would not provide the necessary information of addresses and names from which either a random or a purposive sample could be drawn. The thirty-seven respondents, themselves extremely helpful and eager, were chosen simply because they were accessible through informal contacts. The Sena was the only party contacted by this author in Bombay which was unwilling to make the names and addresses of its party workers available.

4. The fact that most of the Sena's active party workers are native to Bombay supports the contention, made in some migration literature, that the people attracted to protest movements are more frequently the native or second-generation migrants rather than the migrants themselves. Whereas the Maharashtrian migrant living in Bombay likely compares his lot with his earlier and probably less secure position in his home village, the native Bombayite expects to improve his position, not over the farmer-peasant, but over the factory worker.

shakha and party activists reads like a directory to lower-middle-class occupations, excluding professionals (teachers, doctors, lawyers) and big businessmen on the one hand and simple, unskilled laborers or menial workers on the other. The job descriptions—accounts clerk, bookshop owner, salesman in bookshop, clerk in bank, towing operator, assistant supervisor in auto works—suggest that Shiv Sena organizational leaders were predominantly of middle- and lower-middle-class backgrounds.[5]

This impression is further confirmed by the types of property and possessions owned by those interviewed. Few respondents lived luxuriously, but none lived without some amenities. Of the fourteen *shakha pramukhs*, for example, all had radios, all but one had gas stoves, three had refrigerators, two had telephones, and two owned cars.

The typical activist in the Sena organization, then, could be readily identified. He was young, in his late twenties to early thirties; he was at least a matriculate; he was Maharashtrian,[6] native to Bombay; he came from a middle or lower-middle occupational and class status.

Order and Discipline of Party Organization

If youth was the hallmark of the party activist, discipline was the trademark of the organization. The Sena leader, Bal Thack-

5. The caste background of the *vibhag* and other Sena activists suggested the strongest representation to be of the middle- and upper-caste groups but with a sizable percentage from lower and scheduled castes as well. Of the seven *vibhag pramukhs*, five belonged to the middle and upper castes; two were from backward castes (one was a lawyer). Of the thirty-seven lower-level leaders interviewed, slightly under one-third were from one of the Brahmin castes; 14 percent were from the CKP or other closely related urban caste; one-third were from the middle-level Maratha caste (none of the respondents indicated whether they came from the Maratha or Kunbi-Maratha caste). Fifteen percent were from the lower or scheduled castes and the remainder declined to report their caste group.

6. The seven *vibhag pramukhs* as well as the thirty-seven party activists interviewed reported their mother tongue to be Marathi. The most prominent non-Maharashtrian Shiv Sena worker, by this criterion of mother tongue, was Arun Mehta, head of the Sena trade union organization and Gujarati by ancestry. The Sena insisted that the organization was not exclusively Maharashtrian; one Shakha was reported to be a Muslim from the south and Parsees, Christians, and Punjabis were found among the ranks of active workers. Within the Sena hierarchy, however, non-Marathi-speakers were the exception.

eray, and his few close confidants engaged in deliberate and careful planning which laid down the blueprint for party organization. Within six months of the June 1966 meeting, sixty branch offices had been established which Thackeray and a handful of party organizers had created. They carefully chose the seven *vibhag pramukhs*, who in turn, in consultation with Thackeray and his close associates, appointed three assistants each. The branch leaders, or *shakha pramukhs*, were then selected, each with either the initiation or approval of Thackeray or his chief organizer.

This top-down hand-picking process of leadership selection distinguished Shiv Sena from other parties in Bombay politics of the 1960s. Since 1971, the Congress—and at earlier periods the extreme Left and Right—have followed similar selection methods. But in the 1960s, this process was singular to Shiv Sena. The leadership of the Congress (O)—the dominant municipal party of the 1960s—was composed of people nominated and elected by the local ward committees or by their elected representatives. With the smaller parties which had difficulty establishing committees throughout Bombay, in certain wards, whoever was willing to volunteer the time and effort was gratefully voted into office.

The centrally controlled nature of the Sena's leadership selection was equally evident in the procedures of its leadership demotion. In choosing the *vibhag* and *shakha pramukhs*, the Sena selected many without previous political experience whose qualities as political leaders could not be easily judged in advance. The performance of newly appointed leaders was closely watched and poor appointments were quickly rectified. In the initial appointment, particular attention was given to the individual's personal qualities, his loyalty, speaking ability, the extent of his acquaintance and contacts, his ability to relate easily with young people, his interest in physical activity; when judgments about these qualities proved incorrect, remedial steps were promptly taken. While reprimands or disciplinary action rarely reached the ears of the public, in some cases the incidents were used by Thackeray or other organizers to remind the public and the Sena rank-and-file that party indiscipline would not be tolerated. One occasion occurred in a Sena public meeting: Reporting that he had fired the *malad shakha* and would deal similarly with others in the Sena ranks who veered from Sena principles, Thackeray declared that he did not mind being thought of as a dictator since only a dictator could save India.[7]

Order, discipline, and the centralization of authority best describe the conduct of Shiv Sena meetings and the mode of communication between different levels of the party hierarchy. The *shakha* meetings, led occasionally by Thackeray but more often by one of his chief organizers, were reportedly run with clocklike precision. It is said that the seating was in order of the *shakha* number (1 to 140), *shakhas* were called upon in turn to report on their branch activities, votes were never taken, and controversial matters were either settled beforehand or were not opened for discussion at the meeting.[8]

The order of the ward level replicates that of the Bombay-wide organization. In one of the very active *shakhas* of Girgaum, leaders were appointed from each street or major *chawl* in the neighborhood and were instructed to report into the ward office each week to check the bulletin board for notices and announcements. The financial accounts and books noting the *shakha* activities and meetings were regularly inspected by the higher party organizers. And similar to the higher-level party meetings, in the ward meetings, votes or show-of-hands were never entertained and controversial topics were reserved for the pre- or post-meeting conferrals among the *shakha* and his several assistants.

Communication with the individual *shakhas* took place with amazing speed and messages or directives from Thackeray and his cohorts reached the ward office almost instantaneously. It is

---

7. See account in *Link*, "Shiv Sena: Incipient Fascism," Aug. 27, 1967.

8. Open splits among the personnel are very rare. One such incident, interesting because of its near uniqueness, was reported in the *Times of India*, Jan. 10, 1974, "Bombay Poll Drive Gathers Tempo." In this incident, Thackeray declared his support for the Congress candidate while a prominent Sena activist in the area supported the "right-wing" Hindu Mahasabha candidate. Even more recently, the papers reported a clash between Shiv Sena party workers in the city of Pune. Thackeray had expelled several Sena members from Pune, according to the newspaper account. The expelled members issued a statement saying that "The Shiv Sena is not the personal property of Mr. Thackeray or any other leader or person," *Times of India*, Jan. 7, 1976.

sometimes satirically observed that the only more efficient network of communications in Bombay is *matka*, the illegal numbers game. Discrediting the notion that rapid communication requires sophisticated technology, the game of *matka*, operating in a city of over 5 million, requires mere minutes for bets to be reported to the central office and for the results to be circulated throughout the city. It is no mean feat to have constructed, as the Sena has, a communications network of similar efficiency, stretching from party heads to the lowest branch office.[9]

Not only were the communications between party personnel impressively efficient and disciplined; but also, and more astonishing, the Sena public meetings exhibited a similar order and precision. According to one Shiv Sena leader, the meetings held in outlying rural areas, although subject to the uncertainties of roads and transportation, convened at the scheduled hour; questions were solicited by workers in advance and sometimes submitted in writing before the meeting. In Bombay the massive rallies held in Shivaji park attracting tens of thousands functioned with rare disturbance. Young volunteers were stationed in the crowds to keep people seated and the speakers were almost never interrupted by shouts or even audience chatter. Through one meeting (Diwali, 1970), interspersed by a downpour of rain, the audience remained seated and seemingly oblivious. The contrast between the orderliness of the Sena meetings and other party rallies was extreme. For other party rallies, constant chatter, shouts from the back for those in the front to sit, and throwing of pebbles at the speaker proved the rule. For Shiv Sena, shouts of disruption were not even the exception.[10]

Perhaps the occasion that best illustrates the supreme orderliness of the Sena's organizational machinery was the preelection parade during the important bye-election contest in Parel (the textile district of Bombay) in 1970. The procession, two days

9. The rapidity of Sena communications was witnessed personally by this writer, whose interview with one *shakha* was reported to the Sena organizational leader and instruction about the conduct of future interviews issued and received the next day by nearly all *shakhas* in Bombay.
10. It should be noted, however, that the *aftermath* of Sena rallies often included violent disturbances, looting, and clashes provoked by those who attended the meetings.

before the election, was scheduled to follow a route several miles long and to collect finally in one large park at the end of Parel where speeches would be made and the campaign terminated. The participants in the procession itself—not including those who lined the sidewalks—numbered in the tens of thousands. Many were children and young adults. Shiv Sena volunteers manned the parade route, handing out water to the thirsty and holding signs announcing the chants and slogans that would be shouted by the long lines of marchers in perfect unison. But more significant still, as one Shiv Sena worker commented, was the fact that in a society where beginnings and ends of meetings and events or even personal appointments do not always follow the precise dictates of the clock, the procession began one minute later than scheduled and arrived at the end of the route exactly five seconds earlier than had been planned.[11]

Shiv Sena's ability to mobilize young party workers through the creation of a disciplined party organization suggests comparisons with other selected political parties. The structure of Shiv Sena, for instance, bears a strong resemblance to that of the once powerful "right-wing" organization Rashtriya Swayamasevak Sangh. Several of the words for the organization's institutions and personnel, such as *shakha* (branch), were common to both parties and were not standard terminology for the equivalent positions in other Maharashtrian parties. The centrally imposed decisions and the code of discipline in the RSS were also a major aspect of the Sena's procedures. J. A. Curran, in his study of the RSS, writes:

Through the *Shakha* the organization administers its internal affairs. Such matters as doubts over ideology and infractions of discipline are handled by the *Shakha* quietly and expeditiously. Loyalty to the *Shakha* becomes so ingrained that mere disapproval of "un-Sanghly" actions by comrades in the *Shakha* usually brings an erring member back quickly into line. The morale of the Shakha is normally high. Through this unit, the R.S.S. leadership exacts unquestioning obedience to its dictates.[12]

11. See *Maharashtra Times* account, Oct. 16, 1970.
12. J. A. Curran, *Militant Hinduism in Indian Politics: A Study of the R.S.S.* (International Secretariat, Institute of Pacific Relations, 1951), pp. 45–46.

Curran's observations on RSS discipline could serve perfectly as a description of Shiv Sena.

Like Shiv Sena, the RSS traditionally drew its membership heavily from the young and from the lower middle class. Both organizations, moreover, placed emphasis on paramilitary preparedness and physical fitness. Regular physical training and exercise were a part of RSS activity. Like the RSS, the Sena attempted to build an all-Bombay paramilitary guard. Military and physical prowess were central to the ideology of both organizations. The very name, Sena, means army. The choice of Shivaji, a martial hero, as the party symbol and the Sena's periodic efforts to steer young Maharashtrian boys into army careers[13] are further indication of the shared concern of the Sena for military virtues.

Similarly, the Sena has not shied away from violence. On several public occasions, Thackeray vowed that it was only by being willing to retaliate in kind that the violence of the Sena's archrival, the Communists, could be checked. Newspaper stories perpetuated this reputation by carrying frequent articles on violent clashes between Sena volunteers and those of other parties, on the burning of shops and South Indian (*Udipi*)[14] eating places, and by giving coverage to more spectacular items such as the conviction of young men, said to be Shiv Sena volunteers, for the murder of a communist state legislator.[15]

The Sena's adoption of the paramilitarism, discipline, and organizational style of the RSS is not entirely accidental. Many of the most active organizers in the RSS were Maharashtrian and several Sena leaders are said to have had experience in the RSS. The party's chief organizers, several of the *vibhag pramukhs* and corporators, and Thackeray himself were—with varying de-

13. See, for instance, the editorial in *Marmik*, May 9, 1971, which advises Marathi youth to join the armed forces. Posters in *shakha* offices advertise the army and provide instructions about application procedures.
14. "Udipi hotels" are small Bombay eating places run by persons from the Udipi region of Karnataka. Their cleanliness and good, inexpensive, vegetarian food makes them very popular among Bombay's middle-class office workers. Their South Indian ownership, however, has made them the target of Sena ire and of a Sena-instigated but not very successful boycott. On the burning of Udipi hotels, see, for example, *New York Times*, Jan. 13, 1974.
15. MLA Krishna Desai. See *Free Press Journal*, Feb. 16, 1971.

grees of involvement—supporters or members of either the RSS or the Hindu Mahasabha.[16] Whether directly borrowed or independently conceived, it would be difficult to overlook the similarities of style and organization between those of the Sena and the erstwhile RSS.

The highly centralized and structured nature of the Sena organization distinguished the party from its Bombay counterparts of the 1960s. As shall become clearer in the following section, the structured nature of the Sena organization lent a discipline and order to Sena activities—a feature that drew large numbers of youths into Sena ranks.

Party Activities

Program and party activities as well as the specific style of election campaigns seemed designed specifically with the purpose of involving youthful Maharashtrians. Emotions rather than material incentives provided the central impetus for mobilizing the young party activist.

A number of *shakhas* organized gymnastic and exercise classes; some of the more active branches, such as the Lamington Road Shakha in Girgaum, formed committees which volunteered help for constituents with minor drainage, housing-repair, and other problems. *Shakha* offices also engaged the energies of youthful members in organizing religious festivals or special projects such as the blood drive during the Bangladesh war.

The importance of noneconomic issues for Shiv Sena organizational personnel was further suggested by the history of Shiv Sena political demonstrations. The Sena demonstration which marked the party's perhaps greatest display of power was the so-called Bombay *bandh* (shutdown) of February 1969. The citywide *bandh*, which involved extraordinary numbers of Sena workers, was held to protest not the incursions of outsiders into

---

16. Thackeray is said to have been an RSS member as a student, as were large numbers of young Maharashtrians at the time. The erstwhile Shiv Sena chief organizer, Pradhan, is also reported to have been an active organizer in the RSS. The Sena openly supported Pandit Bakhale, who ran as an independent for the municipal corporation although his affiliation with the Hindu Mahasabha was widely recognized.

the Bombay economy, but rather the issue of the boundary dispute between the two states of Maharashtra and Karnataka. While this issue was clearly of a nonmaterial nature, the Sena party workers gave as much of their full and committed energies to this demonstration as to other Sena activities.

Not surprisingly, most of the Sena's organizational energies were directed toward electoral campaigns. There were elections almost every year since the Sena's founding in 1966. The 1967 elections in Thana, the municipal elections in 1968, the Parel assembly bye-election in 1970, the parliamentary elections in 1971, assembly elections in 1972, municipal elections in 1973, and more recent bye-elections involved much of the Sena's organizational finances and time.

The election campaigns and demonstrations were planned in such a way as to appeal to youthful energies. The discipline of the marching, chants, and slogans, evident in the Parel election campaign of 1970, clearly stimulated enthusiasm among young Sena workers. Other campaign techniques such as the Sena trademark of decorating Bombay walls and buildings with political cartoons, or the bicycle march of 1971 in which hundreds of Sainiks wearing Shiv Sena armbands or insignia came together in droves on owned or borrowed bicycles, were clearly intended to engage the energies of the young Maharashtrian.

Before 1968, the Sena had little of material worth to offer prospective party members. It was not that the Sena organization operated its initial campaigns in Thana or in Bombay on shoestring budgets: the campaigns with their numerous rallies and marches required expensive sound equipment and rented trucks; the voluminous flags, posters, and cartoons that covered the walls and buildings of Bombay were also evidence that the Sena had raised substantial sums for the campaigns.[17] One estimate suggests that more than 50,000 flags were made, costing ten rupees apiece, and that those who participated in the demonstrations were given transportation and pocket money for the

17. It is generally acknowledged that industrialists who saw the Sena as a force to combat the communist unions gave liberally to the party. Bajaj and Mahindra were names often associated with these contributions, but many other industrialists clearly also donated funds.

day.[18] While such estimates may, indeed, be correct, they do not indicate that Shiv Sena won its large and powerful following of party workers through financial incentives. The long hours put in by the large, active rank-and-file Shiv Sainik were volunteered even if remuneration was offered for occasional participation in a day of campaigns or parades.

After 1968, patronage no doubt figured in the party's mobilization of workers. With forty-two municipal councilors elected in 1968, the Sena could claim significant powers of patronage and job appointments included in perquisites of all corporators.[19] In a 1971 survey of Bombay voters, it is interesting that over 14 percent claimed that they knew personally someone who had found a job "through Shiv Sena."[20] Such figures would suggest that after 1968–69 at least, when the Sena had secured a place in the corporation and had established itself as a powerful force in Bombay politics, the ranks of active Sena workers could have been inflated by those seeking jobs and material gain.

By 1968, moreover, *shakhas* began to organize activities that provided concrete material incentives to Sena members. Again, these activities were of a kind to be of special appeal to the young of the middle or lower-middle class. Nearly each *shakha*, for instance, maintained an employment register in which those seeking jobs listed their name, qualifications, and type of post sought. When jobs were brought to the attention of the local corporator or *shakha* office, the register was consulted and the individuals were advised of job vacancies. In the case of certain *shakha* offices, advice was given to the youths about how to complete the necessary application form, how to appear at interviews, etc.

18. *Link*, Apr. 7, 1968.
19. Although it is impossible to pinpoint the exact number of such patronage positions, some idea may be gained from the Bombay Corporation Rules, which requires all appointments with a monthly pay of greater than 500 rupees to be approved by the appropriate standing committee of elected representatives. All appointments at lower pay are to be made by the commissioner (a civil servant) and do not need the approval of elected officials. With people on the employment rosters of the corporation numbering between 65,000 and 80,000, the extent of jobs over which corporators have some influence is not inconsequential.
20. Voter survey, 1971, conducted by the author and Kartikeya Sarabhai. The survey included about 450 Maharashtrians and an equal number of South Indians resident in Bombay.

Since contracts, application forms, and interviews were key aspects of the hiring process for white-collar jobs, middle-class youths had reason to find Sena services of interest.

In addition, several *shakhas* planned, although few actually implemented, programs to offer typing, stenography, and English instruction for neighborhood youths. A further activity that elicited the interest and support of the young, middle-class constituent is the encouragement the Sena gave, in its early years, to small business ventures. The Sena central office provided small amounts of money to individual *shakhas*, which in turn lent the funds out as capital to young Shiv Sainiks desiring to try their hand at small business ventures; coconut, *bhel-puri*, and potato-*wada* (types of snacks) carts and refreshment stalls, a truck to help vendors transport goods collectively, and various other small undertakings were sponsored.[21]

Other services were also provided by the Sena branches. Several *shakha* offices maintained small libraries, mostly of student texts. Others, such as the active Lamington Road branch, attempted to assist students in other ways. A brochure which recounts the activities of this particular *shakha* notes:

Taking into consideration the difficulty in finding adequate study space for the many deserving students in the ward, the Shakha has taken the lead to arrange a room in a local school. Nearly 100 to 150 students took advantage of this facility. Further, in order to encourage good and scholarly students, the students who have shown remarkable success in the SSC as well as degree examination are felicitated and given prizes by the Shakha. We have also decided to give fees for the whole year to four poor and deserving students in each standard from standard VIII to standard XI.[22]

Although after 1968 these activities may have motivated already active and potential Sainiks toward further commitment and party work, the spirit of party involvement was not dampened; in fact, there is reason to believe that even after 1968 it

21. As the party began to encounter difficulty in collecting repayment for the loans, the Sena leadership ceased using party funds and instead tried to encourage individual businessmen to lend money to deserving Sainiks.
22. *Lamington Road Shakha Souvenir*, 1970, Ward 38.

was that spirit rather than the ideology of the party or the material perquisites associated with party work that maintained a committed corps of party workers.

In contrast to the Sena voter, for instance, economic reasons were not foremost in the image the party activist held of Sena objectives. In the questionnaire administered to the thirty-seven Sena activists, the respondents were asked to state the principles for which Shiv Sena stood. Multiple responses were allowed and were frequently offered. Interestingly, however, only 21 percent of all answers mentioned that Shiv Sena sought to help Marashtrians secure jobs. The largest percentage (52 percent) made the much vaguer claim that Shiv Sena stood for the principle of "Maharashtra for Maharashtrians." An additional 25 percent of the responses stated that the major principle of Shiv Sena was to combat "antinational" forces. These responses are in marked contrast to the distribution of answers in the survey of 450 Bombay voters mentioned earlier. Responding to the identical question, 59 percent of the answers mentioned jobs specifically, 22 percent cited the principle of "Maharashtra for Maharashtrians," and 8 percent noted Shiv Sena's intention to combat "antinational" forces. Shiv Sena's image as a champion of specifically economic injustices did not, then, appear to take primacy in the eyes of the Sena party activist.

Mobilization of Youth and the Exhilaration of Belonging

What evidence is there that Maharashtrian youths were drawn into Sena ranks less out of ideological commitment or a promise of concrete material benefits than out of a desire to be involved and directed? On what grounds is it possible to claim that it was the exhilaration of being part of an ordered, militant organization that caused Maharashtrian youths to enter the Sena fold?

"Hard" evidence in support of this contention is limited. Two factors cited earlier bear repeating: (1) The mobilization of party cadres in the period of enormous Sena activity between 1966 and 1968 cannot be explained by material incentives since the Sena party offices did not have access to resources and patronage prior to the party's entrance into municipal politics. (2) Interviews with Sainiks indicated that Shiv Sena activists were less impressed by the party's claims about economic injustices than by its more generally xenophobic image.

But these two points hardly clinch the case. The argument must admittedly be inferential, resting more on observation and anecdote than on surveys or concrete events. To even a casual observer, what distinguished the Sena organization from other Bombay parties was the zeal and enthusiasm of those engaged in its activities. An almost clublike, fraternal spirit was exhibited in the way Shiv Sena activists talked among and about each other and the party. The occasional boyishness and constant exuberance obtained at the highest level of the organization as well as among the young Shiv Sainiks working in the *shakha* office. In a remark suggestive of this spirit, Arun Mehta, former leader of the Sena trade union movement, noted: "We have a little joke among us. The trade union movement began on August 9, 1968. August 9, 1942, was the date of the Quit India movement and forty-two is a lucky number for Shiv Sena. There were forty-two corporators elected; Thackeray was forty-two when the Shiv Sena began. My first union number ended in 42. We have these little jokes."[23]

In the *shakha* offices the highly charged atmosphere and excitement were almost always in evidence. There was constant laughter. Talking, crowds of young boys, arms on each others' shoulders, and excited shouts interspersed the hushed conferences of several Sainiks huddled on benches or chairs.

Perhaps the best way of illustrating the distinctive character of the Sena organization and its activists is to contrast two visits made to the Shiv Sena and Communist party (CPI) offices the day of the Parel bye-election in 1970.

The Parel Assembly bye-election was being held to fill the seat vacated by the death of the Communist state legislator, Krishna Desai. Desai had been murdered by a band of youths who were reported, although the report was denied by the Sena organization, to have been Shiv Sena volunteers. The Communist candidate was Desai's widow, a woman who, like the Sena nominee, was a Maharashtrian from the district of Ratnagiri. In the two-

23. Interview with Arun Mehta, Nov. 10, 1970.

way race, the Sena had received the support of all the "rightist" parties—Jan Sangh, Swatantra, Hindu Mahasabha, and Congress (O). The Communist candidate was supported, officially, by Congress (R) and the socialist parties. Even at the moment immediately preceding the election, it was not clear who would emerge the victor, and when the results were announced the closeness of the race was confirmed by the tiny margin of the Sena victory (1,679 of 62,662 votes cast).[24]

But despite the predicted close competition, the party offices two days before the elections appeared to indicate that the results were a foregone conclusion. The Sena offices were jubilant, crowded, and noisy. The CPI office was half-empty, the workers muted. The contrast could not have been more stark. At the Sena office, the first object to meet the eye—as in most Sena offices—was a garlanded print of Shivaji, the seventeenth-century Maharashtrian hero. The walls were plastered with photos and posters of Mahadik, the Sena candidate, and of Thackeray, as well as with the ubiquitous cartoons. The place was crowded with tables, chairs, and hordes of workers. Only a couple of those present appeared older than forty. The rest were young boys in their teens and early twenties. Constant chatter—all in Marathi —jokes, and an occasional excited command filled the office. A few workers exclaimed in a manner reminiscent of the ebullience of an athletic competition: "We'll show them—the red flag will never fly again in Bombay." The journalists quizzed one of the workers about the campaign. After running down the several reasons why the Sena was assured of victory in the quick-fire manner of a preassembled speech, the worker went on to deliver the often-quoted Sena slogans about the "antinational" character of the Communist party, the unreliability of the "red monkeys," etc.

The visit to the CPI headquarters revealed an entirely different scene. A half-dozen workers sat around a table; several others stood in an adjoining room. A handful of children and young teenagers came in—and were introduced as the children of several of the party workers. The workers were almost all in

24. Election results reported in *Maharashtra Times*, Oct. 20, 1970. The visit to the party offices occurred several days previously.

their forties and fifties. On the walls were several posters, including one, slightly yellowed at the edges, of Lenin as a young man. Another poster bore the party insignia. The party workers sitting in the office included several women—a marked contrast to the all-male group of the Sena office. The atmosphere was somber and studied. Two men debated a point about campaign procedure—in English, although both were Maharashtrian. The visitors were quickly asked to sit down and tea was immediately brought. No one appeared too busy to be bothered by extensive questions. Those gathered around were uninterested in making predictions or even in engaging in the usual campaign denunciations of the other party; instead, a tense discussion was struck up about the historical role of the party in the Bombay trade union movement. Two workers vehemently and openly disagreed—an occurrence almost never witnessed in public view in a Shiv Sena office.

A case might be made that Maharashtrian youth in particular are susceptible to the appeal of an organization such as Shiv Sena. Maharashtrian history, both early and recent, is studded with the rise and fall of militant movements. The military exploits of Shivaji, whose military prowess underlay the founding of the Maratha Empire, has parallels in only a few of the historical annals of other regions of India. Two recent movements, usually termed "extremist"—the Hindu Mahasabha and the RSS—received perhaps their strongest support in the region of Maharashtra. The Hindu-communalist assassin of Gandhi, Godse, and other widely known Hindu extremists were Maharashtrian by birth. In its early years the RSS had an enormous following among students and youth in Maharashtra.

A study of Bombay University students provides additional support for the idea that Maharashtrian youth is particularly receptive to extremist or militant appeals. In the study, students from India's many linguistic communities at the University of Bombay were ranked according to the score on a questionnaire designed to identify "antidemocratic and fascist" attitudes. A scale was constructed by combining the results of a number of questions covering a range of attitudinal sets. They included questions on compulsory military training, belief in religion and the supernatural, the inherent superiority of certain communities, etc. The mean scores on the scale were highest for the Hindi- and Marathi-speaking student groups and lowest for the Tamilian and Gujarati communities.[25]

Whether or not Maharashtrian youth may be more susceptible than youths of other communities to the appeals of order and discipline is an open question. But it is likely that the sense of "compatriotism" and the excitement inherent in the discipline and order of the Sena organization were factors that attracted large numbers of youths to Sena ranks as to those of other highly disciplined political organizations such as the RSS. The strength of these emotive appeals, rather than the attraction of either monetary incentive or a particular ideology, seems to have provided the central force that mobilized Maharashtrian youths into Sena ranks.

Shiv Sena succeeded within the space of several years in forming a highly disciplined, hierarchical, and effective party organization. Recruited by a small group of organizers around Bal Thackeray, the numerous party activists were a visible and enthusiastic core of Shiv Sena support throughout Bombay. The pool of support from which these activists were drawn included largely the young, middle-class Maharashtrian youth.

Shiv Sena success in mobilizing a large cadre of party activists was due to the party's ability to elicit a strong sense of involvement among its active supporters. After 1968, material incentives may also have played a subsidiary role in attracting an ever-increasing number of supporters. But the disciplined, structured, and vibrant quality of the Sena organization and activities, more than anything else, was central in recruiting young party workers. The exhilaration, the sense of importance, and the self-involvement experienced by Shiv Sainiks held out enormous appeal for youth as a whole and perhaps for middle- or lower-middle-class Maharashtrian youth in particular.

Other parties have successfully mobilized youthful cadres

25. P. K. Muttagi, "An Investigation into the Cross-Community Attitudes of Undergraduates and Postgraduate Classes in the University of Bombay, 1970," unpublished dissertation, University of Bombay.

through the similar appeal of a disciplined, directed party organization. The RSS in Maharashtra is one such case.[26] More distant but no less analagous is the appeal of the Nazi youth groups. As one member of that organization put it: "Without really trying to get new members, the Thalburg Hitler Youth grew rapidly. I think most of the boys joined for the same reason I did. They were looking for a place where they could get together with other boys in exciting activities. . . . I don't think the political factor was the main reason boys joined. . . . We weren't fully conscious of what we were doing but we enjoyed ourselves and felt important."[27]

A remark of a Bombay journalist visiting one of the *shakha* offices in 1971 illustrates particularly well the greater importance of organizational style over ideology as an instrument for mobilization. The reporter, a Maharashtrian, is known for articles which reflect a general sympathy with the ideologies of the Left. Ten years earlier, he had been active in the Praja Socialist party. Visiting one of the Shakha offices, and struck by the exuberance of the young Sainiks who talked jubilantly in Marathi of the *shakha* activities and Sena exploits, the reporter noted: "They are just like we were ten years ago. The same vitality and involvement was there in the PSP. If I were ten years younger today, I would be a Shiv Sainik."[28]

26. See S. H. Deshpande, "My Days in the R.S.S.," *Quest*, 96 (July–August 1975), pp. 19–30.
27. William Sheridan Allen, *The Nazi Seizure of Power* (Chicago: Quadrangle Books, 1965), p. 73.
28. February 1971. The comment was not made for attribution.

7 | Shiv Sena's Front Ranks: Political Stability and Interethnic Relations

"Manohar Joshi, Mayor of Bombay?" one of Joshi's youthful acquaintances exclaimed with evident disbelief as he read the headline announcement of the April 6, 1976, *Times of India*. "He was with me at Ruia College. He was a nice sort of guy who used to joke a lot; he was never a serious student—maybe he got a third class. Later when he became a Shiv Sena councilor, people used to call him Principal Joshi. I was surprised when I heard that phrase until I learned that the institution of which he was the principal was either a driving school or tutorial classes in Dadar."[1]

Manohar Joshi is, by his own admission, a self-made man. Although from a high-caste Brahmin background, he claims to come from a poor rural family. When he was young he moved from his native village in Colaba to Bombay, where he stayed with an uncle. He went to school and college in Bombay, became involved in some small business concerns, and was able to acquire his own driving school. Before Shiv Sena, he was not really active in politics, although he helped out in some of the local Congress campaigns.

Joshi says he has worked hard to advance himself. Now he can enjoy some of the fruits of that hard work, for instance, the neatly kept rooms into which he and his family have recently moved. The apartment is in a newly constructed multistoried dwelling overlooking a green open area, a rare sight in the otherwise crowded (predominantly Maharashtrian) section of Bombay

---

1. Ruia is one of the well-respected colleges in the Bombay University system, although it does not have the prestige of the older St. Xavier's or Elphinstone colleges. The comment, not for attribution, was made by a Maharashtrian from Bombay now living in the United States.

called Dadar. Now, other people say, Joshi has become quite well-to-do. From his origins in a Colaba village to the mayoral office in Bombay, Joshi has come a long way.

Joshi's political views are not easily characterized. Although Shiv Sena's main purpose is to restore Maharashtrians to their rightful place in Bombay, Joshi explains, Shiv Sena's ideology encompasses a broad range of issues. Shiv Sena is concerned with the common man. That is why the party is dedicated to rooting out corruption. Bootlegging, the prevalence of hawkers (vendors), the illicit draining of water lines—all these practices must stop if Bombay is to be made livable. To eliminate corruption and to clean up the city are two of Shiv Sena's dearest goals. These goals can be achieved through various methods. Preventing so many people from flooding into the city is one important step, but it cannot be done by coercive measures: they would be illegal, Joshi has been told. Some lawyers he knows, however, are exploring this question. Other measures can be taken—self-help projects in the slums, more efficient management of municipal projects. Shiv Sena is also determined to combat the Communists and other antinational forces. In doing so, Shiv Sena is ready to use any means. Joshi's statements are not products of reflection or analysis. They are emphatically made assertions that pick up on truths of the moment.

Shiv Sena Corporators: Social and Political Background

Manohar Joshi is typical in many ways of his Shiv Sena colleagues on the municipal corporation. Like Joshi, they are for the most part political neophytes, young men of lower-middle-class background, often upwardly mobile.

One of the consequences of Shiv Sena's formation has been the mobilization of a new political elite. Projected into the political limelight from positions at the margin of politics, the Sena leadership represents a type of politician previously scarce in Bombay politics. A comparison of the political and socioeconomic background of the Sena leadership with that of Bombay politicians from other political parties illustrates the different roots of the new arrivals. The profile is based on data collected in 1970–71 from interviews with 107 of the 140 members of the

Bombay Municipal Corporation. The interviews included 39 of the 42 Shiv Sena councilors, 18 of 19 Congress (R) party leaders, 10 of the 11 Praja Socialist party (PSP) leaders, and 40 of the 47 Congress (O) representatives.[2] These interviews demonstrate that the municipal corporation underwent significant change when Shiv Sena was elected for the first time in 1968.

The Shiv Sena is not, as is characteristic of other parties in India, a group split off from an older party which has formed its own organization. Rather, the Sena corporators are new to the ranks of municipal politics. Not one Sena councilor held elective, citywide office at any time prior to 1968.[3]

The newness of most Sena councilors to the halls of political debate is noted by other party leaders. In the view of more venerable practitioners of corporation politics, the Sena leaders are political upstarts whose behavior on the corporation floor is an affront to rules of parliamentary procedure and proper conduct. The catapulting to political prominence of Sena councilors appears to explain the boyish exuberance and jests which frequently attend the party caucuses and exchanges on the floor among Sena leaders. In sharp contrast to Shiv Sena, a large per-

---

2. The Congress parties and Praja Socialist Party (PSP) were selected because they represented with Shiv Sena the four largest parties in the corporation. The 107 councilors on whom the analysis is based represent all corporators from the four parties who were willing or available to be interviewed. Several interviews were also held with members of the Republican, Jan Sangh, and Communist (CPI) parties. These interviews do not figure, however, in the above analysis. All statistics on corporators cited in this chapter, unless otherwise indicated, are based on this survey. (The numbers and party affiliation of the councilors is drawn from party standing as of March 1970.) Interviews were oral but based on the identical questionnaire.

3. Only five of the thirty-nine Sena leaders interviewed mentioned having held an official position within a party organization prior to contesting office on the Sena ticket. Three were secretaries/presidents of the Congress Ward Committees in Bombay; two were office holders in PSP, including one councilor who managed the campaign in his ward for Krishna Menon. Menon was then (1967) contesting against a Shiv Sena-supported candidate of the Congress party. Of the thirty-three Sena corporators who mentioned earlier sympathy with another party, 52 percent mentioned Congress and 21 percent PSP. The last figure may be low. At least one corporator (interview with S. N. Acharya, March 1971, Bombay) claimed that close to 80 percent of Sena corporators had been Congress party members.

centage of councilors from the other parties in the corporation claim long political experience. Thirty-five corporators, or nearly one-third of non-Shiv Sena councilors, served on the corporation prior to 1968[4] and, unlike Shiv Sena councilors, many had their first political experience in some facet of the nationalist movement.

The Sena's role in mobilizing new elites into politics replicates that of opposition parties elsewhere in India. As Angela Burger observes, opposition parties may serve this function more effectively than Congress since "A party of national independence tends to have its leadership frozen in those social groups which were mobilized at that time."[5] Partly for this reason, the likelihood is slight that the Congress party would give choice opportunities, such as municipal seats, to political unknowns. In Bombay, however, other opposition parties—the Jan Sangh, PSP, etc.—also reflect the marks of age: a tendency to be locked into certain established leadership groups. Because it was new in 1968 and was not yet beholden to long-time party workers, the Sena, alone among Bombay parties, was able to convoy large numbers of people with limited political experience into higher levels of leadership.

The Sena leadership is "new" not only in the sense that it comprises people lacking earlier political notoriety; it is also new with respect to the socioeconomic groups it represents. The Sena leadership, as elaborated below, is decidedly younger, less cosmopolitan, and from a lower socioeconomic strata than the elite of the other municipal parties, and it is overwhelmingly Maharashtrian.

The youngest Sena member in 1971, three years after the elections, was twenty-four years old. At that time, no one in either of the two Congress parties or in PSP was under thirty. In the Sena, 15 percent were thirty years or under and only 12 percent were older than fifty, while in the PSP, Congress (O),

---

4. Statistic cited in G. S. Badhe and M. U. Rao, *The Bombay Civic Election of 1968* (Bombay: All-India Institute of Local Self-Government, 1970), p. 132.
5. Angela Sutherland Burger, *Opposition in a Dominant-Party System* (Berkeley and Los Angeles: University of California Press, 1969), p. 270.

Table 21. Educational background of Bombay municipal councilors

	Shiv Sena (n = 39)		C(O), C(R), PSP combined (n = 68)		Congress (O) (n = 40)		Congress (R) (n = 18)		PSP (n = 10)	
	#	%	#	%	#	%	#	%	#	%
Advanced degree	5	13	24	35	13	33	5	28	6	60
BA (graduate)	5	13	12	18	8	20	2	11	2	20
First or second year of college completed	8	20	5	7	4	10	—	—	1	10
Diploma	4	10	5	7	3	7	2	11	—	—
Matriculate	12	31	17	25	8	20	8	44	1	10
Primary	5	13	5	7	4	10	1	6	—	—

and Congress (R), taken together, less than 3 percent were thirty years or younger and 35 percent were over fifty.

The occupational background of both Shiv Sena councilors and their fathers also distinguished the Shiv Sena membership of the corporation from their colleagues in other parties. Thirteen percent of Shiv Sena, compared with 21 percent of the other party members, reported themselves to be professionals (lawyers, doctors, etc.).[6] Of the Sena councilors, 23 percent claimed to own small businesses, while 37 percent, on the average, of the two Congress parties and PSP claimed business as their chief occupation.[7] Clerical workers made up 21 percent of the Sena corporation party and 6 percent on the average of the other parties. Skilled and supervisory factory workers made up 21 percent of Shiv Sena and 19 percent on the average of the other three parties.[8] The election of forty-two Shiv Sena members clearly marked the entrance into municipal politics of a less professional group from less established occupational backgrounds than those of councilors from other political parties.

The information on father's occupation clearly shows the poorer roots of Shiv Sena's leadership and their concomitant upward mobility. The fathers of nine of the thirty-nine Sena workers (23 percent) were blue-collar factory workers. None of those interviewed from the other corporation parties claimed a father whose chief occupation had been blue-collar factory labor.

As might be expected on the basis of the occupational background of the Sena councilors, the party leadership was less highly educated than councilors from other political groups. Sixteen percent of the Sena councilors had a B.A. or more advanced degree, compared with 51 percent of the other three parties combined. As is indicated in Table 21, a larger percentage of Shiv Sena councilors had completed only a primary edu-

6. Those reporting themselves as "social workers" were asked to state their most recent occupation, hence the unusually small number of social workers.
7. Forty percent of this group claimed to own "large" businesses.
8. The 19 percent figure for Congress/PSP councilors is explained by the large number of PSP corporators who report themselves as factory workers although they are (middle-class) union organizers.

cation. The schooling of the councilors' children was equally revealing and indicated that although Shiv Sena councilors were upwardly mobile, their children had not ascended to the educationally privileged status of the children of other party members. Only four (10 percent) of the Sena councilors had sent at least one child to an English-medium school. (English education, offered primarily in private and church schools, is still to a large extent an indication of privileged status). This figure compares with the 54 percent in Congress (O), 50 percent in Congress (R), and 40 percent in the Praja Socialist party who had sent at least one child to an English-medium school.[9]

The election of Shiv Sena corporators produced a group of municipal councilors with a somewhat less "cosmopolitan" experience. In their travel, linguistic abilities, and political tutelage, Shiv Sena councilors appeared to be of a more circumscribed background. Fully one-third of Shiv Sena councilors had never traveled outside Maharashtra. The experience of other party leaders was more extensive: on the average, 5 percent had trav-

9. The less-advantaged socioeconomic background of Shiv Sena councilors is further underscored by the household amenities that councilors claimed to own. From the items included in a property checklist citing radios, telephone, tape recorder, air conditioner, refrigerator, motorcycle, and car, two simple scales were formulated which measure common and luxury consumer durables. Shiv Sena councilors were markedly less affluent than the other parties' representatives, scoring 2.0 as against 2.5 for the others combined with respect to common goods (Scale 1) and 0.74 compared to 1.03 for the combined parties' representatives with regard to luxury items (Scale 2).

The first scale was computed by scoring the possession of a radio as 1, or a radio and telephone *or* refrigerator as 2, and of a radio, telphone, *and* refrigerator as 3. The second scale was calculated by scoring the ownership of a tape recorder *or* air conditioner *or* motor cycle as 1, ownership of a car as 2, of a car *and* tape recorder *or* air conditioner *or* motorcycle as 3.

One attribute which does not identify Sena leadership as a new, less privileged group is caste. As Table 25 demonstrates, there are only slight differences, as measured by broad caste categories, among the parties. This is not to suggest, however, that there are no caste differences between Shiv Sena and other parties, but rather that they are not revealed in the broad rankings of high, middle, and low caste. Shiv Sena (and the PSP) include a disproportionate number of the urban castes (CKP, etc.), Congress (O) a disproportionate number of non-Hindus (Jains, Muslims, etc.), and Congress (R) a disproportionate number of Marathas. The category "high caste" includes Brahmins as well as CKP and SKP. The middle category which includes Marathas does not distinguish between Marathas and Kunbi-Marathas. The category "low" includes both low and scheduled castes.

Table 22. Travel experience of Bombay municipal councilors

	Shiv Sena #	Shiv Sena %	C(O), C(R), PSP combined #	C(O), C(R), PSP combined %
Only in Maharashtra	13	34	3	5
Outside Maharashtra but not extensively	14	37	11	16
Outside Maharashtra and widely throughout India	10	26	43	65
Outside India	1	3	9	14

eled only within Maharashtra, while 14 percent had been abroad (see Table 22).

In language skills, the Sena leadership was less "cosmopolitan" as well. While twenty-four (62 percent) of the Sena corporators interviewed could claim fluency in English, 80 percent of Congress (O) members, 72 percent of Congress (R) members, and all of the PSP leaders interviewed were demonstrably fluent in English. This lesser degree of fluency in English was reflected in the choice of newspapers that councilors regularly read. Compared to 46 percent of Shiv Sena corporators who reported receiving English-language newspapers at home, 73 percent of Congress (R), 61 percent of Congress (O), and 80 percent of PSP corporators claimed to subscribe to English language dailies.

Perhaps the most outstanding difference of the new elite brought into office by the Sena's 1968 successes was their language background. All forty-two Shiv Sena councilors claimed Marathi as their mother tongue. Not only were Marathi-speakers found in far fewer numbers in other parties, but there was also a much lower representation of Marathi-speakers in the previous corporation. As is evident in Table 23, the number of Maharashtrians increased markedly with the 1968 election.

The sharp rise in the number of Marathi-speakers in the 1968 corporation can be traced directly to the emergence of Shiv Sena. No other party, with the exception of the PSP (which had an electoral adjustment with the Sena in 1968), approaches the Sena in its representation of Marathi-speakers. As is indicated in Table 24, the Shiv Sena's 1968 victories placed a sizable block of Marathi-speakers in power in the municipality.

Table 23. Mother tongue of Bombay municipal councilors, 1961 and 1968

	1961 #	1961 %	1968 #	1968 %
Marathi	57	43.5	78	56
North Indian	20	15.3	24	17
South Indian	11	8.4	7	5
Gujarati	36	27.5	25	18
Others	7	5.3	6	4
Total corporators	131		140	

Sources: 1961 data from B. A. V. Sharma and R. T. Jangam, *Bombay Municipal Corporation: An Election Study* (Bombay: Popular Book Depot, 1962), p. 116. 1968 data from G. S. Badhe and M. U. Rao, *The Bombay Civic Election of 1968* (Bombay: All India Institute of Local Self-Government, n.d.), p. 131.

Table 24. Marathi component of political parties in Bombay Municipal Corporation

Shiv Sena (n = 42)		Congress (O) (n = 47)		Congress (R) (n = 10)		PSP (n = 11)	
#	%	#	%	#	%	#	%
42	100	11	23	6	60	10	91

The disproportionately high representation of Shiv Sena councilors who are young, of lower-middle-class status, and have little political experience might possibly be an artifact of the high Maharashtrian representation in the Sena's ranks. That is, because the Maharashtrian population in Bombay is in general of a less well-established socioeconomic strata, it could be that Shiv Sena has mobilized not a new class of Maharashtrians but simply *more* Maharashtrians, thus changing the political and socioeconomic profile of the corporation. This is not the case, however. Shiv Sena has not only propelled more Maharashtrians into office but it has also mobilized a section of the Maharashtrian community not previously well represented in the corporation. As summarized in Table 25, the Maharashtrians who have ridden into office with Shiv Sena are younger, less "cosmopolitan," of a younger political generation, and of a lower economic strata than the "average" *Maharashtrian* in the other corporation parties.

As against the mean age of 39.9 for Shiv Sena corporators, the mean age of Maharashtrians in the other three parties is 44.7. The socioeconomic background of the two groups is also distinct: professionals (doctors, lawyers) are fewer (13 percent in the Shiv Sena) than in the other parties (23 percent). These differences also carry over to the educational qualifications. A high 39 percent of non-Shiv Sena Maharashtrians claim an advanced

Table 25. Background profile of Maharashtrian councilors in Bombay Municipal Corporation

	Shiv Sena (n = 39)	Maharashtrian Congress (O), Congress (R), PSP corporators (n = 23)
Differences		
Age (years)	39.9	44.7
Property		
Index 1	2.00	2.35
Index 2	.74	1.28
Education (%)		
Primary	13	13
Matriculate	31	21
Diploma	10	4
College-unfinished	20	9
BA	13	17
Advanced degree	13	39
Fluency in English (%)	62	73
Travel (%)		
Only Maharashtra	33	16
India—some	36	64
India—extensively	26	60
Outside India	3	20
News (% receiving English newspapers)	46	85
Educating at least one child in English medium (%)	10	43
Political experience (% participating in nationalist movement)	33	74
Similarities		
Place of birth (%)		
Bombay	51	54
Elsewhere in Maharashtra	49	46
Caste (%)		
High	30	33
Medium	46	28
Low	23	29
Other	—	—

degree beyond the B.A. level, as distinct from 13 percent among the Shiv Sena corporators.

Shiv Sena corporators are also, as indicated by several factors, less cosmopolitan than their Maharashtrian counterparts in other parties. While 20 percent of Congress and PSP corporators have traveled outside of India and 61 percent widely within India, the comparable figures are only 3 percent and 26 percent for Shiv Sena councilors. A further 62 percent of Sena corporators claim ease in speaking English, compared with 73 percent of the leadership of the two Congress parties and the PSP. Only 46 percent of Sena corporators report receiving an English newspaper at home, as distinct from 85 percent of their Maharashtrian counterparts in the other three parties. The political experience of Shiv Sena corporators is also different from that of Maharashtrians in the two Congress parties and PSP. Far fewer Sena councilors gained their first political experience in an India-wide (nationalist) event: one-third of Shiv Sena councilors as distinct from 57 percent of Congress (O) and Congress (R) and 90 percent of PSP corporators report having participated in the Independence movement.

The emergence of Shiv Sena in 1968 promoted into positions of political power a group of Maharashtrian councilors substantially different from leaders of the other major Bombay parties. Not only did this new elite constitute a group with less political experience; it also represented a class much younger, less established financially, and more limited in cultural contacts and experience. Finally, and perhaps most important, the emergence of the Shiv Sena carried into office a group of politicians whose initial contact with political activity lay not in India-wide events nor in the nationalist movement but in regional, Maharashtrian or "parochial" issues.[10]

Shiv Sena, Political Stability, and Interethnic Relations

The consequences emanating from Shiv Sena's mobilization of this new elite are not self-evident. The emergence of a relatively youthful middle- and lower-middle-class Maharashtrian political

10. See Ram Joshi, "The Shiv Sena: A Movement in Search of Legitimacy," *Asian Survey*, 10 (November 1970), 973.

elite, drawn from a section of the population with limited, perhaps parochial, political and educational experiences would appear to spell political disorder and greater hostility between ethnic communities. Shiv Sena's entry into municipal politics has not, however, brought political disruption. And although Shiv Sena may well have intensified interethnic tension, even in this area the party's impact has been less deleterious than is generally assumed.

The general portrayal of Shiv Sena as antidemocratic derives from the often startling pronouncements of Bal Thackeray and other Sena leaders decrying democratic institutions and invoking the occasional "necessary" use of violence. Thackeray's admiration for the forcefulness of Hitler gained prominent coverage in the press, both in Western and in Indian journals.[11] In Thackeray's own publication, *Marmik*, praise was offered for Hitler's leadership: A cartoon appearing in a 1968 issue portrays Patkar of the Communist Party questioning Thackeray as to his plans to defeat communism in India. The reply instructs Patkar to seek the answer from Hitler and Mussolini in their coffins. The cartoon then goes on to picture Hitler and Mussolini rising from their graves and saying, "What we were not able to do, Thackeray has done."[12] The barrage of criticism that Thackeray's comments invited caused the Sena leader to amend his earlier remarks. Thackeray hastened to insist that his praise for Hitler

11. See, for instance, the Marathi paper *Nawa Kal*, Aug. 19, 1967, which reports Thackeray as saying, "Yes, I am a dictator. Why should we have so many rulers? It is a Hitler that is needed in India today." Thackeray's position is stated more fully in an article of May 5, 1968, in *Marmik*, "Weak Democracy or Strong Dictatorship?" in which he disavows his admiration of Hitler but speaks instead of the need for an enlightened dictatorship:

Considering the present situation in India and taking into account the disgrace made to democracy and mistakes in politics, we have to say with regret that our democracy has become paralyzed and no doubt is left in our mind that a strong dictatorship is better than this present paralyzed diseased democracy for the good of the nation. We want to make it clear that we are not opposed to democracy as an institution. No one can deny that democracy should be given the first preference among the many forms of government man has evolved out of his experience. . . .

On uttering the word "dictator" the present people can only see Hitler in front of them. They should be reminded of the Dictator Atatürk Kemal Pasha.

12. *Marmik*, Feb. 11, 1968.

did not encompass "the Nazi and Jewish part," and that he did not mean a "Hitler-style" dictator but rather an "enlightened dictator" such as Atatürk or Nasser.[13]

The idea of an enlightened dictatorship is one to which most of the Sena leadership subscribes. In the survey of municipal corporators, respondents were asked to describe what they felt in general to be the best form of government for India, both in the short and the long run. Twenty-three of the thirty-nine Sena corporators responding mentioned that some form of dictatorship, described variously as "military rule," "enlightened" or "benevolent" dictatorship, "democratic dictatorship," and "guided democracy," was most appropriate for India at the moment. One councilor suggested that many people were attracted to Shiv Sena because they had felt "betrayed by democracy."[14]

The difference between the ideology of Sena leaders and those of other parties in this regard is patent: only one of the Congress and PSP respondents replied that dictatorship might be appropriate for India—even in the short run. While a few others mentioned the importance of a strong government, a much larger number explained that democracy, although slow, was still the only form of government appropriate for India.[15]

It is clear, however, that this idea of the need for some form of dictatorship to solve India's current problems is not one that sits entirely securely with many Sena corporators. In a party where differences and especially dissension from opinions of the top leadership are heavily discouraged, it is some measure of the strength of feeling that sixteen corporators persisted in noting

13. Interview with Bal Thackeray, Jan. 18, 1971.
14. Interview with W. Mahadik, Dec. 7, 1970. Sena leaders explained their advocacy of dictatorship in various ways. One commented: "In India a Hitler is wanted. It is an evil to give illiterates the vote. . . . Only when people are educated and have minimum needs met, then will dictatorship not be necessary." Several others echoed this elitist position: "Dictatorship is necessary because the common people do not have abilities. They must be led." "India needs a government of experts."
15. Most corporators articulated their support for democracy less in terms of moral imperatives than of the impracticability of other forms of government. One Congress (O) Corporator, Mr. Panchal, commented that many military governments, of which Pakistan was one example, could not perform more effectively than electoral political systems.

democracy as the form of government most appropriate to India's current needs. Of these, three explicitly volunteered that they differed from Thackeray in this respect while five others explained their position by alleging that Thackeray himself did not really believe in dictatorship.

The lack of total conviction about the benefits of dictatorship is further manifested by the reply of thirty-seven Sena corporators that democracy is "in general" the best form of government. Thirty-six of the thirty-nine Sena corporators felt, moreover, that for India in the "long run," democracy is preferable.

This division surfaced during the Emergency when Mrs. Gandhi suspended parliamentary procedures. Thackeray declared his support of the Emergency, consistent with his earlier pronouncements that democracy was inappropriate to India's present needs. He did not, however, have the full support of the party, as became clear when a strong faction in Shiv Sena urged him to support the Janata in the spring 1977 elections.

The difference between Sena and other party councilors is apparent, nevertheless, in a variety of areas related to normative issues of politics. Not only are many more Sena than Congress or PSP corporators attracted by nondemocratic forms of government; but also, on a range of issues concerning the use of physical force or violence, the Sena leadership can be distinguished from that of other municipal parties. The more outspoken of the Sena elite, for instance, have clearly tried to create the image that the party will not shy away from the use of violence. On a number of public occasions, Thackeray has admonished the audience that the violence of the "Left" can only be countered effectively through reciprocal measures.[16]

Shiv Sena's willingness to put such threats into practice is suggested by numerous incidents, many of which are reported in the Bombay press. The murder of Communist MLA (member of the legislative assembly) Krishna Desai and the numerous clashes and violence between Sena and Communist union personnel are only some of the widely cited examples.

16. "Crossing the New Frontier: Election Manifesto of the Shiv Sena," 1971, mimeographed.

Table 26. Attitudes toward the use of force among Bombay municipal councilors

	Shiv Sena (n = 39)		Congress (O), Congress (R), PSP (n = 60*)	
	#	%	#	%
Against property				
Yes, without qualification	29	74	8	13
Yes, with qualification	7	18	3	5
No	3	8	49	82
Against persons				
Yes, without qualification	26	67	1	1
Yes, with qualification	9	23	4	7
No	4	10	55	92

*Six councilors did not reply.

It is also clear that the use of force is a concept accepted by Sena corporators in numbers far exceeding that of other municipal party councilors. In the interview schedule, respondents were asked two questions concerning the use of force: (1) Under present circumstances, in Maharashtra, would you say the use of physical force, *such as the destruction of property*, is an appropriate means to political ends? (2) Under present circumstances, in Maharashtra, would you say the use of physical force, *such as the threatening or injuring of persons*, is an appropriate means to political ends (italics added)? Of the thirty-nine Sena councilors interviewed, twenty-nine replied affirmatively and without qualification to the first question. Close to half of this number volunteered that they were not Gandhians, or that a Gandhian philosophy was no longer appropriate. Only one Shiv Sena councilor, in addition to the three who disagreed with the use of force against property, felt that the employment of force against persons could not be justified. This 10 percent contrasts markedly with the 92 percent of Congress (O), Congress (R), and PSP councilors who stated that the use of force against persons was unacceptable. The divergence between Shiv Sena and other councilors on the appropriateness of using force is clearly displayed in Table 26.

Again, although a clear difference exists between Shiv Sena and other party leaders concerning the political use of force, it should be recognized that Shiv Sena corporators are not unanimous on the role that force should play in the political strategy of the party. A number of party leaders are concerned about "rowdies" who, they say, associate with the party, activate the youth, and draw them into violent acts for which the Sena should not be held accountable. One councilor apologized for the violence in the party, noting that in a city of Bombay's magnitude there will be all types: In Kurla, a slum area, there will be the less educated elements who join the party; in Girgaum, a middle-class constituency, there will be the intellectuals. But such remarks are chiefly those of individuals demurring at the main line of Sena thought—an ideology that countenances dictatorship and the extreme use of force.

It is a mistake, however, to infer from the Sena's advocacy of dictatorship and force and from its own nondemocratic party structure that it plays a highly disruptive role in Bombay politics. Despite the antidemocratic rhetoric of the Sena and its somewhat violent demeanor, the party has not attempted to undermine the stability of Bombay politics. While "leftist" parties and the so-called antinationalist Muslim and South Indian groups have been frequent targets of Sena violence, the party has almost never directed its denunciations at national, state, or local governmental institutions.[17]

In the light of Shiv Sena's antidemocratic pronouncements, the party's obeisance to national symbols and to national causes —to the point of chauvinism—is striking.[18] During the Bangla-

17. The party on public occasions takes care to distinguish between what it considers to be the legitimate use of violence (against the "Left") and the illegitimate use of violence (against government). In a statement released to the press Feb. 18, 1968, listing the principles of Shiv Sena, note is made that "the Shiv Sena is opposed to violence and the destruction of *national* property and will never incite people to indulge in such antisocial and subversive acts [italics added]." The reason, however, that Thackeray and other Sena leaders feel justified in openly exhorting violence against the Left is their perception of leftist parties as "antinational."

18. In Thackeray's case, support for national institutions has not meant the consistent lauding of national political leaders. He was critical of Nehru for the latter's support of Krishna Menon and his presumed tolerance of leftist views. Thackeray also periodically leveled cutting asides at Mrs. Gandhi. For example, see his unflattering reference in the Diwali issue of *Marmik*, 1970, to the lady in Delhi with a white forehead (a crude reference to her widowhood).

desh conflict, the Sena was among the more active groups organizing blood drives in Bombay. In public addresses and in *Marmik* editorials, Thackeray has enthusiastically urged Maharashtrian youth to seek careers in the military. Notice boards in the office of the Sena student organization, Vidyarthi Sena, and in *shakha* offices contain information about army service and application procedures. In one display of nationalist fervor, the Sena stationed its volunteers at the doors of movie houses to prevent the audience from leaving before the national anthem had been sung. At times, Thackeray's commitment to nationalism has been directed at quashing the growth of regionalism elsewhere. In protest against the refusal of Madras cinema houses to show Hindi films, Sena leaders succeeded in forcing Bombay houses to cease showing films made in Madras. When Madras theaters rescinded their decision, Thackeray's campaign ceased and Bombay houses resumed their showing of Madras films. As one journalist remarked:

> The economics of the celluloid has triumphed over the politics of the DMK. The screening of Hindi films has been resumed in Madras state simply because, if this is not done, the Shiv Sena will not allow the exhibition in Maharashtra of Hindi films made in Madras studios. The answer to the Annadurais of this world, evidently is the Bal Thackerays. This may not be the most desirable way of ordering our affairs, but I fail to see what else there is to be done.[19]

Not only does the Sena make extensive efforts to demonstrate its nationalist credentials, but the party also has endeavored to show its support for state and local political institutions. The Sena has not been known for burning government property, for *gherao*-ing (encircling) ministers, or for disrupting parliamentary debates, as have other groups.

Thackeray's refusal to discredit or oppose the government was most pointed in the protest of Class III and IV government employees during November 1970. While most political parties supported the employees' demand for increased emoluments, Thackeray, despite the fact that the strikers were overwhelming-

---

19. "The Moving Hand Writes," *Eastern Economist*, 50 (Apr. 19, 1968), 835.

ly Maharashtrian and lower-middle-class—and thus the Sena's natural constituency—urged the government employees to return to work and accept a settlement.

The demonstrations of May 1968 against the presence of hawkers, the attacks on South Indian residences, the burning and looting of Udipi hotels, the break-in at the Communist party (of India) union headquarters, the violence perpetrated against neo-Buddhists, the *morcha* (public procession) protesting the shifting of the atomic energy establishment from Trombay to Hyderabad, the Sena-led *bandh* (shutdown) calling attention to the presumed ill-treatment of Maharashtrians in Karnataka—all may well be countenanced as disruptive. But it is striking that in only one of these instances (protesting the atomic energy move) was the government the target.[20] More important is the fact that the Sena has contested two municipal elections and repeatedly entered legislative and parliamentary contests: the party's espousal of authoritarian and extremist principles does not detract from its own willing participation in the parliamentary process.

What impact has Shiv Sena had on interethnic relations in Bombay? In the late 1960s and early 1970s there were numerous instances reported of attacks on South Indians by presumed Shiv Sena volunteers. That such assaults took place is clear; what is less evident is what long-term impact these violent incidents may have had on the lives of both South Indians and Maharashtrians in Bombay. Particularly in the early years of Shiv Sena, the party's critics predicted that there would be an exodus of non-Maharashtrians from Bombay. Isolated reports cited cases of non-Maharashtrian businesses threatening to transfer their establishments to other states.[21] These reports, however, were followed by stories citing incidents of those who decided against

20. For accounts of Udipi attacks see *New York Times*, Jan. 13, 1974; on the CPI break-in, see *Link*, Jan. 7, 1968; on the Trombay atomic energy *morcha*, see *Link*, Aug. 27, 1967. (An article in *Enlite*, Apr. 1, 1967, argues that the atomic energy *morcha* strengthened Naik's hand in his move to prevent the transfer.) The clashes between Shiv Sainiks and neo-Buddhists occurred in the Worli slums in Bombay. Certain party members, such as Pramod Navalkar, have tried to "cleanse" Shiv Sena's image. See "We Don't Want Anarchy," *Himmat*, Aug. 3, 1973.
21. "Why Did Bombay Burn?" *Frontier*, Mar. 8, 1969.

134 | *Ethnicity and Equality*

leaving or who left, only to return shortly to Bombay. Official reports such as police bulletins emphatically denied that non-Maharashtrians were leaving the city.[22]

Accurate estimates of recent migration trends are handicapped by the unavailability, as yet, of mother-tongue and migration data from the 1971 census. However, a sample survey conducted in 1971 by CIDCO (the City and Industrial Development Corporation) of 1,500 households in Greater Bombay contains information on recent migration trends. The CIDCO survey estimates that the Maharashtrian share of migration in 1971 has risen to 47 percent from 42 percent in 1961. Given the fact that the 1961 out-of-state migration figures were inflated by Maharashtrians moving back to Bombay from other states after the 1960 separation of Maharashtra and Gujarat and the location of the state capital in Bombay, the decline in out-of-state migration figures for 1971 does not seem substantial.[23] Evidence is not yet available to suggest that the percentages of South Indians migrating to Bombay substantially declined.

In other areas where the Sena's impact might be most starkly registered, such as in language patterns, little change seems to have taken place. There is not, for instance, any evidence to suggest that more non-Maharashtrians are sending their children to Marathi-medium schools.[24] It may be that more non-Maharash-

22. See, for instance, *Swarajya*, Sept. 2, 1967.
23. City and Industrial Development Corporation (CIDCO), New Bombay Draft Development Plan, October 1973, Appendix S, Table S-23. This explanation is reinforced by the CIDCO estimate which shows that the state which has declined the most in its percentage of migrants sent to Bombay is Gujarat—from 17 percent in 1961 to 14 percent in 1971.
24. If more people were sending their children to Marathi-medium schools, an increase since 1966 in the percentage of students enrolled in Marathi-medium streams would be registered. This increase could be expected to show up particularly in the younger grades (standards I and II) since parents would be more inclined to place a non-Maharashtrian child in a Marathi-medium school when the child is entering school rather than in the course of his education. However, as Appendix IX, Table A3 shows, no such development appears to have taken place.
Some changes in fluency in Marathi as a second language may well have happened. Ram Joshi, former principal of a well-known Bombay College (SIES), reports that the student audience shows greater comprehension of Marathi dialogue or jokes in school plays or talks than in earlier years.

Table 27. Attitudes of Congress and Sena voters toward South Indians

	Noneducated*				Educated†			
	Shiv Sena (n = 116)		Congress (R) (n = 169)		Shiv Sena (n = 44)		Congress (R) (n = 31)	
	#	%	#	%	#	%	#	%
Positive	71	61	129	76	25	57	12	39
Negative	45	39	40	24	19	43	19	61

*Below matriculation.
†Matriculation, diploma and/or college education.

trians are learning Marathi as a second language than was earlier the case, but this could be as much a function of the states' reorganization and the establishment of the unilingual state of Maharashtra as it is of any effort by Shiv Sena.

There is some indication, further, that Maharashtrians do not view other ethnic communities in Bombay with the hostility that might be expected from Shiv Sena's xenophobic image. If Shiv Sena had exacerbated Maharashtrian hostility toward other ethnic groups, Sena followers might be expected to demonstrate less favorable attitudes toward non-Maharashtrians than would supporters of other Bombay parties. When in the voter survey of 1971 respondents were asked to describe South Indians, however, Sena supporters were not uniformly more critical than, for instance, Congress voters. As Table 27 illustrates, while a higher percentage of noneducated Sena voters made negative observations about South Indians, the educated middle class of Sena supporters (readers presumably of *Marmik* and other Sena literature) expressed in fact somewhat less hostility toward South Indians than did supporters of Congress (R).

The migration and language patterns of non-Maharashtrians and the survey of Maharashtrian voters do not indicate, then, that Shiv Sena's emergence has generated great hostility between ethnic groups. Three explanations can be suggested. The first is the dilution (largely for political reasons) of the anti-outsider element in the Sena's ideology. The second explanation is the duality, present from the beginning, in Shiv Sena's pronouncements, alerting Maharashtrians to the positive as well as the weaker qualities of other ethnic groups. Finally, the Sena, even in its most belligerent aspects, has not posed a threat to the *cultural* self-identity of non-Maharashtrian groups.

Shiv Sena's campaigns against non-Maharashtrians began to subside after 1968 and the party's election to municipal office. The sensitivity of Shiv Sena nativism to the requirement of procuring votes superseded the party's predisposition for or against particular communities. While the anti-"outsider" campaigns helped secure the Sena numerous seats in the 1968 municipal elections, it became obvious to Sena personnel that the party could not hope to move out of its opposition status without gaining the support of non-Maharashtrians in Bombay. The party managed to win one-third of the municipal seats by presumably gaining a large section of Maharashtrian support. But since Maharashtrians constitute only about 40 percent of the Bombay electorate, the Sena recognized that to improve its political fortunes within the city, it needed to broaden its electoral base. Beginning in 1968, therefore, the Sena's disparagement of non-Maharashtrians was markedly quieted. In 1971, the Sena supported a South Indian, Cariappa, for parliament. Sena slogans written in South Indian languages began to appear on Bombay walls. In *Marmik*, campaigns against outsiders became increasingly scarce. In 1971, from January until June, not one article appeared denouncing non-Maharashtrians. Even the support of Muslims, who after 1968 appeared to replace the South Indian as the Sena bête noire, was sought when political expediency demanded. As a *Times of India* editorial noted, a "bizarre parody" occurred in the Sena's courting of previously denounced "enemies":

How the politicians are able to lead their followers by the nose has been shown by the alliance that Shiv Sena and the Muslim league—ranged against each other earlier over the Vande Mataram [a patriotic song] controversy—found with each other so that the former could get its candidate elected as Mayor while the latter will be represented in some important civic committee.[25]

25. "A Bizarre Parody," Apr. 4, 1973.

The Sena's sensitivity to political exigency is one aspect of the party's experience that is often overlooked. The identification of the Sena as a "fascist" organization, a term used with frequency in journal articles and political manifestos, alleges a similarity between Nazi persecutions and Sena aggression against non-Maharashtrians. The analogy is a careless one not only because of the far greater degree of violence employed by the Nazi party, but also because the Sena, unlike the National Socialists, has perceived a need to garner the political support of the minorities it formerly attacked and has been forced to restrain its xenophobia. The tempering of Sena ideology, brought about by the ethnic composition of Bombay and the demands of electoral politics, is an important development in the history of the party.

The abatement of Shiv Sena's antimigrant campaigns is not the only explanation of the absence of greater hostility between ethnic groups. The nature of Sena ideology, even in the early phases, called attention to the "good" as well as the negative side of the migrant communities. *Marmik* and other Sena publications, particularly through 1967, made frequent disparaging references to non-Maharashtrians. South Indians in early *Marmik* writings were portrayed as "Yes, sir" men, ready to accept orders, compliant to the point of obsequiousness, willing, in sum, to do anything to get ahead. Gujaratis were shown as practical people of inconstant principles—eager to please clients and customers when profits are at stake. The actual words used to describe non-Maharashtrians are frequently mocking. South Indians are referred to as *"lungiwallas," "yandugunduwallas,"* "leeches," and "jungle people."[26]

But even in these years when such slighting references to

26. *Lungiwalla* refers to one who wears a lungi—South Indian dress. *Yandugunduwalla* is a nonsense word imitating the syllables of South Indian languages.
  In 1969 the Government of Maharashtra filed a complaint with the Press Council of India deploring the allegedly abusive language used in a *Marmik* article of May 11, 1969. The passage read: "A part of Mysore is called Coorg where human beings do not live. Wild Satans live there . . . and nowadays the progeny of outsiders is noticed giggling in an indecent manner, uttering words through the pot-like mouths and smoking cigars." The press council's report, printed in *Marmik* itself Apr. 23, 1970, noted that this type of writing was apt to inflame passions and pose a danger to the country's unity.

138 | *Ethnicity and Equality*

non-Maharashtrians occur repeatedly, there is concomitant appreciation of the admirable qualities of "outsiders" which Maharashtrians are urged to emulate. Gujaratis, Punjabis, and even South Indians are cited mostly for their superiority in work-related endeavors. In a letter printed in *Marmik*, for instance, one Maharashtrian business manager writes: "Recently I had to employ two Keralite laborers. They are clever, and very hard-working. As soon as they complete their work, they come and ask for the next work. My other laborers should follow their idea. That is my only wish."[27]

The potential impact of this "demonstration effect" on the attitudes of Maharashtrians is recognized by at least one Sena corporator. Commenting that it would be better for Marashtrians to live in mixed housing (along with members of other ethnic communities), he notes: "In a mixed group, people learn from each other. The Parsees and Christians are very neat; the South Indians are hard-working. We see this and we will pick it up."[28]

In *Marmik*'s pages, along with the castigation of non-Maharashtrians are criticisms of Maharashtrians themselves for not emulating the qualities which enable the other ethnic communities to succeed. Articles such as "Beneficial Advice to Marathi People by a Gujarati," "Awake Marathi Man," "Losing a Customer Is a Specialty of Marathi Shopkeepers," all exhort Maharashtrians to acquire the skills of non-Maharashtrians.[29]

Finally, a third explanation for the lack of deeper mutual enmity may lie in the fact that in the cultural sphere, the Sena has not been very demanding. The Sena's position on language usage in Bombay is a case in point. It is not that the Sena refrains from pressing the cause of Marathi: the party does voice demands that municipal and governmental affairs be conducted in Marathi.[30] The party, too, issued statements that all those recruited into the state services should know Marathi and that the

27. "A Justifiable Complaint of a Maharashtrian Factory Owner," *Marmik*, May 1, 1966.
28. Interview with Khedekar, Feb. 5, 1971.
29. May 1, 1966, May 8, 1966, and Apr. 10, 1966.
30. This has also been the ambition of the PSP and SSP in the corporation for many years.

Hindi signs and announcements used on radios, in railway stations, and in other public places in Bombay should be replaced by Marathi.[31] But none of these demands, even if implemented, would alter the cultural or economic position of Bombay's different ethnic groups. In the area of greatest potential importance to the position of Bombay's non-Maharashtrians—the medium of education—the Sena refrains from making any threatening demands. Unlike such ethnic movements as the Parti Quebecois in Canada, which demands that immigrants be enrolled in French-language schools, Shiv Sena officially supports the use of mother tongue as the medium of both private and government-funded schools and advocates the use of English or the mother tongue as the medium of higher education. Even informally, few Sena leaders appear to believe that Marathi should replace English or the many other languages now being used as the medium of instruction in Bombay schools.

Although the Sena recognizes that Maharashtrians are at a disadvantage in college admissions and later in job recruitment because of a poorer facility in English, the Sena solution is the least threatening to outsiders: rather than changing English instruction to Marathi, Maharashtrians are urged to improve their English. The burden of the Sena's linguistic demands falls most heavily on the Maharashtrian himself.

With Shiv Sena's rise to power, numerous politicians, academics, and journalists charged that democratic procedures and the delicate balance in the relations between ethnic groups in Bombay stood in danger of being undermined. Phrases such as "fascist menace," "orgy of terror," "eruption of subnationalism," accompanied periodical and newspaper accounts of Shiv Sena activity.

These epithets allude to only part of the Shiv Sena story. In

---

31. Mahadik, a Sena corporator, has complained on the floor of the corporation that Maharashtrian street signs such as Ranade Road, although written in Devanagri script, do not use Marathi words (see Municipal Agenda, Nov. 27, 1968, p. 1352). He also deplored the fact that a Maharashtrian wakes up in Bombay to turn on the radio and hears the news broadcast begin with "This is Bombay," in Hindi rather than Marathi.

mobilizing a young, lower-middle-class cadre of Maharashtrian leaders, schooled in more parochial political and educational settings than their colleagues from other parties, Shiv Sena did alter the face of the Bombay municipality. To some extent these Shiv Sena leaders, as the epithets suggest, brought with them attitudes unreceptive to democratic procedures and intolerant of a plural society. But less often acknowledged is Shiv Sena's other side: even as Shiv Sena espoused authoritarianism, the party participated in elections and championed nationalist causes. Even as it ridiculed outsiders, the party applauded many of their qualities. And even as the party must be held responsible for violence perpetrated against non-Maharashtrians, Shiv Sena never sought to exact non-Maharashtrian conformity to Maharashtrian language or culture. The "army of Shivaji" turned out somewhat more civilian than most observers predicted.

8 | *Preferential Policies and
Their Impact: The Bombay Case*

> In order to rescue Maharashtrians from the rut of poverty and consequent frustration on all fronts of life, 80 percent [of all] jobs, skilled or otherwise, must be reserved in governmental, semi-governmental, private, and public undertakings. Existing concerns should be persuaded to meet this demand, and licenses to new undertakings should be issued only on this condition.
>
> *Shiv Sena Speaks*

This call for the preferential treatment of Maharashtrians in all levels of jobs in both the private and the public sectors led the list of Shiv Sena demands. The fulfillment of these demands would require, the Shiv Sena manifesto declared, "the warm support and cooperation of the Government of Maharashtra."[1]

Shiv Sena did not leave the task of soliciting employer compliance to the government alone; nor was the party disappointed in its efforts to secure government backing. On the issue of the preferential treatment of Maharashtrians, Shiv Sena and the state government found common cause.

The Sena conducted a broad campaign to pressure businesses to hire Maharashtrians. Part of this campaign was carried in the columns of *Marmik*. In the weekly "exposés" that were features of the *Marmik* issues in the mid-1960s, Shiv Sena identified the firms and its top officers all by name. Sometimes the *Marmik* attacks were highly personal, as in the case of a Maharashtrian officer in the atomic energy division who was singled out for refusing (according to *Marmik*) to hire Maharashtrians. No mention was made of the fact that atomic energy was an all-India public sector establishment mandated by central government policy to recruit an India-wide pool of applicants. The *Marmik* columns listing firm after firm, week by week, served several functions.

---

1. Kapilacharya, *Shiv Sena Speaks* (Bombay: Marmik Cartoon Weekly Office, 1967), p. 47.

142 | Ethnicity and Equality

They alerted employees of the firms themselves to the low ratio of Maharashtrians in top positions; they embarrassed, or at least attempted to, those firms or officers cited in *Marmik* columns; most importantly, they politicized the *Marmik* readership, even those who had no connection with the firms themselves. At the height of the *Marmik* exposés, young Maharashtrian readers were said to be able to recite by memory the "statistics" on the percentage of Maharashtrians in Bombay's top firms.

With the founding of Shiv Sena, the campaigns moved from the columns of *Marmik* to the streets of Bombay. Shiv Sena leaders led *morchas* or public processions to Glaxo, to the Fertilizer Corporation of India, to the State Banks of India, and to many other firms.[2] In one instance, now part of Shiv Sena lore, a prominent Sena leader called on an executive of Indian Oil. Delivering Shiv Sena's ultimatum that more Maharashtrians must be hired, the Sena leader threatened, "You are sitting inside the office but your oil tanks are outside."[3] In the procession to Glaxo, according to the account of one Sena leader, Thackeray and a small group of his cohorts were ushered into the office of a Glaxo manager, where they demanded to know why so few employees were Maharashtrian. The manager insisted that most employees were Maharashtrian and proceeded to get out company records to show the Sena leaders where the employees were born. The Sena leaders retorted that Shiv Sena wanted to know how many employees were *really* Maharashtrians (Maharashtrian by mother tongue). "We made it clear what we meant."[4] Shiv Sena's formation has spawned an abundance of such stories.

2. Accounts have been cited of such encounters with International Tractor, Indian Oil, Glaxo, Sarabhai Chemical, Jayanti Shipping Corporation, New India Insurance, Burmah Shell, and many other companies. For a newspaper report of the state bank *morcha*, see *Times of India*, Jan. 26, 1974.
3. Recounted by a Shiv Sena *shakha* in Parel, January 1971.
4. Recounted by a Shiv Sena municipal councilor, February 1971. Glaxo reputedly has a large number of (Bombay-born) Christians on its employment rosters who, as this incident suggests, are (with individual exceptions) not considered Maharashtrians by Shiv Sena. When told by businessmen, these stories are sometimes related with bemusement or contempt. One of the executives of the Godrej companies recounted with some disdain that Thackeray's sister had visited one of the showrooms to inspect refrigerators for purchase. After

In other ways, less likely to be publicized, Shiv Sena pressure has made itself felt. Small groups of workers have approached the managements of individual firms; Shiv Sena municipal councilors have telephoned and called on executives and personnel officers of firms in their constituencies; and many of the Shiv Sena neighborhood *shakhas* have maintained employment registers. Constituents are invited to list themselves in the registers, and when an employer (or Shiv Sena worker) notifies the *shakha* of a vacancy, individuals from the lists are alerted and coached as to how they may submit an application.

Notwithstanding the *Marmik* columns, processions, and all the other pressures brought to bear on employers by Shiv Sena leaders, Shiv Sena's demands would have carried little clout without the backing of the Maharashtra government. But for many reasons, the Maharashtra government has looked favorably on the Sena demand for preferential treatment.

Preferential Treatment and Maharashtra Government Policy

The Maharashtra state government was initially cautious in pursuing the policy of preferential treatment. Until 1973, it operated within the guidelines suggested by the National Integration Committee that had met in Kashmir in 1968. Accordingly, the government advised that preferences be extended to local persons (those resident in Maharashtra for fifteen years), in Class III and Class IV government jobs, and semiskilled and unskilled positions. In 1968, the Maharashtrian government circulated a directive to large businesses and government offices in Bombay, urging employers to hire local labor.[5] The government argued that local employees were more stable and that with presumed lower absenteeism, profits would be enhanced. The directive further reminded employers of their obligation to com-

---

looking about, she asked the salesperson to show her a list of the Godrej board of directors. Inspecting the list, she remarked caustically that she would never buy a refrigerator from a company that had no Maharashtrians on its board of directors. By this executive's account, it was nevertheless clear that Thackeray's sister was politely received and that all such Sena visitations are treated with circumspection.

5. Signed by M. A. Dhumal, Industries and Labor Section, Circular No. M.S.C. 2468-55003, dated Feb. 4, 1968.

ply with the Notification as to Vacancies Act. The tone of the directive and the fact that the Vacancies Act does not mandate the hiring of local people were indications that the government's advocacy of preferential policies was still tentative.

By 1973, the Maharashtrian government's position on the employment issue had become much more resolute. In a directive to government and business establishments, the commissioner of industries exhorted employers to set aside a quota in managerial as well as in subsidiary jobs.[6] The directive also broadened the definition of local persons to include not only those who were locally domiciled but also all who were native Marathi-speakers. This marked an escalation in the state government's interest in the nativist cause. When quotas were limited to blue-collar and lower white-collar jobs, the government's policy called for little change, for Maharashtrians predominated in lower-class jobs although they did not make up the 80 percent called for in the earlier directives. Since the quotas were to be applied to local persons as defined by residence rather than language, it was likely that many firms could make a strong case that their employment rolls already complied with government stipulations.

The 1973 directive marked a sharp departure from the earlier policy. The *Times of India* reacted indignantly. In an editorial entitled "Parochialism," the *Times* conceded that it was understandable that the Maharashtra government was anxious to provide additional jobs to the people of the state who did not always have a fair deal. Nevertheless, the editorial exclaimed, the recent policy was "going towards the other extreme."[7]

The state's directive of September 1973 urging employers to hire personnel officers whose mother tongue was Marathi was in fact legally justifiable on the grounds that the Factory Act of 1948 required labor officers to speak the language of the majority of their workers. But the directive nevertheless aroused considerable anxiety. In March 1974 questions were raised in the national parliament.[8] Communications were sent from the cen-

6. Signed by P. A. Sabnis, Joint Director of Industries for the Commission of Industries, in Order N. ELP/Undertaking/7934, dated Sept. 25, 1973.
7. *Times of India*, Oct. 15, 1973.
8. See *Lok Sabha Debates*, vol. 36, nos. 11–16, 5th series, March 5–13, 1974,

tral government to the government of Maharashtra and in the next month, the state redefined the term "local person."[9] The redefinition dropped the reference to mother tongue, retaining only the criterion of domicile in Maharashtra.

Despite this retreat, the Maharashtra government's policy, in its inclusion of upper-level as well as semiskilled and unskilled jobs, went well beyond the central government policy of advocating preferences for only lower-salaried jobs. It remains one of the strongest statements of nativist policies at this level of government in India.

The strength of the Maharashtrian government's policy depended not only on its pronouncements but also on the degree to which the government was willing to enforce them by the use of incentives and sanctions. Even with the measure of frankness contained in the government's 1973 directive, resolutions and appeals would not have been effective unless followed by considerable pressure. Resistance among employers against hiring from local labor pools is attributable to several factors. The attraction of recruiting from "outside," according to some industrialists, lies in the traditional specialized skills of particular migrant groups (e.g., Kamathis in construction, "Bhaiyas" in special areas of textiles such as carding). Recruiting migrant workers is also considered desirable when employers are confronted by a troublesome labor situation, since bringing in outside groups weakens the cohesiveness of labor and its susceptibility to organization. Resistance to hiring local labor is, further, in some cases specific to the Maharashtrian worker, who according to prevailing belief is less diligent and less eager than outside workers.

Given such perceptions, the disinclination among employers to accede to government appeals is strong and is overcome only by forceful application of governmental pressure. State government personnel observe that the government has made only appeals to business and that there is no question of coercion. The sanctions that can be and are applied to unreceptive business-

Lok Sabha, Secretariat, New Delhi, March 5, pp. 175–93, and March 13, pp. 71–74.
9. *Times of India*, Apr. 24, 1974.

men represent strong encouragement, however, if not mandatory directives.

In interviews with a large number of industrialists it was eminently clear that government pressures have been intense enough to exact vigorous efforts on the part of companies to comply with governmental policy. As one businessman remarked in a typical comment, "Now at the very least, when all things are equal, we hire the Maharashtrian."

Pressure from government takes many forms. All sizable businesses are required to submit a statement to the government showing the linguistic and geographic origins of persons at different levels of work in the company. This information is usually collected by the company (particularly in the case of white-collar workers) at the time of an employee's application. Officially the government's directive encourages employers to hire local persons, those resident in Bombay for fifteen years; but the form that businesses must submit to the government also calls for information on the linguistic composition of company employment rolls. Sometimes company officials are lax in reporting; the personnel officer from one company claimed to have submitted a form to the government stating that by the company's definition (length of residence), all its workers were Maharashtrian. But on the whole most business managements attempt to avoid offending governmental sensibilities.

The costs incurred by irritating state government personnel are considerable and are particularly high when licenses, permits, or ministerial favors are required. A business intending to expand needs governmental permission. For a water or electricity connection, particularly if it is to be expedited, governmental approval is required. The state government may likewise choose to enforce to the letter the health or safety regulations, thereby penalizing the company for minor infractions.

Such penalties are not often invoked. One manager recounted his inability to secure government permission for plans for a hotel because he could not show that the majority of the laborers were to be Maharashtrian. More commonly it is the anticipation of such sanctions that accounts for their effectiveness. Almost all businessmen interviewed mentioned at least one encounter with the government over the issue of recruitment in which such pressure was informally applied. The following responses are representative:[10]

[Manager of a pharmaceutical company:] The government cannot enforce anything. But it is in our own interest to comply with them as far as possible. The government can create problems for us otherwise. Indirectly we are affected. We may have a licensing problem; or say we want to run a third shift; it's worthwhile keeping the government away.

[Labor and welfare officer, textile mill:] Sometimes the government is insistent. For example, when we apply for additional spindles or machines. Once when we applied for power, government required information from us on the numbers of local persons we employ. But since we were within the rules there was no problem.

[Manager, rayon factory:] Some years back, the government called attention to the fact that labor officers in the company are not Maharashtrian. We told the government that there were no vacancies. Did they want us to sack the officers at their responsibility? We agreed that future vacancies would be filled with Maharashtrians. This is necessary as it may be a question of our needing facilities, water power, etc.

[Personnel officer, cigarette/cigar factory:] The government applies pressure indirectly, when applying for licences, power, etc. They don't call them Maharashtrians, but rather "local people." I had to go there personally; it wasn't enough to send by mail, to make a statement that we would employ 80 percent locals; but they have no check as such.

There are exceptions to this pattern. One instance, reported by an officer formerly with Hindustan Lever, involved a call from a minister of the state government who warned the company that it was not employing sufficient numbers of Maharashtrians. The minister then hastily added that he intended to communicate this to the manager publicly, that his constituency demanded it, but that privately he felt that it was the company's

10. Interviews conducted in 1972 by a research assistant, Ritu Anand, then a senior at Wellesley College.

own affair whom they hired. Generally, however, as the above comments illustrate, government pressure is sufficiently strong to be taken seriously.

Municipal-Level Government Policy

The active policies pursued by the state government are not replicated at the municipal level. Most of the legislation relating to the position of Maharashtrians considered or adopted in the municipal corporation has been entirely unrelated to the issue of preferential treatment of Maharashtrians. One measure adopted by the municipal body, for instance, called for the alteration of several street and road signs from their erstwhile Hindi and English names to Marathi names. Other resolutions aimed at Maharashtrian concerns also involved linguistic reform. These have veered only somewhat less than in the instance of the street signs from concern for Maharashtrian economic prospects. In another instance, the corporation, reaffirming an earlier resolution, announced the compulsory teaching of Marathi as a second language in Bombay schools. This measure had been adopted years earlier and almost all but Gujarati-medium schools had introduced Marathi. Even had the measure been a new one, its acceptance would not have materially affected the position of Maharashtrians in Bombay.

Language legislation may, of course, be of much more than symbolic importance. Were the medium of Bombay University changed from English to Marathi, giving advantage in admissions and performance to Marathi-speaking students, the economic status of Maharashtrians in Bombay would clearly be affected. But the language legislation passed by the municipal corporation was not of this nature.[11]

The municipal corporation's educational legislation, despite initial appearances, is also not designed to affect the economic position of Maharashtrians. At first, with the support of the Sena, the corporation issued a regulation requiring that 75 per-

11. Most of the language legislation passed by the corporation concerns the translation of the municipal agenda, journal, and other records into Marathi and the question of which language to use in corporation debates. The *Bombay Civic Journal* has included a Marathi section since 1970–71.

cent of all seats in the three corporation-run medical schools be reserved for those who had passed their school matriculation in Bombay City. This law made the earlier requirement of having to pass the college interscience examination at a Bombay college more restrictive. But as the Sena legislators soon realized, the regulation did not shift the balance in favor of Maharashtrian applicants at all, but rather discriminated both against migrants from out of state *and* against migrants from elsewhere in Maharashtra itself. As one Sena legislator wryly commented, "It is ironic. Our legislation has probably kept out more Maharashtrians from medical school than ever before."[12]

Legislation concerning employment is clearly of greater direct importance than education to the future status of Maharashtrians in Bombay. Yet in this area the municipal corporation has been mostly silent. One resolution concerning jobs for local persons in the municipal body was proposed by a Shiv Sena corporator. It read:

> In view of the fact that the government of Maharashtra has issued directions that 90 percent of posts in state government in Bombay as well as government offices in *mofussil* (outlying areas) be given to local residents, the same should be done for all posts under municipal administration at all levels.[13]

The last phrase is of particular importance. Although lower-level posts in municipal employment are overwhelmingly Maha-

---

12. Interview in the municipal corporation office of Shiv Sena, January 1970. State-financed medical colleges have requirements that do not simply favor Maharashtrian residents over non-Maharashtrian. They cater almost entirely to their immediate geographic region within Maharashtra by giving preference to graduates of local colleges. The policy of regionalization was recently challenged in the courts and upheld on the grounds that the policy has a rational connection to government objectives. See decision in *Shirang Ganpati Pandit* v. *State of Maharashtra*, A.I.R. 1972, Bom. 242, reported in *Yearly Digest of Indian and Selected English Cases* (Madras: Madras Law Journal Office, 1972,) p. 438.

13. Proposal of W. Mahadik, Apr. 10, 1969 (Municipal Agenda, p. 32); in addition, the corporation has considered (but as of 1971, rejected) the Sena demand to allocate city market stalls by lottery rather than auction, a change which would benefit Maharashtrians who are at times unable to put up sufficient fees in the auction competition. Thackeray has also sought the adoption of a system where up to 80 percent of shops would be allocated to Marathi-speakers and the remaining 20 percent to domiciled persons.

rashtrian, the percentage declines at the semiskilled and skilled levels. Yet although the resolution was phrased to refer to "local people" rather than Maharashtrians and although its passage would have been no guarantee of implementation, the measure was not even adopted by the corporation.

Despite the inaction of the elected body of the corporation, there has been, according to several administrative officials, a growing trend, intensified by the Sena's emergence, to give increasing preference to Maharashtrians at higher levels of employment. Some consideration, it is further reported, has been given to requiring fluency in Marathi as a condition of employment. But if such a trend or development is occurring, it is doing so without the official sanction of the municipal body.

The difference in responsiveness to Maharashtrian claims for preferential treatment on the part of the state and municipal governments can be accounted for by two factors. The first is ethnic affinity: state government personnel in both the state assembly and the bureaucracy are predominantly Maharashtrian. By contrast, the municipal corporation and municipal bureaucracies are ethnically far more heterogeneous (see previous chapter, Table 23). The second factor is that of political interests. The state government stands to profit in a number of ways by Shiv Sena activity. The state government can use the Sena's threats of violence to exact consideration from the central government on issues involving interstate disputes. Shiv Sena has, for instance, organized demonstrations around the Maharashtra-Karnataka boundary disagreement, providing the state Congress government with the grounds for claiming that its own position in the state will be jeopardized unless the issue is resolved in favor of Maharashtra. The state government also stands to gain by Shiv Sena's animosity toward the Left, particularly the communist unions. The Sena is widely seen by the business community as an effective force against communist unions, a view which has led to charges that the Sena receives financial backing from Bombay's large industrialists. Not only is it plausible that the Congress party shares the businessmen's satisfaction with Shiv Sena's union role, but it is also clear that at least in the early years of Shiv Sena, the Congress saw the party as an important electoral ally.[14]

The possible benefits to be reaped from a Sena-Congress understanding at the municipal level were much more problematic. Prior to the Emergency, the two parties were often in direct competition for political power in the corporation, particularly after the Congress (O) decline in the corporation in 1971. Moreover, the position of the Congress in the municipal corporation has been much more tenuous than at the state level, where it was until recently virtually unchallenged. The municipal Congress party therefore could not hope to offer the rewards that attend a strong political position and that would favor an exchange of political support between the Congress and the Sena.

The Changing Employment Status of Maharashtrians

How has government policy affected the actual economic status of Maharashtrians in Bombay? Or, to begin with a prior question, how has the economic status of Maharashtrians changed?

Measurement of the economic progress of different groups in Bombay is made difficult by the paucity of published data. Recent census and citywide surveys do not record the ethnic breakdown of occupational categories. Consequently, it is only possible to offer suggestive observations about employment changes. These observations, based on three studies of public and private employment in the city, point to a clear pattern of rising occupational status among middle-class Maharashtrians.

The first study was conducted in 1970 by a group of Bombay

14. The argument that Shiv Sena is the "brainchild" of the Congress or, less explicitly, that Congress and Shiv Sena cooperation has been mutually advantageous, is often made. See, for instance, Vasant D. Rao, "Shiv Sena—A Case Study in Regionalism in India," *Quarterly Review of Historical Studies* (Calcutta), 13:1 (1973–1974), 136–37; also "And Now Bombay," editorial in *Hindustan Times* (Delhi), Feb. 27, 1974. Most often cited is the example in 1967 when the Congress candidate, S. G. Barve, opposed Krishna Menon for a parliamentary seat. The Congress welcomed Shiv Sena's support in its effort to defeat Menon, standing as a Communist. Barve's victory and, after his death, the election of his sister-in-law, was due in large part to Shiv Sena. Congress and Shiv Sena also cooperated in the parliamentary bye-election in Bombay's Central Constituency, January 1974.

Table 28. Recruitment of managers in twenty-five Bombay companies

Mother tongue of executive	Hired before 1950		Hired 1950–1960		Hired after 1960	
	#	%	#	%	#	%
Marathi	0	0	5	12	10	21
Gujarati	9	56	14	34	21	44
South Indian	4	25	12	29	6	12
North Indian	2	13	5	12	9	19
Sindhi	1	6	5	12	2	4

students at a management training institute who interviewed 125 managers from twenty-five Bombay companies. As Table 28 illustrates, the percentage of Maharashtrian managers hired by these companies has grown steadily over the last two decades, largely at the expense of South Indian and Sindhi personnel.

The percentage of Maharashtrian managers is very low, particularly when cast against the percentage (42 percent) of Bombay's population that is Marathi-speaking. It is nevertheless striking that the growth in Maharashtrians recruited by the twenty-five companies far exceeds that of any other ethnic group.

The second study, an analysis of Bombay telephone directories,[15] reveals a pattern of change in the status of the Maharash-

---

15. In its listing of private firms and government offices, the Bombay telephone directory includes the names, positions, and telephone exchanges of a firm or establishment's officers. From the names, it is possible to identify the linguistic background of the individual and thus to estimate the numbers of Maharashtrians and non-Maharashtrians employed. Some names are not readily identifiable; the surname Desai, for example, could be either Maharashtrian or Gujarati. But when the identification is done by native speakers familiar with Maharashtrian names, there is probably a greater than 85 percent accuracy.

This analysis was done by two research assistants, Neelam Kanodia and Mrs. T. C. Daswani, both natives of Bombay. The Bombay telephone directories used were for 1962, 1967, and 1973. The central government establishments included were Air India, Atomic Energy Department, Indian Oil, Indian Airlines, Directorate General of Shipping, New India Assurance, Posts and Telegraphs, Western Railway, Bombay Telephones, Reserve Bank of India, and Life Insurance Corporation. State and municipal offices included the Directorate of Employment, Industries, Labour and Employment offices, Western Railway Police, Finance Department, and Transport Undertaking (BEST). The private firms included Podar Mills, Shree Ram Mills, Shree Niwas Cotton, India United Mills, Phillips, Mafatlal, Larsen and Toubro, Bajaj, Burmah Shell, Caltex, Glaxo,

Table 29. Maharashtrians in higher-level positions in Bombay establishments

	1962	1967	1973
Public Sector			
Central government			
(11 establishments sampled)			
Total employment (n)	398	677	672
Percent Maharashtrian	19	25	29
State and municipal government			
(7 establishments sampled)			
Total employment (n)	70	102	114
Percent Maharashtrian	64	75	82
Private sector (15 establishments sampled)			
Total employment (n)	55	68	73
Percent Maharashtrian	7	12	16

trian middle and upper classes consistent with that indicated by the manager survey. The findings are reported in Table 29.

The results are unambiguous: the percentage of Maharashtrians in high-level and middle-level positions in both the private and public sectors had risen continuously, beginning before Shiv Sena's emergence and continuing in the years following.

The third study, a survey of 126 clerical workers in twelve private and government organizations, reveals a similar pattern. Of those hired during or before 1971, Maharashtrians accounted for 45.6 percent. Of those hired after 1971, Maharashtrians represented 61.7 percent.[16]

CIBA, Forbes, Forbes and Campbell, Indian Express, and Crompton, Greaves and Co.

For a fuller discussion, see Mary Fainsod Katzenstein, "Governmental Response to Migration," Migration and Development Study Group, M.I.T., c/76-11.

16. This study was done by a marketing research organization in Bombay which the author and colleagues from the Migration and Development Study Group at M.I.T. commissioned in 1976. Similar observations about the improved occupational position of Maharashtrians have appeared in occasional journalist reports. In one report, for instance, on Udipi hotels in Bombay, B. Subha Rao notes that whereas it was once undeniable that these South Indian restaurants employed few Maharashtrians, "importing their near and distant relations from their home districts," now considerable numbers of Maharashtrians work in them: "Indeed, the Satkar group of restaurants, the biggest name in the vegetarian catering business, boasts that nearly 70 percent of its staff is Maharashtrian." B. Subha Rao, "Flourishing Businesses of Udipi Hotels," in *Hindustan Times, Sunday Standard* (Delhi), Jan. 6, 1974.

Perceptions of progress among Maharashtrians appear to bear out the changes suggested by the above data. By 1970, only four years after Shiv Sena's founding and two years after the party's election to the municipal council, sentiment was widespread among Maharashtrians that their status in Bombay was improving. As was perhaps to be expected, this feeling pervaded Shiv Sena offices and party meetings. But it also seemed to be a sentiment echoed by the ordinary voter, Shiv Sena supporter and nonsupporter alike.

Exuberance among young workers pervades Shiv Sena offices. In the tones of the true believer, young Sainiks relate stories of Maharashtrian success. The tales share a common theme. Whether it is the Bank of Baroda, Voltas, Glaxo, or any other of the numerous well-known Bombay firms, Maharashtrians, the account begins, had enjoyed few opportunities. One young Sainik with typical enthusiasm told the story of a friend employed at CIBA. The friend had been called, along with other Maharashtrian workers, to speak with one of the managers after threats from Shiv Sena leaders. The manager requested their help in recruiting Maharashtrians and shortly thereafter more were hired.

One factor that may contribute to such perceptions is the obvious upward mobility of key Sena leaders. In 1970, for instance, Manohar Joshi, a prominent Sena figure who by his own account was raised in poverty, planned a European vacation—his first trip outside India. While such meteoric improvements in lifestyle are hardly unique to Shiv Sena political leaders, they still help to reinforce the idea among Sena party followers that the lot of Maharashtrians is improving.

A distinct exception to such optimism is found within the Communist party. Most Communist party leaders and workers are strongly convinced that Shiv Sainiks are strikebreakers, "bourgeois lackeys," and that Maharashtrians have been offered mere tokenism with the intent of dividing the working class by rewarding a selected few.

The ordinary Bombay voter seems to agree much more closely with the Shiv Sainiks than with the Communists. In a survey of over 450 Bombay voters conducted after the parliamentary elections in 1971, 51.5 percent of the population said that they felt more Maharashtrians were getting jobs than ever before, 19 percent felt that more Maharashtrians were not getting jobs, 25 percent replied that they were unsure, and 4.5 percent declined to respond.[17]

In answering another question, 14 percent of those asked claimed that they personally knew of people who had found jobs through Shiv Sena. While Shiv Sena supporters who felt prospects for Maharashtrians had improved outnumbered those who did not by four to one, the ratio among Congress party supporters was two to one. The figures are a compelling indication that among Maharashtrians in Bombay, including those who do not support Shiv Sena, there has been a sense of improving job possibilities.

The manager survey, telephone book analysis, office survey, and voter interviews are not as comprehensive as census data. But it is striking that each accords with the conventional Bombay wisdom which sees Maharashtrian job opportunities as improving.

Preferential Treatment as an Instrument of Public Policy

To what extent can the improvement in the job status of Maharashtrians be traced to governmental policy? The chronology of events is revealing: The improvements in Maharashtrian status noted in the managerial, telephone directory, and clerical surveys demonstrate that Maharashtrian job mobility began well before the Sena's founding in 1966. Since the surveys draw on pre-1973 data, they also indicate that marked advancement of Maharashtrians occurred prior to the stringent policy measures adopted by the state government in that year.

Can it be argued, then, that government policy and Shiv Sena pressure have been largely irrelevant to the enhancement of job

---

17. Results drawn from a survey conducted by the author and Kartikeya Sarabhai in Bombay in 1971. The survey, as indicated in Chapter 5, included interviews with 479 Maharashtrian voters and an approximately equal number of South Indian voters living in Bombay.

opportunities among middle-class Maharashtrians? Can other factors, such as the expanding educational system and the growing number of educated Maharashtrians, or simply Bombay's growing economy, account for Maharashtrian improvements in recent years?

The underrepresentation of any social group in white-collar positions is sometimes attributed to a scarcity of supply. Such an explanation in the Bombay case would presume an earlier shortage, and in more recent years a growing pool, of educated Maharashtrians. There has been an enormous growth in school enrollments in Maharashtra. Secondary enrollment rose from slightly under 2 million in 1950 to 6.5 million students in 1965.[18] Between 1963 and 1970, enrollment in primary schools rose by 31 percent, in secondary schools by 60 percent.[19] At the University of Bombay alone, enrollment has risen nearly 300 percent, from 24,000 in the early 1950s to almost 90,000 students in 1971.[20] Not all of these are Marathi-speaking students, and there is in fact some indication that the *proportion* of Maharashtrians in higher education may have declined relative to other linguistic groups. The newer constituent colleges built since the 1960s in Bombay seem to cater more to the Gujarati than to other ethnic groups; and in one prestigious Bombay college (Elphinstone), Maharashtrian enrollment fluctuated from an estimated 38 percent in 1956 to 21 percent in 1965 and 30 percent in 1975.[21] But even as the percentage of Maharashtrians may have declined, the number of Maharashtrians receiving B.A. degrees grew with the rapid expansion in college enrollment throughout the 1960s. Thus it is by no means clear that there has been a shortage of educated Maharashtrians, although it is patent that their numbers have rapidly grown.

It is a widely accepted maxim that job opportunities for previously underrepresented groups are greatly enhanced in peri-

18. Government of Maharashtra Education Department, *Educational Development in Maharashtra State, 1950–51 to 1965–66* (Bombay: Government Central Press, 1968), fol. p. 90.
19. Educational Department, Maharashtra State, 1971, p. 2, mimeograph.
20. Statistics taken from annual reports of the University of Bombay.
21. Calculations made by examining Elphinstone enrollment rosters.

ods of general economic growth. If it could be shown that Maharashtrian occupational status improved markedly in a period of general recession, it might be possible to identify government pressure as a critical force explaining the change in Maharashtrian status. But such a disjunction between policy and economic forces has not taken place. Instead, employment appears to have increased throughout the 1960s and early 1970s except for a single brief slump in 1967–68 (see Appendix IX, Figure A).[22] Although employment in certain industries, most notably textiles, has declined, it appears that white-collar job opportunities in other sectors have been expanding.

In addition to expanding job opportunities and the growing numbers of educated Maharashtrians, one other factor has favored job mobility among Maharashtrians. In 1960 the multilingual state of Bombay was divided into two states, Gujarat and Maharashtra. As with linguistic reorganizations elsewhere in India, the separation has encouraged the transition to greater use of the regional language. This development has probably resulted in Maharashtrians facing less of a disadvantage in job recruitment than was the case earlier.

An explanation of the growing proportion of Maharashtrians in middle-class jobs must incorporate a combination of factors. The establishment of a separate Maharashtrian state in 1960 and the accompanying linguistic changes, the expanding economy, and the growing numbers of educated Maharashtrians have all favored the upward mobility of middle-class Maharashtrians. Given these other favorable circumstances, it is virtually impossible to identify the extent to which governmental policy is itself responsible for Maharashtrian advancement.

The experience of preferential treatment in Bombay is important to a normative evaluation of preferential policies. One argument sometimes used to weigh the desirability of preferential treatment revolves around an assessment of whether such policies can work. In a 1976 court case in the United States, *Alevy* v. *Downstate Medical Center of New York State* (39 NY 2nd 326), the court unanimously held that "reverse discrimination" was con-

---

22. For data on economic growth in Bombay, see Appendix IX, Figure A1.

stitutional "in proper circumstances." One justice on the court admonished, however, that because the consequences of preferential treatment were sometimes so undesirable, preferential policies should not be adopted if they did not work. Similarly, he noted that "if such practices really work, the period and extent of their use should be temporary and limited."[23] This study of Bombay suggests, however, that efficacy is poor grounds on which to evaluate the desirability of preferential treatment. Even in Bombay, where it is clear that the government has applied considerable pressure to exert compliance with preferential policies and where the data to evaluate the changing economic status of the target population do exist, it is difficult to assess the role that policies have played. Because the question "Does it work?" is rarely answerable, the value of preferential treatment may have to be judged on other grounds.

An even more important lesson emerges out of the Bombay experience, a lesson which underscores the political rather than the moral basis of the decision to institute preferential policies. The Maharashtra government's decision grew out of Shiv Sena pressure, out of the shared political interests of the party and state government, and out of the ethnic ties which linked the Maharashtrian community of Bombay to the Maharashtrians who governed the political affairs of the state. It is not that normative considerations were irrelevant to the pursuit of preferential policies. The state government's recognition that the constitution both guarantees freedom of movement and prohibits discrimination based on place of birth probably did influence the formulation and enforcement of preferential policies: directives which might otherwise have extended preferential treatment to Maharashtrians were phrased to confer special privileges on "local" persons. Preferential employment, moreover, was deemed voluntary rather than compulsory by government circulars and instructions. Although the constitution may have thus set limita-

23. Quoted in Robert L. Hardgrave, "Defunis and Dorairajan: Protective Discrimination in the United States and India," paper delivered at the 1976 Annual Meeting of the American Political Science Association, Chicago, September 2–5, 1976, p. 12.

tions on the extent and nature of preferential treatment, constitutional authority did not prevent the government from reaching its decision to promulgate preferential policies. One lesson of the Bombay experience, then, is that the decision to adopt preferential policies was grounded less in moral considerations than in political imperatives.

9 | *Preferential Policies and Judicial Response: The National View*

The Maharashtra government is not alone in the support it accords the policy of preferential treatment for local persons. Although the type of policy varies, there is not a state in India that does not now proffer, in such areas as jobs or university admissions, preferences for local persons.

The practice of providing special reservations for disadvantaged groups in employment or universities finds an acceptance in India far more widespread than in the United States or Western Europe. Policies of preferential treatment have met strong resistance in the United States, as illustrated by the controversy over the DeFunis and Bakke cases.[1] In India, however, the practice of "reverse discrimination" is explicitly prescribed within the constitution itself. Departing from the nineteenth-century liberal notion of equality defined as equal opportunity, the authors of the Indian constitution advanced instead the precept of unequal opportunity or preferential treatment for disadvantaged groups as the very requisite of equality. Based on the premise that legal equality is meaningful only in the presence of social and economic parity, the guarantee of equality of opportunity and the

---

1. *De Funis et al.* v. *Odegaard et al.* (416 U.S. 312, 1974) and *Bakke* v. *Board of Regents, University of California* (76-811). The cases involved the preferential admissions of minority students in the University of Washington Law School and University of California Medical School at Davis, respectively. The De Funis case was declared moot by the Supreme Court. Justice Douglas, however, wrote a lengthy opinion which advances a classical liberal argument: "The key to the problem is the consideration of each application in a racially neutral way" (p. 334). "Whatever his [De Funis's] race, he has a constitutional right to have his application considered on its individual merits in a racially neutral manner" (p. 337). "So far as race is concerned, any state-sponsored preference to one race over another in that competition is in my view 'invidious' and violative of the Equal Protection Clause" (p. 344).

proscription of discrimination in the Indian constitution are modified by stipulations which permit the extension of preferential treatment to scheduled castes, tribes, other backward classes, women, and children.[2] Defending this perspective on preferential treatment, former supreme court justice A. N. Ray has reflected, "Equality of opportunity for unequals can only mean aggravation of inequality. Equality of opportunity admits discrimination with reason."[3]

Although the preferential treatment of such groups as scheduled castes and tribes is directly mandated by the Indian constitution, the extension of reservations to local persons is on a less sure constitutional footing. Most articles in the constitution that relate to residence or place of birth prohibit discrimination rather than mandating preferential treatment. The constitution, for instance, guarantees all citizens the right to move freely throughout the territory of India and to reside and settle in any part. Constitutional assent for preferential policies for local persons can be found only in Article 16(3); and that article gives parliament *alone* the right to prescribe residential requirements for employment in government services exclusively.

But policies of localism persist both in the absence of parliamentary approval and outside government service. State domicile restrictions are reported as having existed as early as the 1950s.[4] In the last fifteen years, as employment possibilities and admissions to universities have tightened, state governments have seized the initiative and have exhorted public and private employers to hire from the local labor force. In the late 1960s and early 1970s, these policies became more widespread and more exacting. The late 1960s brought a wave of state directives which urged employers and universities to favor applicants who had resided in the local area for ten or fifteen years.

How have the courts reacted to these policies? Have the courts endeavored to arrest their momentum? The political logic of preferential policies is such that the state governments have a

2. Particularly Articles 15(3), 15(4), and 16(4). See Appendix 3.
3. *State of Kerala* v. *N. M. Thomas*, 1976(1) *Service Law Reporter*, p. 807.
4. *Report of the States Reorganization Commission* (New Delhi: Government of India Press, 1955), p. 230.

strong interest in their maintenance. Because state governmental personnel are often from the ethnic group that stands to gain from preferential policies, the political incentives encouraging preferential treatment are strong. Only the courts and possibly the central government are in a position to curtail the promulgation of preferential policies. What measures the courts have— and have not—taken is the subject of this chapter.

The reaction of the courts must be examined in the light both of the historical debate over preferences in India and of the present national and state policies. In the sections that follow, this chapter will describe the debate over residential requirements that occupied several of the Constituent Assembly sessions in the 1940s, explore the present policies of both the central and state governments with regard to sons-of-the-soil claims, and analyze the development of judicial opinion on the issue of residential requirements by reviewing court decisions since Independence.

Residence Requirements: The Constituent Assembly Debates

Reservations for communal and class groups in government jobs, in the legislatures, and in educational establishments go back in India to the nineteenth century. In the 1880s, special schools and scholarships were established for "depressed classes" in the regions of Madras, Baroda, and Travancore.[5] In 1909, the British set up separate electorates for the Muslim community, bringing to four the number of recognized communal and class divisions within the electorate. By 1935, the number of separate electoral constituencies reached seventeen.[6] A system of special reservations in government jobs was also gradually instituted in many regions. In Madras, for example, the First Communal Government order of 1921 established six categories (Brahmin, Non-Brahmin, Christian, Muslim, European, and Anglo-Indian) from which recruits for government service in Madras were

---

5. Lelah Dushkin, "Scheduled Caste Politics," in J. Michael Mahar, ed., *The Untouchables in Contemporary India* (Tucson: University of Arizona Press, 1972), p. 170.

6. Kamlesh Kumar Wadhwa, *Minority Safeguards in India* (Delhi: Thomson Press, 1975), p. 25.

drawn.⁷ In the Punjab, similarly, 20 percent of government positions were reserved for the Sikh community at the time of Independence.⁸

The arguments for such reservations involved one of three justifications: (1) the egalitarian intent to secure protection for disadvantaged groups whose interests would otherwise be neglected; (2) a pragmatic view which supported such concessions in the interest of political stability; (3) the divisive purpose, attributed to the British, of weakening the unity of the nationalist movement.

The members of the Constituent Assembly initially voted to retain the widespread system of reservations developed under the British. Partition, however, brought the system of reservations into disfavor since separate Hindu and Muslim electorates were thought to have precipitated communal tensions. The assembly, therefore, abandoned the early proposals and made exceptions only for scheduled castes, tribes, other backward classes, and Anglo-Indians.⁹

Sons-of-the-soil claims for constitutional recognition aroused mixed reactions in the Constituent Assembly. The draft constitution initially proscribed any preferential treatment of sons-of-the-soil. Proposals sympathetic to residential requirements in the state public services were not incorporated in the draft.¹⁰ Article 10 of the draft constitution banned, outright, discrimination based on place of birth. During discussion of the draft, Jaspat Roy Kapoor of the United Provinces sought to strengthen the stricture by adding "residence" to the grounds on which discrimination would be prohibited.¹¹ According to Kapoor's amendment, Article 10 was to read: "No citizen shall on grounds only

7. See Eugene F. Irschick, *Politics and Social Conflict in South India: The Non-Brahman Movement and Tamil Separatism* (Berkeley: University of California Press, 1969), pp. 236–67.
8. B. Shiva Rao, *The Framing of India's Constitution* (Nasik: Government of India Press, 1968), vol. V, p. 194.
9. Ibid., pp. 741–80, or Wadhwa, *Minority Safeguards*, pp. 64ff.
10. See summary of statements by Panikkar, Tyagi and Patel in B. Shiva Rao, *The Framing*, pp. 193, 195.
11. *Constitutional Assembly Debates* (hereafter referred to as *CAD*), Nov. 30, 1947, p. 676.

of religion, race, caste, sex, descent, place of birth or residence or any of them be ineligible for any office under the state."

Alladi Krishnaswami Ayyar, however, contended that residential qualifications should be allowed only under given circumstances and sought to amend the article to permit parliament to set residential requirements for state employment.[12] B. R. Ambedkar, charged with the major responsibility for drafting the constitution, successfully urged the acceptance of both the Kapoor and Ayyar amendments (see Article 16, Appendix 3).

A number of different arguments were advanced in support of extending preferences to local persons. One argument, proffered by Mahavir Tyagi, cited the sovereign impulses of the separate regions. Tyagi proposed that residential qualifications were not an unreasonable concession to the desire on the part of the states to be self-governing: "If there are open chances for the residents of one province to serve in another, it means that the residents of that province shall not be able to enjoy self-government." The absence of residential requirements, Tyagi argued, "will go against the real spirit of Swaraj."[13] A second argument took a simple, pragmatic position, contending that such preferences were then widespread and that their abolition would be "impracticable."[14]

A third argument, submitted by Ambedkar, made reference to the inequalities of the different regions and the need to protect the job interests of people from the less advantaged states. Although Ambedkar conceded that residential qualifications detracted from the value of a common citizenship, he urged the assembly to recognize that: "At the same time it must be realized that you cannot allow people who are flying from one province to another, from one state to another as mere birds of passage without any roots ... just to come, apply for posts and so to say

12. As Kartikeya Sarabhai has commented, it is ironic that the argument to accept residential restrictions on state employment was made by Ayyar and Rajgopalachari, two Tamil Brahmins, members of a community which in the 1960s was to become one of the chief targets of nativist protest in Bombay. "Unity among Diversity, Public Policies and the Evolution of India's Goal of National Integration," draft of Ph.D. thesis, M.I.T., pp. 2–7.
13. *CAD*, Apr. 30, 1947, vol. 3, p. 448.
14. Shiva Rao, *Framing of India's Constitution*, vol. II, p. 186.

take the plums and walk away." Moreover, Ambedkar observed, "We are merely following the practice which has been already established in the various provinces."[15] Permitting parliament rather than the different states to lay down residence requirements had at least the advantage, Ambedkar noted, of imposing a uniformity on the highly disparate policies of the various states.

Governmental Policies on Preferential Treatment

The uniformity of which Ambedkar spoke has remained elusive. At times the absence, and on occasion the disregard, of central government direction has allowed the states to pursue a wide range of preferential practices. The central government's policies on preferential treatment sought to protect meritocratic principles in recruitment even as some concession was made to nativist claims for special treatment.

Just as Ambedkar's constitutional formulation represented a compromise between protagonists and opponents of preferential policies, the central government has had to respond to similarly conflicting pressures. On the one hand, the central government is cognizant of the view articulated most commonly in Delhi and within the all-India services in the states that preferential policies introduce inefficiency. On the other hand, the government is sensitive to the high-pitched demands which have fulminated in the states out of the sense of inequalities suffered by local ethnic groups.

The government's policy, formulated by the National Integration Committee which met in Kashmir in 1968, reflects the effort to respond to concerns of both efficiency and equality. In an effort to accommodate ethnic claims without doing damage to meritocratic principles, the committee urged that high-level jobs be recruited on an all-India basis and that lower-level positions be filled through local channels. Based on the committee's recommendation, the prime minister (then Indira Gandhi) wrote to the minister for industrial development and the minister of labor and rehabilitation, directing them to implement the Na-

15. *CAD*, Nov. 30, 1948, vol. 7, p. 700.

tional Integration Committee formula. The minister of industrial development in turn issued instructions to public-sector undertakings that recruitment to posts carrying a basic salary of not more than 500 rupees per month should be made through the National Employment Service (e.g., the local employment exchanges, which are reputed to favor local applicants). The minister of labor and rehabilitation also issued appeals to the (private sector) All-India Organization of Employers to adhere to the same policy.[16]

The formula advocating an all-India employment competition for higher-level positions and a localized selection procedure for less skilled jobs sought a balance between the desire to further national productivity and the need to respond to claims for regional equality. As Mrs. Gandhi explained, preferential policies were promulgated by the central government with reluctance:

This is a matter in which one has to have a certain balance. While we stand for the principle that any Indian should be able to work in any part of India, at the same time, it is true that if a large number of people came from outside to seek employment . . . that is bound to create tension in that area. Therefore, while I do not like the idea of having any such rule, one has to have some balance and see that the local people are not deprived of employment.[17]

Spokesmen for the central government justified their advocacy of preferential policies in several ways. But the dominant viewpoint in the central government was that expressed by Mrs. Gandhi. Noting on the one hand that national integration and productivity required a mobile labor force to which domicile restrictions would be inimical, she conceded the need for prefer-

---

16. See speech by F. H. Mohsin, *Rajya Sabha Debates*, 89:1–4 (July 25, 1974), p. 211. For other speeches by government spokesmen, see R. K. Khadilkar, Minister of Labour and Rehabilitation, in *Rajya Sabha*, 80:10–18 (May 25, 1972), p. 88; Siddeshwar Prasad, Deputy Minister in the Ministry of Heavy Industry, in *Lok Sabha Debates*, 29:6–10, Aug. 2, 1973, p. 191; M. H. Choudhury, Minister of Industrial Development, in *Rajya Sabha*, 77:12–15, Aug. 9, 1971. Also see account by A. G. Noorani, "Legality of Local Recruitment," *The Indian Express*, New Delhi, Apr. 2, 1974.

17. *Lok Sabha Debates*, 22:21–25 (Dec. 13, 1972), p. 13. See also speech by F. H. Mohsin, n. 16, p. 213.

ential policies, stating: "And I do stand by this: that where there is any big industry or project it should be seen that those local people who cannot travel around seeking employment elsewhere should be given full opportunity. Otherwise tension will be created."[18]

State policies have often veered from both the letter and the spirit of the central government's directives. While some states, such as West Bengal, have expressed reluctance to adopt policies of localism, other states, such as Maharashtra and Tamil Nadu, have issued outright directives urging employers to hire a given numerical quota of local persons, not simply in the less skilled positions, but at all levels of employment.

There are at least six methods by which states have practiced discrimination against nonresidents: (1) by prescribing proficiency tests in the regional language as prerequisites for recruitment to the public services; (2) by setting domicile tests requiring residence for a certain number of years in the local region; (3) by restricting outsiders from acquiring property; (4) by channeling recruitment through government employment exchanges, where the practice is often to give preference to local persons in registration and placement; (5) by devolving on local bodies responsibility for recruitment, and thus effectively narrowing the pool from which applicants are drawn; (6) by setting educational or other requirements, such as receiving the previous degree or certification from a local educational institution as a prerequisite for admission to a higher level of education.[19]

In most states, preference is given to state residents, particularly in medical and technical education. In some cases, admission to educational institutions is even more narrowly confined to those within a particular area of the state. Preferential admission is based on requirements either that an applicant produce a domicile certificate (notarized evidence that the individual has

18. *Rajya Sabha Debates*, Feb. 28, 1974, p. 93.
19. The first three are cited as well in the States Reorganization Commission Report. See the comment on this by Lawrence Ebb, "Inter-State Preference and Discriminations," in Lawrence Ebb, ed., *Public Law Problems in India: A Survey Report: Proceedings of a Conference Held at Stanford Law School, July 15–August 16, 1957* (Stanford: School of Law, Stanford University, 1957), p. 163.

resided in a given locality for a certain period of time, ranging usually from five to fifteen years) and/or that the applicant has passed the previous level of education (interscience or matriculation) from a local college or school. The precise restrictions vary widely from state to state and it is difficult even for the central government to keep current on the particular requirements of the different states. In the aftermath of the National Integration Committee meeting in 1968 in Kashmir, a question was asked in the Rajya Sabha about what was being done to implement the committee's recommendations. On November 26, 1969, the government submitted a reply which reports the responses of different states to the government's inquiry about domicile restrictions (see Appendix VII). The enumeration of requirements (Appendix VIII) gives an indication of the wide range of residential restrictions.

Although it is difficult to document state by state, there is some evidence to suggest that domicile requirements in educational admissions have become increasingly more restrictive. For example, in Maharashtra State medical schools in Bombay, a rule was adopted in 1969 which required that in addition to passing the qualifying examination from the local university, an applicant must produce evidence of having completed secondary education in the state.[20] Medical school admissions procedures elsewhere indicate that although a domicile requirement of five years was once usual, states are now moving to set domicile qualifications at ten or fifteen years.

Preferential policies are not found exclusively in the realm of education. Since the late 1960s, many of the state governments have begun instituting measures to protect the employment opportunities of the local population. These measures include formal bills passed by the state legislatures as well as directives issued by the state governments. Examples follow of the kinds of

20. In 1969–70, the State of Maharashtra medical colleges introduced a ruling that "in addition to the qualifying exam mentioned above [interscience] only those students will be eligible for admission to medical colleges who have passed also the SSC or Senior Cambridge of the Indian School Certificate . . . from any of the recognized schools in Maharashtra state." See "Medical Colleges of the Government of Maharashtra, Rules for Admission," 1973–1974 (MO-A 0219-1), p. 2.

preferential policies pursued by some of those state governments which have been most active in this area.

Maharashtra

As the previous chapter detailed, in a circular dated September 25, 1973, the director of industries of the Maharashtra State government called on the public and private sectors to employ local persons in all categories of jobs. The circular urged that in all future recruitment, 60 percent of top managerial jobs and 90 percent of subordinate staff be drawn from among an applicant pool of local persons. The personnel or recruitment officer, the circular stated, should be Marathi-speaking. The term "local" was initially defined as referring to people domiciled in Maharashtra for fifteen years or those whose mother tongue was Marathi. Later, in response to central government and other pressures, the Maharashtrian government redefined the term, removing all reference to mother tongue and defining "local persons" only by residential qualifications. Employers were asked to report periodically to the state government regarding progress in recruitment.[21]

West Bengal

In 1972, when the Congress government came to power in West Bengal, it made several declarations that in lower-level jobs, preference should be given to local persons. Nothing was done to implement such a policy until October 1972, when the state employment committee met to discuss the question for the first time. Labour Minister G. D. Nag noted that government policy was to give preference to local persons, defined as those whose mother tongue was Bengali or who had been domiciled in West Bengal for ten to fifteen years. When this issue came up before the state cabinet, there was considerable reluctance to take any active measure. The chief minister at the time, Siddhartha Sankar Ray, was known to oppose the pursuit of any

21. See "Parochialism," *Times of India* (Bombay), Oct. 15, 1973; Order No. ELP/Undertaking 7934, Sept. 25, 1973, signed by Joint Director of Industries; and "Maharashtra Ticks but West Bengal Still Toys with Idea," *Hindustan Standard*, Oct. 27, 1973.

policy of localism. While the government has been said to have urged employers privately to hire local persons, the West Bengal government has been more reticent than its Maharashtrian counterpart on this issue.[22]

Tamil Nadu

The Tamil Nadu government circulated a directive after the Maharashtrian model in August 1974, urging employers to hire local persons to not less than 80 percent of the jobs in technical, nontechnical, supervisory, and nonsupervisory categories. Like the Maharashtrian directive, the circular also stated that personnel or recruitment officers should be local persons. The Tamil Nadu government maintained, however, that its appeal to employers was more liberal than its Maharashtrian counterpart in that the official definition of local persons was strictly a residential one and made no reference to mother tongue. "Local persons," the directive said, should be interpreted to apply to those residing in Tamil Nadu for fifteen years or more.[23]

Meghalaya

The distinctive feature of the Meghalaya government's policy is that it has been formulated not only through administrative fiat but also through legislative action. The legislature in 1974 passed a residence permit bill which required that those who seek to stay in Meghalaya longer than four months secure a spe-

22. See ibid.; "Jobs for Local People," *Times of India* (Bombay), Sept. 13, 1973; "Sons of What Soil?" *Finance*, June 7, 1975; and "Sons of the Soil: Report from the States," *Illustrated Weekly*, Nov. 3, 1974, p. 22. The latter article reports that the West Bengal state assembly passed a resolution saying that anyone who had lived ten years or more in West Bengal should get preferential treatment in employment. It is interesting that one of the first actions of the present communist chief minister, Jyoti Basu, was to issue a statement repudiating policies of localism.

23. See "Jobs for Local People: T. Nadu Govt's Appeal to Employees," *The Hindu*, Aug. 6, 1974; "DMK Demands 80 p.c. of Jobs for Locals," *Times of India*, July 8, 1974; and "Sons of the Soil," *Illustrated Weekly*, Nov. 3, 1974. Another article in the same issue of *Illustrated Weekly*, "Who Are the Sons of the Soil?" by K. P. Nayar, reports that legislation was passed in the state implementing the directive; however, there is no mention of such legislation in the other *Illustrated Weekly* article nor in the newspapers of other periodical sources consulted.

cial permit. The bill further specified that only those who had lived continuously in Meghalaya for twelve years or more and who had made Meghalaya their fixed and permanent home would be considered true locals.[24]

Andhra Pradesh

The Telengana case in Andhra Pradesh is different from those mentioned above in two ways. First, it involves a controversy between people of two regions of the same state rather than between those migrating between states. Second, the preferential treatment of local persons in Telengana has roots in the history of the region which are absent in the other areas described above. Prior to Independence and the incorporation of Telengana (formerly the princely state of Hyderabad) within the Indian Union, the Nizam of Hyderabad had made a practice of offering special privileges in the state services to *mulkis* (those local to the Telengana region).

Preferential policies were extended to *mulkis* after Independence through a parliamentary act, the Andhra Pradesh Public Employment (Requirement as to Residence) Rules, passed in 1959. This legislation followed by two years a law which had been passed pursuant to Article 16(3) of the constitution, permitting parliament to set residential requirements. The 1959 act, renewed in 1964 and placed before parliament again in 1968, made provision for the preferential hiring in jobs and university admissions of Telengana residents. In 1969, the supreme court declared such provisions, and the original residential requirement act in particular, *ultra vires* the constitution, ruling that the constitution does not allow such discrimination by one region against another region of the same state.

The supreme court's rejection of the *mulki* provisions was fol-

24. See "Road to Ruin," *Times of India*, Jan. 10, 1974, and editorial in *Statesman*, Jan. 7, 1974. According to the *Statesman*, the restrictions do not apply to the cantonment and municipal limits of Shillong. In the rest of the state the law will prohibit a stay of longer than four months, without prior official permission, of anyone who has not already taken up fixed and permanent habitation in Meghalaya for twelve years or more. The article points out that the rules do not refer to buying land or to getting employment but simply to *being* in Meghalaya.

lowed by the central government's appointment of the Wanchoo Committee, which underscored the correctness of the supreme court's ruling, observed that regional preferences within a state could only be legitimized by a constitutional amendment, which the report advised against, and recommended the decentralization of recruitment. "There is no constitutional bar to such a procedure for recruitment to local offices to fill class III and class IV posts for there is no impediment to any one competing for such appointment," the committee suggested. But in actual practice the experience has been that the recruitment being made for local offices by the heads of those offices and the vacancies in each case being small, the persons who compete for such posts are by and large local people."[25] Subsequently, the *mulki* rules were revived by a supreme court decision (A.I.R. 1973 SC 930). The 32nd Constitutional Amendment, however, which became effective in the spring of 1974, abolished the *mulki* rules but made way for a series of presidential orders which "regionalized," by zone and district, university admissions and employment. The recommendations of the Wanchoo Committee proved prescient: preferential policies in Andhra Pradesh are now formulated largely through the decentralization of recruitment.

Policies of preferential treatment in educational admissions and employment have, thus, varied from direct legislative enactments (Meghalaya) and explicit administrative orders (Maharashtra) to a more indirect expression of localism (West Bengal). The policy of most state governments goes well beyond the recommendations of the national government. Unlike the central government's policy as represented by the 1968 National Inte-

25. Shriram Maheshwari, "Regionalism in India: Political and Administrative Response," *Indian Journal of Public Administration* 19:4, 457. See also Myron Weiner, "Changing Conceptions of Citizenship in a Multi-Ethnic Society: Migration, Protected Labor Markets, Law and Citizenship in India," Migration and Development Study Group Working Paper MDG/75-4, c/75-6, M.I.T., Cambridge, Massachusetts; and Hugh Gray, "The Failure of a Demand for a Separate Andhra State," *Asian Survey*, 14 (April 1974), 338–49. See also K. V. Narayana Rao, "Mulki Rules in Telengana: A Study in Internal Migration Policy with Respect to Employment," Hyderabad, National Institute of Community Development, October 1975, unpublished.

gration Committee recommendations, many state governments have requested not simply that recruitment be done through the local employment exchanges but rather that domicile or residence requirements be made mandatory for employment. Many of the state governments, moreover, have directed employers to hire local persons not only in lower-grade jobs but at all levels of employment.

Leaving aside the special case of Andhra,[26] the central government has rarely acted to curb state policies of localism. Partially in response to the outcry in parliament that followed the Maharashtra government's circular of 1973, the central government did succeed in pressuring Maharashtra to alter its definition of local persons; but the government has infrequently taken public issue with the states' setting of quotas or with the states' assertion that preferences be extended in skilled and managerial as well as semi or unskilled jobs.[27] Because of the confusion that arose from the divergence in policies, several state officials urged that the central government convene a conference of chief ministers. This recommendation has not yet been acted upon.

The lack of central government direction does not mean that the states have pursued policies of preferential treatment without restraint. But the restraint is at least partially self-imposed. Knowing that the constitution bars discrimination on grounds of birthplace or residence (except, in the latter case, where parliament has legislated otherwise), the states have not sought to pass bills compelling employers to adopt preferential policies. Rather, states have issued instructions through *executive orders* which solicit *voluntary* compliance. It is possible that this practice has

26. This case is special because, unlike Bombay or the other nativist localities, it involved the demand for a separate state and thus elicited the direct involvement of the central government.
27. In his appearance in the Rajya Sabha on July 25, 1975, Deputy Minister of Home Affairs F. M. Mohsin observed that the state directives were probably unconstitutional; but his statement was very mildly worded: "It is doubted very much whether it would be constitutional legally because a particular period of residence shall not be the criterion for getting employment. It may hit against the fundamental rights of the constitution. That legal position apart, I do appreciate the sentiments behind it or the principle behind it." *Rajya Sabha Debates*, July 25, 1974, p. 211.

weakened preferential policies; if nothing else, it has meant that the policies are pursued indirectly and sometimes covertly rather than in a direct or open manner.

Preferential Treatment and the Courts

In confronting state preferential policies, the courts have faced a complex set of constitutional issues. Most constitutional provisions are inimical to preferential policies. Article 14 provides generally for equality before the law. Article 15 sets out more specifically the grounds on which discrimination is prohibited, including among them place of birth, but not residence. Article 16(1) and (2) bar discrimination in state employment on grounds of both birthplace and residence. Article 19(1, d) and (3) guarantee to all citizens the right to move freely, reside, and settle anywhere in India. Only Article 16(3) would suggest an opening for the preferential treatment of local persons by allowing parliament (not the states) the right to set residential requirements in state services (see Appendix 3).

Because of this apparent opposition between constitutional provisions and policies of preferential treatment, it seems likely that the courts would seek to counter the states' adoption of preferential policies. The courts, however, have not played this role. In the area of employment, they have ruled on only a very limited number of cases and have not formulated any identifiable doctrine. In the area of educational admissions, courts have rejected state preferences in some areas and upheld increasingly restrictive policies in others.

Very few cases challenging sons-of-the-soil policies have involved matters of employment. Among the few that have reached the courts, there are a number that seek the abolition of language requirements favoring local persons. An early case in Orissa involved both a language and a residence requirement. A governor's resolution stipulated that applicants to the Orissa administrative service must be permanent residents of the state. Permanent residence could be established if the applicant or one of the applicant's parents could provide evidence of having lived in the state for twelve years and could show evidence of a certain standard of fluency in Oriya. Interestingly, the court upheld the requirement until such a time as parliament were to make a law under Article 16(3).²⁸ Later, in 1969, the Orissa High Court upheld a policy which made knowledge of Oriya mandatory for appointment to the position of district judge.²⁹

As described earlier in the chapter, parliament did pass a law in 1957 under which such rulings as the Orissa government's resolution would have been held unacceptable. Nevertheless, domicile rules like those enunciated in the governor's resolution have been replicated in orders issued by a number of state governments in the late 1960s and early 1970s. Challenges to these executive orders, however, have not yet been brought before the courts. Although there have been a number of cases, related to the *mulki* rules in Andhra Pradesh, which have held as unconstitutional any discrimination in public employment between people of regions of the same state, the constitutionality of statewide domicile rules in employment has not been tested in the courts.³⁰

In contrast to the paucity of job-related cases, there has been a large amount of litigation related to sons-of-the-soil policies in educational admissions. Here, the trend in court decisions since Independence has been to uphold increasingly restrictive residential requirements.

The articles of the constitution bearing on educational admissions include Article 29(2), which bars discrimination in admissions on grounds of religion, race, caste, and language. No mention is made in this article, however, of either birthplace or residence. Residence or domicile restrictions in educational admissions are usually challenged, therefore, under the more general strictures of Articles 14 or 15. The latter bars discrimination on grounds of birthplace but not residence. Residential classifications in university admissions can be challenged only under Article 14 and must be justified on grounds of "reasonableness" —demonstrating that the residential restrictions have a reasonable nexus to the object of the classification.

28. *Raghun Rao* v. *State of Orissa, A.I.R.* 1955 Orissa 113.
29. *Radha Charan* v. *State A.I.R.* 1969 Orissa 237.
30. *AVS Narasimha* v. *State of Andhra*, decided by Supreme Court 28/3/69, 1970 S.L.R.

Reservations for specified classes of people are very common in admissions policies of Indian universities. In medical and technical institutions particularly, an elaborate system setting aside a proportion of seats for specified groups has become commonplace. The groups to whom reservations are most usually extended are scheduled castes, tribes, other backward classes, women, athletes, children of people who served in national causes, Colombo Plan scholars, and a range of other classes.[31] A fairly typical arrangement is that of the Punjab Medical College, which reserves 50 percent of the seats by the following categories:[32]

20%	Scheduled castes/tribes
2%	Backward classes
10%	Backward areas
2%	Sportsmen/women
6%	Central government nominees (including from Jammu and Kashmir)
1%	Women candidates
2%	Children of political sufferers of the freedom struggle with Punjab domicile
5%	Candidates from border areas of Punjab
2%	Children of defense personnel who have lost their lives in emergency / Children of defense personnel who have been disabled during National Emergency and released from service / Children of personnel of the Border Security Forces killed/disabled during enemy action
50%	Total reserved seats

In most medical and technical colleges, preference is given to persons domiciled and/or residing in the state. The courts have consistently barred reservations based on place of birth but have sustained domicile and residential requirements, which are defined in terms of an individual's intention to make the state the

---

31. Terms used often in admission procedures are "lady students," "sportsmen," and "children of political sufferers." The Colombo Plan provides for the exchange of students among various "Third World Countries."

32. See *Gurinder Pal Singh and another* v. *State of Punjab and others*, A.I.R. 1974 Punjab and Haryana 125. The number of seats effectively if not officially reserved may go above 50 percent in some cases. A 1973 decision, *Subhash Chandra* v. *State of U.P.*, upholds a reservation of 49 percent *in addition to* the places reserved for nominees of the central government who qualify through a different examination system (*A.I.R.* 1973 Allahabad 295).

locality of future residence and/or ability to provide evidence of previous residence (five to fifteen years) within the state.

In an early landmark case, *D. P. Joshi* v. *State of Madhya Bharat* (1955), a tuition differential for state and out-of-state residents was upheld. (The actual term used is "capitation" fee.) The challenged ruling governed the admission fees requirement of the medical college at Indore. It stipulated that for all students who had bona fide residence and original domicile in Madhya Bharat, no special admissions fee would be required. "Bona fide residents," the rules allowed, included citizens of India whose original domicile was not in Madhya Bharat but who had acquired a domicile in the state and had resided there for not less than five years. Justice Ayyar, writing for the majority of the court, noted that residence and place of birth were "two distinct conceptions with different connotations both in law and in fact." While Article 15(1) prohibited discrimination based on place of birth, it did not prohibit discrimination based on place of residence. Justice Jagannadhadas, dissenting, argued that the phrases "bona fide residence" and "original domicile in Madhya Bharat" could only have meant place of birth and were thus in contravention of Article 15(1).[33]

The five-year requirement necessary for the establishment of domicile under the Madhya Bharat rules appeared at the time quite restrictive. This requirement, however, has since been followed by far more exacting requirements of ten and fifteen years.[34] In an essay on interstate preferences and discriminations written in 1956, Lawrence Ebb observes that such a five-year rule made the acquisition of state domicile equivalent to the five-year naturalization period required to attain national citizenship.[35] In his opinion, if there were constitutional doubt as to the propriety of a state's use of the national five-year naturalization period in formulating its local residence rule, there would

33. *D. P. Joshi* v. *State of Madhya Bharat*, A.I.R. 1955 S.C. 334, p. 334.
34. Some states had extremely restrictive requirements even earlier. *Sudhir Ch. Nag* v. *State of Assam*, A.I.R. 1958 Assam 25 concerns an Assam education department rule of the mid-1950s which made permanent residence in Assam a condition for scholarship eligibility.
35. "Inter-State Preference and Discriminations," p. 167.

be serious doubt as to the constitutionality of a longer residence requirement.

Since the mid-1950s, however, several cases have been decided which sustained residential requirements of ten and fifteen years. State courts as well as the Supreme Court of India have taken a position which, while barring discrimination on grounds of place of birth,[36] nevertheless upholds lengthy residential requirements.

In 1971, for instance, the supreme court handed down a decision which sustained Rule 3 of the rules for selection of candidates for admission to the state medical colleges of Mysore, framed by the state on July 4, 1970. The rule stated that "no person who is not a citizen of India and who is not domiciled and resident in the state of Mysore for not less than ten years at any time prior to the date of the application for a seat shall be eligible to apply."[37] The court held that a domicile requirement (met by demonstrating the intention to reside in the state) and, in addition, the ten-year residential rule were not in contravention of Article 14. In a brief decision, Justice Dua, delivering the judgment of the court, conceded the likelihood of some cases of hardship under the impugned rule but noted that "cases of hardship are likely to arise in the working of almost any rule which may be framed for selecting a limited number of candidates for admission out of a long list."[38]

A later case challenged the applicability of the same rule to private colleges in Karnataka. In this case, *Arun Narayan* v. *State of Karnataka*, decided in the Karnataka High Court in 1976, Justice Chandrashekhar concluded in a forceful decision that "the right to move freely throughout the territory of India . . . and to reside and settle in any part of India . . . do not by themselves ensure that every citizen of India will have all the advantages and privileges in every state available to citizens domiciled or residing therein and that no kind of preference is permissible to

36. See *A.I.R.* 1969 Orissa 80. The case, *Abodha Kumar* v. *State of Orissa*, involved the selection of candidates on the grounds of their district of birth. The court held the rule to be violative of Article 15(1).
37. *N. Vasundara* v. *State of Mysore, A.I.R.* 1971 SC 1439, p. 1440.
38. Ibid., p. 1443, para. 19.

citizens who are domiciled in or residents of that state."[39] Alluding to a possible distinction between essential and nonessential claims, the justice argued that residential or domicile requirements infringing on rights to the protection of life, property, water facilities, and other basic needs would not be reasonable. But other preferential policies applied in granting agricultural lands, house sites, or in university admissions would not necessarily be violative of an individual's constitutional rights.

The court's position on the susceptibility of private educational institutions to constitutional guarantees prohibiting discrimination is not yet clearly evolved. In the 1976 Karnataka case mentioned above, the court held that it would be too technical to dismiss the petition solely on grounds that the respondent university was a private institution. Since the university "feels obliged to obey the direction of the government," the opinion stated, "the petitioner is entitled to ask for a writ restraining the State of Karnataka from enforcing its ruling on the respondent university."[40]

The Karnataka ruling made no mention of the deliberations of an earlier case in Andhra Pradesh which had reached quite different conclusions.[41] This 1972 decision had concerned a private medical college which required fifteen years' domicile in the state of Andhra Pradesh. The Andhra court held that, because the medical college was private, Article 14 was not applicable. (Although the college received a grant-in-aid from the government and was attached to a government hospital, and although membership of its executive committee included ministers and other officers of the government, it was still considered a private institution.) The court, however, went on to observe that even if Article 14 could be invoked, the admissions rule requiring *fifteen* years' domicile was reasonable and in consonance with Article 14.

The Andhra decision stands out because of its strict view of the immunity of private institutions, because of the exacting *fif-*

39. *A.I.R.* 1976 Karnataka 174, p. 185.
40. Ibid., p. 178.
41. *Nookavarapu Kanakadurga Devi* v. *Kakatiya Medical College, A.I.R.* 1972 Andhra Pradesh 83, p. 90.

teen-year residential requirement that the decision supports, and because the residential requirement pertains to domicile within one *region* of the state rather than within the state as a whole.

There has been judicial disagreement over the legitimacy of domicile regulations that distinguish between persons from different regions of the same state. Most of the decisions upholding within-state reservations in university admissions have been decided by the Andhra Pradesh courts. Three cases that came before the Andhra bench (in 1959, 1962, and 1972) all held preferential treatment of students from the Telengana region of the state to be consonant with Article 14 of the constitution.[42]

Outside of Andhra Pradesh, however, the courts have tended to strike down classifications that distinguish between students from different regions of the same state. In *State of Kerala* v. *R. Jacob Mathew* (1964) and *P. Rajendran* v. *State of Madras* (1963), the court declared unconstitutional university procedures admitting students on the basis of the district in which they resided. Two other cases involving admissions procedures that apportioned places according to region and territorial units were also held to be in contravention of Articles 14 and 15.[43]

Although the courts have rejected most selection procedures which require residence in a particular district or area of a state, they have allowed admission procedures which favor the university's own students. In *Sidappa* v. *State of Mysore* and *Chanchala* v. *State of Mysore*, such a requirement was held not to be violative of Article 14.[44] In delivering his opinion, Justice M. Shelat noted that the preferential treatment of a university's own students

---

42. *Murlidhar* v. *State of Andhra Pradesh*, A.I.R. 1959 Andhra Pradesh 437; *Ramakrishna* v. *Osmania University*, A.I.R. 1962 Andhra Pradesh 120; and *N. K. Devi* v. *Kakatiya Medical College*, A.I.R. 1972 Andhra Pradesh 83. A number of decisions discussed subsequently in the chapter sanction reservations for people from particular regions of a state (hill and rural areas and the Uttarkhand division of Uttar Pradesh). These are not really analogous to the Andhra Pradesh cases since they involve regions outside the area where the university is located. Thus the issue is not one of "localism."

43. I.L.R. 1964 (2) Ker. 53, rev'g A.I.R. 1964 Ker. 39; A.I.R. 1963 S.C. 1012; *Abodha Kumar Mohapatra* v. *State of Orissa*, A.I.R. 1969 Orissa 80; and *A. Periakaruppan* v. *State of Tamil Nadu*, A.I.R. 1971 S.C. 2303.

44. A.I.R. 1967 Mysore 67; A.I.R. 1971 S.C. 1762.

"does not have the disadvantage of districtwise or unitwise selection as any student may pass the qualifying examination in any of the three universities irrespective of the place of his birth or residence."[45]

Although the legal distinction Shelat makes between residential and intrauniversity preferences is a sharp one, the de facto result of an admissions policy favoring the university's own students may not be greatly different from reservations drawn up by district or region. Under both schemes, university enrollment would probably be composed largely of those from the immediate region in which the university is located. Since the qualifying examination to some medical colleges can include P.U.C. (preuniversity course) or even S.S.C. (secondary-school-certificate) results, a student wishing to qualify for a medical school outside his or her area of residence may have to leave home and enroll in a secondary or preuniversity course at a young age (sixteen to eighteen years). Thus, even university admissions procedures which require that a student qualify in the university's own examinations pose a barrier to the ease of enrollment outside a student's area of residence.

A related issue which has proved controversial in the courts is the question not only of whether university admissions can be apportioned by unit or district but also whether the presumed backwardness of a territorial unit can be considered in granting preferential admission. In northern India, several cases have reached the courts which question the practice of extending preferences to persons from rural areas or from designated backward regions of a given state. In the Uttar Pradesh medical colleges, for instance, the admissions process has set aside a number of places for candidates from rural and hill areas and from the Uttrakhand area, an impoverished region of the state. In 1973, in *Subhash Chandra* v. *State of U.P.* the Uttar Pradesh high court (Allahabad Bench) upheld the practice.[46] Curiously, the very same year, the same high court (Lucknow Bench) in another case struck down the reservation for candidates from

45. *A.I.R.* 1971 S.C. 1762, para. 22.
46. *A.I.R.* 1973 Allahabad 295.

rural and hill areas, arguing that there was insufficient justification to consider those areas backward.[47] The decision, however, did not denounce the principle of territorial restrictions. Justice D. S. Mathur, writing for the court, observed that "from the limited viewpoint of admission in medical colleges, classification based on areas may not be proper; but another object which can be kept in mind is that the services of qualified doctors be available to all the residents of the country."[48] A territorial classification aimed at achieving such an objective, Mathur commented, would not be unreasonable. A later case, also argued before the Allahabad courts and subsequently brought before the supreme court, *State of Uttar Pradesh* v. *P. Tandon*, partially overruled the Chandra case, declaring that reservations of seats for candidates from rural areas was unconstitutional while that for the hill and Uttarkhand areas was valid.[49] Chief Justice A. N. Ray, in his opinion, declared the reservation for rural areas invalid since: "This reservation appears to be made for the majority population of the State. Eighty percent of the population of the State cannot be a homogeneous class."[50] Ray went on to argue, however, that the state had presented sufficient evidence to demonstrate that the people living in the hill and Uttrakhand areas constituted a socially and educationally backward class of citizens.

The Judiciary's Rationale

Judicial arguments over the legitimacy of domicile restrictions revolve around issues of efficiency, equity, and state interest. In reaching a ruling, the courts have dealt with three questions: (1) Are domicile practices in admissions procedures consistent with the selection of the most meritorious student body? (2) Will domicile rules advance the interests of the state? (3) Can domicile rules be justified by a region's claim of backwardness?

It is frequently on the basis of the first question, on forming

47. *Dilip Kumar* v. *State of Uttar Pradesh*, A.I.R. 1973 Lucknow 592. The decision upheld reservations for candidates from the Uttrakhand division.
48. Ibid., p. 595, para. 13.
49. A.I.R. 1975 S.C. 563.
50. Ibid., p. 569.

the most meritorious class, that domicile rules are struck down. A number of decisions have held that domicile rules have no reasonable relation to the object of the admissions rules, namely to admit the most qualified student. A representative instance of this reasoning is found in *Periakaruppan* v. *State of Tamil Nadu*.[51] Striking down a unit admissions policy, Justice K. S. Hegde of the supreme court observed:

Before a classification can be justified it must be based on objective criteria and further it must have a reasonable nexus with the object intended to be achieved. The object intended to be achieved in the present case is to select the best candidate for being admitted to medical colleges. That object cannot be satisfactorily achieved by the method adopted.[52]

In *D. N. Chanchala* v. *State of Mysore*, also decided in 1971, a university-based admission procedure was *upheld* by the same reasoning. Writing the decision for the supreme court, Justice Shelat noted that although a university-based admission process might mean that a candidate with lower marks from the university in question could be preferred over a candidate with higher marks from another university, this would not necessarily mean, given the possible difference of standards, that a less meritorious student was chosen over a more capable one.[53]

The preeminent importance ascribed in these decisions to standards of achievement and meritocracy has been modified on numerous occasions by the claims either of state interest or of equity. The legitimacy of claims of the state was recognized explicitly in one of the early (1955) landmark decisions, *Joshi* v. *Madhya Bharat*. Upholding a tuition differential for in-state and out-of-state students, the supreme court decision noted:

We are in this petition concerned with a Medical College and it is well known that it requires considerable finance to maintain such an institution. If the State has to spend money on it, is it unreasonable that it

51. *A.I.R.* 1971 S.C. 2303.
52. Ibid., p. 2306, para. 12.
53. *A.I.R.* S.C. 1762, p. 1769, para. 22.

should so order the educational system that the advantage of it would to some extent at least enure for the benefit of the State?[54]

Upholding a ten-year domicile rule on similar grounds, the supreme court in a 1971 decision explained that an important objective of admission rules was to select candidates who will serve the people of the state, at the same time paying attention to recruiting qualified students: "The object of framing the impugned rule seems to be to attempt to impart medical education to the best talent available out of the class of persons who are likely so far as it can reasonably be foreseen to serve as doctors, the inhabitants of the State of Mysore."[55] The decision goes on to note that while it is not possible to say with certainty that those admitted to the medical colleges would necessarily stay in Mysore State to practice, and while they have a fundamental right as citizens to settle anywhere in India, the desire of the state to formulate admission rules which will advance the medical interests of the people of the state must be deemed acceptable.

Such "service" justifications for *within*-state residential distinctions have usually been rejected. In the 1975 *Tandon* case mentioned earlier, the Allahabad high court struck down the preferential treatment in admission of students from rural areas that the state justified on "service" grounds:

Medical graduates hailing from rural areas may also be disinclined to return to the villages for medical practice on account of poor facilities and they will also try to build their career in the urban centers where they hope to have a better job satisfaction. The assertion on behalf of the State of U.P. that the reservation of seats for candidates of these areas was with a view to feed the dispensaries of these areas appears to be pretentious and cannot be a justifiable ground for making reservations.[56]

The court has thus tried to reconcile the objectives of meritocracy and of state interest. It has also struggled with the still further conflicting claims of equity. Former supreme court justice

54. *Joshi* v. *Madhya Bharat*, p. 340, para. 15.
55. *N. Vasundara* v. *State of Mysore*, A.I.R. 1971 S.C. 1439, p. 1443, para. 8.
56. *A.I.R.* 1975 Allahabad 1 (full bench), p. 7, para. 13.

M. Hidayatullah has alluded to the role that residential preferences may play in reducing uneven levels of development. Noting that discrimination on grounds of residence may be justified, the former chief justice remarked: "Sometimes local sentiments may have to be respected or sometimes an inroad from more advanced states into less developed states may have to be prevented."[57]

Most decisions that uphold on grounds of equity the preferential treatment of persons from backward areas involve within-state rather than statewide restrictions. In *Uttar Pradesh v. Tandon*, for instance, the supreme court allowed the reservation in medical admissions for people of the hill and Uttrakhand areas of the state on the grounds that those areas were socially and educationally backward. Similarly, the Andhra high court in a 1972 case held that preferential treatment of Telengana students in medical admissions was justified since:

Kakatiya Medical college was started for the spread of medical education mainly for Telengana region, which is educationally backward in the State. If in view of this object, provision is made to cater to the educational needs mainly of that particular region, as it badly requires such assistance, it cannot be said that the object to be achieved has no relation to the classification made by giving larger representation to the Andhra region. The increase in the Telengana quota is consistent with and promotes and advances the object underlying the establishment of the institution.[58]

The recognition in domicile cases of the claims of backwardness has raised two questions: (1) What constitutes backwardness? and (2) How can standards of achievement be upheld while recognizing the special needs of backward groups? Judicial discussion on the first question has revolved around whether the inadequacy of medical facilities in a given region constitutes sufficient evidence of a region's backwardness and, if not, what other evidence must be provided. Although there has been little discussion in domicile cases of the second issue, the court has

57. *Annual Survey of Indian Law, 1970* (New Delhi: Indian Law Institute, 1970), p. 70.
58. *Devi v. Kakatiya Medical College*, p. 93, para. 17.

clearly stated that meritocracy cannot yield entirely to the claims of backwardness. The case of *Kumar* v. *Uttar Pradesh*, decided in 1973, involved, among other issues, a ruling which set aside a number of seats for scheduled caste candidates and for candidates from the rural areas and hill and Uttrakhand divisions. The ruling relaxed for scheduled castes the level of minimum marks below which a candidate could not be considered, from 33 percent in the aggregate to 30 percent. For candidates from the Uttrakhand division, the admission procedure set *no* minimum percentage for candidates,[59] but this total absence of standards was rejected as unacceptable by the court.

The courts have, thus, sought to protect merit-based admissions by generally ruling against the practice of conferring preferences on people of one region of a state over persons from another region of the same state where there is no element of backwardness. The Andhra courts that have upheld preferential treatment in admissions for the Telengana region of the state are, however, exceptions.

Even the court rulings sustaining medical college favoritism of students passing from their own preparatory courses have in some ways also detracted from an admission system which is blind to the regional origins of its students. These decisions, taken together with the decisions approving increasingly stringent statewide domicile requirements, show the emerging pattern of a judiciary which has gone along with rather than resisted the increasing localism of state university policies.

With the trend toward the formulation of preferential policies through executive orders, there remains a small but potentially important unresolved issue: whether executive orders are legally binding. In a 1961 case in Madhya Pradesh, the court ruled that administrative directives could not be questioned under the equality clause of the constitution. The bench questioned the sensible ruling of an earlier Andhra Pradesh judgment which stated that:

The government pleader counters this argument by stating that the rules are only administrative directions given by the Government and

59. *A.I.R.* 1973 592.

that non-compliance with the rules does not confer on the petitioner any right to compel the respondents to proceed in strict conformity with the rules. The contention of the Government is a double-edged weapon and it cuts both ways. . . . The Government, therefore, cannot rely upon the scheme embodied in the rules to sustain the selections and to ignore it to defeat the claims of the petitioner.[60]

The Madhya Pradesh court took exception to the Andhra bench reasoning and noted:

It is obvious and is also not disputed that "Medical Colleges in Madhya Pradesh Rules for Admission, 1960" are merely executive or administrative instructions in a field which is not covered by any statute. If they had been statutory rules, we would not have hesitated to strike down such of those rules as offend against the provisions of Art. 14 or quash any discriminatory action taken.[61]

If administrative orders (the chief vehicle through which preferential policies on sons-of-the-soil issues have been executed) are held neither legally binding nor an admissible subject of litigation, the court may abdicate even the small role it now plays in setting boundaries on the localism of state policies.

Under the Emergency declared in June 1975, sons-of-the-soil demands subsided and the call for central government clarification of preferential policies was muted. The end of the Emergency, however, and the return of a more open political system presages a resumption of the debate over preferential policies.

In summary, the following observations can be made with regard to the judicial position of domicile reservations:

1. No explicit doctrine has developed either through decisions of the high courts or the supreme court. Rather, the rulings have been made on a case-by-case basis.

2. The courts, nevertheless, appear increasingly inclined to accept policies of localism evidenced by: (a) the high courts' acceptance of domicile requirements of ten and fifteen years as stipulations for university admissions, and (b) the courts' acceptance

---

60. *Ramchandra Vishnu* v. *State of Madhya Pradesh,* A.I.R. 1961 Madhya Pradesh 247, p. 250, para. 8.
61. Ibid., para. 10.

of procedures extending preferences to the universities' own graduates (a policy with results similar to those of rulings struck down by the courts which would have extended preferences to persons from particular regions within a state).

3. The courts' role in this area may be shaped as much by their silence as by the decisions taken. The courts have taken no action in response to the state orders of the late 1960s and early 1970s which directed employers to give preferences to local persons.

The Courts and the (Ir)reversibility of Preferential Policies

If any section of the government could be expected to dilute policies of localism, it would most likely be the courts. The state governments, composed of the same ethnic populations that stand to benefit from preferential policies, have a strong stake in the policies' survival. The central government, too, is reluctant to bear down on such policies where intervention might produce greater antagonism from the states. The courts, by contrast, are under fewer constraints. Up to this point, however, the courts have not acted to brake the development of more stringent domicile requirements.

What action might the courts take? It may be instructive to consider briefly the role the courts have played in shaping preferential policies aimed at the uplift of low-caste groups and backward classes. Initially, the courts attempted to bar preferential treatment (outside the constitutionally mandated area of reservations in the legislatures). This attempt, however, was overridden by parliament. In 1951, in the *Dorairajan* case (*A.I.R.* 1951 SC 2266), the possibility of judicial intervention in this area was shown to be limited. In this case, Mrs. Dorairajan, a candidate for admission to the Madras Medical College, challenged a government order that set fixed percentages by caste and community according to which the incoming class was to be selected. Both the Madras high court and the supreme court declared the government order unconstitutional. In reaction to this decision, however, parliament passed a constitutional amendment, Article 15(4), which entrusted the state with the power to make special provision for the advancement of scheduled castes, tribes, and other backward classes. By the early 1950s, as this case illustrated, it was already too late to dismantle the political foundation upon which preferential policies were built.

Another critical event in the development of preferential policies took place in 1963—this time one in which the court played the key role. In 1963, the supreme court handed down a decision on a case, *Balaji* v. *Mysore* (*A.I.R.* 1963 SC 649), in which the court held (among other matters) that reserved places should not exceed 50 percent. This ruling has guided the admissions procedure of most universities throughout India since that time. Whether the line can be held, however, is an issue that will confront the courts in the years ahead.

Similarly, in the area of domicile reservations, the courts could not hope to seek their abolition. But there are open issues where judicial action could prove critical. Will the state government directives setting domicile requirements in employment continue to stand? Will the length of residence necessary to meet domicile requirements be left, as some of the courts have ruled, at ten and fifteen years? What percentage of university seats or employment slots should be reserved for local applicants? These are key issues on which the courts will either by action or inaction inevitably have influence.

Over the last years, the state governments have adopted increasingly stringent restrictions on persons not "local" to the state who seek employment or university admissions. State domicile requirements that once mandated a five-year residence in the state now often require residence of ten or fifteen years. With the issuance of state directives in the late 1960s and early 1970s, moreover, employers were urged to hire local persons not only in the state services but in the private sector as well, and not only in unskilled and menial jobs but also in professional and managerial positions.

Many of these practices, it is recognized, repudiate both central government directives and constitutional principle. And yet, as much by their inaction as by any active assent, the central government and the courts have lent their support to these policies. The explanation for this anomaly is intimated by Indira Gandhi's remark that a "balance" must be sought—a balance that will protect the mobility of citizens and guard against the political disruption which such mobility engenders. As her observations suggest, preferential policies have brought into relief the potentially conflicting nature of national goals. On the one side is the commitment of the states to the economic advancement of their ethnic constituencies, together with the central government's recognition that such advancement is essential to political stability. On the other side is the central government's concern to preserve merit-based recruitment and the free movement of labor. To the extent that present policies prevail, the "balance" that will be struck is one that weights equality and stability over mobility and meritocracy.

10 | Modernization and Meritocracy

Scholars writing on contemporary events run the occupational risk of seeing their subject fade from public view before the study's completion. While Shiv Sena's power has receded, its end is not imminent. Presently the party has no member in either parliament or the state assembly. In the municipal elections of November 1978, the electorate returned twenty-one Shiv Sena corporators, a decline from the thirty-five-member bloc which represented the party in the corporation before the elections.[1] The November election results cut in half the strength that Shiv Sena enjoyed when, in 1968, forty-two of its candidates were elected in the party's first bid for electoral office in Bombay. Nevertheless, the party remains at present, just as it did in 1968, the chief opposition in the municipal body.[2]

Several reasons account for the Sena's diminishing strength. It was unlikely, as indeed the party recognized, that it could maintain the intense pitch of nativist alarm which prevailed when the Sena first rode into power. In attempting to institutionalize its power base, the party has been only partially successful. It stepped up its organizational work within the unions,[3] and it attempted to widen its appeal beyond the party's Maharashtrian constituency by championing a range of causes.[4] The party's inability to sustain its electoral support was due in part

1. The results of this election are reported in the *Times of India*, November 10, 1978. The victorious Janata party secured 85 out of the 140 municipal seats.
2. The Sena's status as the main opposition party presumes the continued division of the Congress and Congress (I) parties in Bombay.
3. This occurred with the appointment of a new leader to head the Sena's union organization, the BKS.
4. In the late 1960s the party attempted to build its "nationalist" image by attacking so-called antinational groups (communists, Muslims, etc.). Later the party took up more routine civic issues, leading drives against corruption, inflation, and the like.

to its progressive inability to distinguish itself from other parties in the eyes of the voter.

The party's difficulties also derived, however, from its ill-chosen alliances. On the eve of the Emergency, Thackeray muted what had been his regular attacks against the Gandhi government and was able to avoid the fate that other opposition groups were to suffer. During the Emergency, Thackeray offered his full support to Mrs. Gandhi. Whether this was rank opportunism or the result of his long-held conviction that only an authoritarian leadership could bring the desired discipline and direction to Indian politics is not clear. When Mrs. Gandhi decided to suspend the Emergency and hold elections, Thackeray threw the party's support behind Mrs. Gandhi, to the distress of a large faction within the Sena. This division caused a number of Sena corporators to resign from the party; its popular support was weakened; and bitter fights ensued within the party.[5] When the state assembly elections were announced for the first month of 1978, the Sena publicly declared its support for the nationally dominant Janata party. Shiv Sena, however, failed to effect an electoral agreement and was unable to secure a single seat.

The importance of Shiv Sena as a subject of study is not measurable, however, by its longevity, by the number of seats it has won or lost, or by the notoriety that the party has on occasion achieved. Rather, its value as a topic for scholarship rests in the salience of the questions the Sena poses about preferential treatment—why such demands arise as the organizing point of an ethnic movement, how such demands are received, and what is gained or lost by the pursuit of preferential policies.

Shiv Sena is a manifestation of India's new ethnicity and the demands for preferential treatment which have recently reverberated in developing and industrialized nations alike. Social movements and political organizations that express this new ethnicity demand not regional autonomy but equality through

---

5. As on previous occasions, the divisions within the party resulted in violent confrontations. In December 1978 the erstwhile chief organizer of the party was assaulted and severely injured.

preferential treatment. Growing out of the heightened importance of the state in the management of the economy and the regulation of society, this new ethnicity is almost entirely modern. The political demands of these new ethnic movements confront liberal notions of equality of opportunity with their own precepts of equality of results. Shiv Sena is an expression both of this new ethnicity and of a new equality.

Shiv Sena's demands for preferential treatment have gained political respectability because they are in line with broader political developments in India which transcend Bombay. Throughout India, state governments have seized the initiative on questions of preferential policies. Although the center has viewed this development with some distaste, it has, by and large, chosen a passive stance. By its inaction as much as by explicit choice, the central government has chosen equality and with it political stability over meritocracy and common citizenship. The tacit political coalition that unites state governments with the center on the question of preferential policy provides the political context in which Shiv Sena has flourished.

This study of Shiv Sena as one sons-of-the-soil movement in India has been organized around three questions: (1) What causes the emergence of a movement whose focal point is the claim for preferential treatment? (2) What has been, and what explains, the nature of the government's response? (3) What impact have preferential policies had on the group they are intended to assist? In addition to summarizing the answers this book provides to these three questions, this chapter also attempts to place the Bombay experience in a broader perspective by comparing Shiv Sena with ethnic movements elsewhere in India and in other parts of the world.

The Emergence of Shiv Sena and the Claim for Preferential Treatment

The formation of Shiv Sena and its focus on the issue of special reservations for Maharashtrians are two distinct issues warranting separate explanations. The first is the origins of ethnic discontent; the second, the reasons this discontent found expression in the demand for preferential treatment.

Shiv Sena's Origins

The origins of Shiv Sena can be found in three sets of conditions, the first of which is demographic. A set of demographic processes—high in-migration and low out-migration—worked to precipitate migrant-native conflict in Bombay. The combination of a high inflow and low outflow of populations intensified competition for employment and resources, creating an environment in which discontent could be readily mobilized. Two-thirds of Bombay's population is migrant. Well over half (57 percent) is non-Maharashtrian. Situated in a state with one of the lowest levels of out-migration among the states of India, Bombay was a likely setting for nativist discontent.

But this set of demographic conditions alone would have been an imperfect predictor of nativist activity in Bombay. It fails to explain the timing of Shiv Sena's emergence or why one ethnic group rather than another became the chosen target. No sudden change in numbers or population ratios preceded the Sena's founding. The percentage of Marathi-speakers prior to Shiv Sena's emergence in 1966 declined only very slightly. Nor do numbers explain why South Indians became the object of Sena antagonism when their population rose only very slightly prior to the Sena's emergence and never reached even one-half the size of the Gujarati-speaking community of Bombay.

A second condition of Shiv Sena's emergence, then, more important than population ratios, was the existence of ethnic conflict among the middle classes of Bombay. In the case of Shiv Sena, the *numbers* of migrants and natives resident in the city did not prove nearly as crucial as the *positions* they held. The position of Maharashtrians in the city of Bombay has undergone a change in the course of the last century. Over the last decades, spurred by Independence and by the establishment of a separate Maharashtra state in 1960, Maharashtrians have acquired increasing political power. With this change in political resources came an inevitable questioning of economic status. In Bombay, the migrant (or more accurately the non-Maharashtrian) population has constituted a substantial proportion of the city's middle class. South Indians, particularly, have been successful at securing the white-collar office jobs so often the preferred occupational choice of educated Maharashtrian youths. Intense job competition between the Maharashtrian and non-Maharashtrian middle classes is critical to an explanation of Shiv Sena's development. It illuminates the reason underlying the Sena's animosity toward South Indians rather than, for instance, toward the more numerous and well-to-do Gujarati community. Competition over jobs also helps to explain the timing of Shiv Sena's emergence. In the years preceding the Sena's 1966 founding, job opportunities in the tertiary sector multiplied but so did the numbers of youths matriculating from Bombay and Maharashtrian schools. Expectations of a profusion of employment openings that had grown with the creation of a separate state in 1960 were partially realized, but the simultaneous explosion of job seekers had not been fully anticipated. Intensified by the India-wide recession of 1966–67, the economic frustrations on which a nativist movement could build were substantial.

The importance of middle-class job competition is joined by a third set of conditions upon which the emergence of Shiv Sena depended: the party's superior organization. The organization was important in two ways. First, the carefully constructed system of *shakhas* and organizational activities, designed to appeal particularly to youth, mobilized a large pool of young party workers on whom the Sena's electoral campaigns depended. The discipline and structure of the Sena created for its young Maharashtrian party activists a sense of excitement and involvement not visible in the other parties of the 1960s in Bombay. It was through these young party workers that voters were contacted, neighborhood activities planned, and electoral campaigns conducted. Party organization was equally important in mobilizing working-class voter support. To win one-third of the city's municipal seats, the party had to secure the votes of a large section of the Maharashtrian working class. Shiv Sena's extremist ideological position found support among a section of the Maharashtrian working class in Bombay and may have drawn voters into the party fold. But the organization of neighborhood *shakhas* in working-class and slum sections of the city, and their ability to deliver needed services, was indispensable to Shiv Sena's electoral victories.

To what extent are these three demographic, economic, and political conditions important to an explanation of ethnic movements elsewhere in India and in other countries?

Demographic Conditions

A number of studies of ethnic movements in India and Western Europe have cited the role that out-migration from a region plays in siphoning off discontent that might otherwise find expression in ethnic conflict. In an article on sons-of-the-soil movements in India, Myron Weiner remarks that the growth of tribal protest in the Chota Nagpur region coincided with the decline in job opportunities and the reduced rates of out-migration in the regions to which tribals had earlier moved. Weiner notes further that the other states in which organized nativist movements have been formed also exhibit relatively low rates of out-migration as compared with other states in India.[6] Similar observations about migration have been made in the context of other country experiences.[7]

But a demographic explanation of migrant-native conflict is troubled by the absence of evidence that any particular *level* of in- or out-migration triggers the organization of protest. In India it is striking that common to most of the cases where organized antimigrant movements have erupted, the native ethnic community is outnumbered. In Bombay, Bangalore, Gauhati, and Chota Nagpur, the nativist organization represents an ethnic community that forms either half or just under half of the local population. But even here there are exceptions: There are areas in India where the "native" population is a minority and no organized nativist movement is present (Coorg or Kolar dis-

6. Myron Weiner, "Sons of the Soil: Migration, Ethnicity and Nativism in India" (Center for International Studies, M.I.T. Working Paper MDG/75-3C/75-5, February 1975), pp. 19–23.
7. J. S. MacDonald, "Agricultural Organization, Migration and Labor Militancy in Rural Italy," *Economic History Review*, 16 (1963–64), 61–75; and Walter Dean Burnham, "A Note on Political Nativism in the United States" unpublished working paper, p. 8.

tricts in Karnataka, for example) as well as an important region (Telengana) where the native population is a numerical majority and yet highly articulate and organized antimigrant movements have been formed.

Outside India, too, there seems to be no numerical formula underlying the emergence of ethnic protest. There is a range of presumptions about the level of ethnic mixture conducive to conflict and these presumptions sometimes inform policy decisions. In France, for instance, Gary Freeman has noted that policy makers and a large sector of the general public came to believe in a "threshold of tolerance"—a level between 10 percent and 30 percent beyond which conflict became inevitable. "In the hospital service," one French official noted, "neither the medical staff nor the French patients react when there are 2, 5, 10, 15 or 20 percent foreigners, even if they are of the same nationality. Automatically when this percentage approaches 28, 29, 30 percent, one observes a new phenomenon."[8] A similar assumption has prevailed at times in Britain when the government provided extra funds and spoke in favor of student dispersal in the cases of schools whose enrollment exceeded an immigrant population of 30 percent.[9] These ideas have also had currency in the United States, as when educational authorities in the early part of the century warned against admitting excessive numbers of Jews. In the words of President Lowell of Harvard, "If their [the Jews] number should become 40 percent of the student body the race feeling would become intense."[10] Whatever might be the prevailing presumption, the actual relation between ethnic ratios and the emergence of conflict or protest is very imperfect.

Middle-Class Job Competition

Competition over white-collar jobs, so important in the case of Shiv Sena, is a frequent although not universal antecedent of ethnic conflict. In India, interethnic competition for middle-

8. Gary P. Freeman, "Immigrant Labor and Racial Conflict in Industrial Societies: The French and British Experience, 1945–1974," draft copy, p. 200.
9. Frederick M. Wirt, "Ethnic Minorities and School Policy in European Democracies: Theory and Case Studies," paper delivered at Annual Meeting of American Political Science Association, Chicago, Ill., September 1974, p. 20.
10. "Jews Facing a Closing College Door," *Literary Digest*, July 8, 1922, p. 28.

class jobs helps to explain the presence of a nativist movement in Bombay and its absence in other Indian cities where the migrant population is large and unemployment is high. In Calcutta, for instance, where there is a sizable migrant population and a serious employment problem, the lack of organized ethnic conflict is striking. What distinguishes Calcutta from Bombay is the relative dominance of the "native" (Bengali) middle class in the city's white-collar professions—a stark contrast to the position of the Maharashtrian middle class in Bombay. In other cases of ethnic conflict, middle-class competition for jobs is a constantly recurring theme. As Donald L. Horowitz has stated in a study of ethnicity in developing countries, "If there is anything universal about ethnic conflict, it is the struggle for predominance in the lucrative, prestigious, white-collar positions originally created by the colonialists."[11] This holds true for sons-of-the-soil movements in India. In Bangalore, there has been competition over white-collar jobs in the city's large public-sector establishments; in Hyderabad and in Chota Nagpur, there has been intense conflict over teaching positions and jobs in the government bureaucracy. In Assam, similar conflict over administrative and clerical positions has revolved around the expanding public-sector and private industrial establishments in the state. Conspicuous by its absence in all localities is any organized protest between ethnic groups over factory and working-class jobs.

The prevalence of middle-class job competition in the emergence of ethnic conflict outside of India is also striking. Historical studies of nativist movements in the United States reveal a social profile of movement activists similar to the lower-middle-class occupational strata (shopkeepers, assistant clerks, office supervisors) of Sena leaders.[12] Summarizing the findings of a series of studies on the contemporary resurgence of ethnicity in

11. Donald L. Horowitz, "Multi-racial Politics in the New States: Towards a Theory of Conflict," in Robert J. Jackson and Michael B. Stein, eds., *Issues in Comparative Politics* (New York: St. Martin's Press, 1971), p. 172.

12. For a description of Know Nothing activists in the nineteenth-century United States, see W. E. Binkley, *American Political Parties* (New York: Alfred Knopf, 1947), p. 189; also see Donald Kinzer, "The American Protective Association, A Study of Anti-Catholicism," doctoral dissertation, University of Washington, Seattle, 1954, p. 241.

Western Europe, Milton Esman notes that "although hard data on this subject are limited, it seems that the activists originate primarily from groups that have benefited from the post-World War II expansion of higher education but that are frustrated by limited career opportunities in the peripheral regions. . . . Many appear to be underpaid teachers suffering both from declining social prestige and low incomes."[13] Similar observations have been made about the disproportionately high middle-class support of the separatist Parti Quebecois in Canada, which receives a high number of votes among white-collar workers, students, and professionals and much lower support among workers, farmers, and the unemployed.[14]

But even generalizations such as the importance of middle-class job competition to the emergence of ethnic conflict have their exceptions. On the one hand, there are cases of ethnic or nativist protest organized by middle-class activists around issues either unrelated to job competition or around causes that may even run counter to the economic self-interest of the middle class. The Swiss referenda held in 1970 and 1974 to decide on the Schwarzenbach and Oehen proposals to curtail the immigration of foreign workers received surprisingly high support among middle-class Swiss voters who were in no way competing for the construction and hotel jobs in which foreign workers predominated.[15] In Sri Lanka, Donald Horowitz has persuasively argued, Sinhalese elite resistance to Tamil regional autonomy persists even to the disservice of their own economic interests.[16] Cases can also be cited, albeit infrequently, of ethnic movements organized around and by working-class populations. Victor and Brett deBary Nee's study, *Longtime Californ'*, documents the nineteenth-century anti-Chinese protests on the West Coast that

13. Milton J. Esman, "Perspectives on Ethnic Conflict in Industrialized Societies," in Milton J. Esman, ed., *Ethnic Conflict in the Western World* (Ithaca: Cornell University Press, 1977), p. 374.

14. Jane Jenson and Peter Regenstreif, "Some Dimensions of Partisan Choice in Quebec, 1969," *Canadian Journal of Political Science*, 3 (June 1970), 310.

15. Henry H. Kerr, Switzerland: *Social Cleavages and Partisan Conflict*, Sage Professional Paper in Contemporary Sociology, Vol. 1, 06-002, 1974, Table 3, p. 11.

16. Horowitz, "Multi-racial Politics," pp. 168–69.

were organized by working-class white San Franciscans.[17] The nativist protests that resulted in the anti-Chinese restrictions of the 1880s had little support among at least the business sector of the middle class, which stood to gain by the low wages Asian immigrants were willing to accept. Middle-class job competition is a recurrent but not universal theme of ethnic conflict.

Party Organization and Youth

In the case of Shiv Sena, the party's electoral strength was dependent on the highly successful party organization, which enabled it to mobilize large numbers of Maharashtrian youths who were crucial to the election campaigns and neighborhood Sena organizations. The importance of party organizations in mobilizing youthful activists is a common foundation upon which ethnic movements in India and elsewhere have been built. Youth, sometimes students and sometimes those newly employed or about to enter the work force, has played a visible role in several of the sons-of-the-soil movements in India. Not only in Bombay but also in Telengana, Chota Nagpur, and Bangalore, many of the organizing tasks, such as painting slogans on the street walls, organizing protest marches, or contacting voters, were undertaken by youthful activists. Like the typical Shiv Sainik, the prototypical activist in the Birsa Seva Dal (Chota Nagpur), the Kannada Chaluvaligar (Bangalore) or the Telengana Praja Samiti was male, young, and a recent matriculate (secondary school graduate).

The often disproportionate representation of youth in many other emergent opposition (ethnic or other) movements is well documented. The 1971 Sri Lanka uprisings, the organization of the Dravida Munnetra Kazahgam (DMK) in India, the Scottish Nationalist movement, and Quebec separatism all record very high levels of support or organizational work among young activists.[18] Indeed, a historian at Boston University has argued

17. Victor G. and Brett deBary Nee, *Longtime Californ': A Documentary Study of an American Chinatown* (Boston: Houghton Mifflin, 1974), pp. 46, 52.
18. See W. Howard Wriggins and C. H. S. Jayewardene, "Youth Protest in Sri Lanka (Ceylon)," in W. Howard Wriggins and James F. Guyot, eds., *Population Politics and the Future of Southern Asia* (New York: Columbia University Press, 1973); Marguerite Ross Barnett, *The Politics of Cultural Nationalism in South India*

that many political revolutions were dependent on demographic changes bringing about the emergence of particularly large youth cohorts.[19] Although evidence on this point is far from satisfactory, there is at least ample documentation for the lesser claim, that disproportionate numbers of youth are often involved in oppositional movements.

Even if this more moderate claim is correct, it is important to consider into what types of oppositional movements youth is drawn. Or, put another way, what forces mobilize youth? The Bombay experience suggests that the substance of ideology is less important than the more intangible factors of involvement and peer compatriotism that a highly disciplined, organized party of any ideology can generate. Ideological factors, particularly in a general apolitical sense, are not unimportant. Marguerite Barnett observes that youth leaders could be found frequently in the DMK because in part, "young people responded most decisively to the dislocations and inequalities of modernization,"[20] which the DMK protested. Maharashtrian, Quebecois, and Scottish youths certainly respond positively to the claims to equality of their respective movements. Given the expected slow pace of economic and social change, it is probably recognized that the young stand to benefit more than their seniors from demands for ethnic equality. But these ideological claims are not the only, and in some cases not even the major, force that attracts young party activists. The ability of a party organization to generate a disciplined, cohesive cadre into which youths can be drawn has proved of compelling importance. In Sri Lanka, for example, in 1971 the Janatha Vimukhti Peramuna (People's Liberation Front) owed its strength in large part to its careful political organization. It created secret study classes, group cells, assault training classes—a close-knit intensive paramilitary organization[21] which resembled in structure, although certainly not

---

(Princeton: Princeton University Press, 1976), p. 188; Milton J. Esman, "Scottish Nationalism, North Sea Oil, and the British Response," in Esman, *Ethnic Conflict*, p. 270; and Jenson and Regenstreif, "Partisan Choice in Quebec," p. 310.
  19. Herbert Moller, "Youth as a Force in the Modern World," *Comparative Studies in Society and History*, 10 (April 1968), 237–60.
  20. Barnett, *Politics of Cultural Nationalism*, p. 189.
  21. Wriggins and Jayewardene, "Youth Protest in Sri Lanka," pp. 347–48.

in ideology, right-wing organizations such as the RSS in India which have been successful for many of the same reasons in mobilizing youth. Although youth cadres are certainly not a crucial part of all ethnic movements, in developing countries (with a large proportion of the population under twenty-five), a movement that can mobilize youth gains an important political resource.

The mobilization of youthful activists, middle-class job competition, and the combination of high levels of ethnic "outsiders" together with low rates of out-migration are, then, three features common to Shiv Sena's genesis and to numerous movements both elsewhere in India and outside. It is, however, not possible to argue that these three political, economic, and demographic conditions are either necessary or sufficient requisites of nativist politics. As two recent studies of ethnicity have commented, in attempting to generalize about the origins of ethnic conflict, we are still "all beginners."[22]

The Demand for Preferential Treatment

In explaining how claims for preferential treatment became the focus of nativist objectives, three conditions can be identified under which the demand for special treatment becomes a compelling political strategy. The first is in a situation where a group is geographically dispersed (scheduled castes in India, blacks in the United States). An ethnic population with its own political territory (Sikhs and Tamils, in India, Basques or Croatians in Europe) may seek economic or political gains through demands for greater regional autonomy. Where a group lacks political control over a territory—even where, as in the case of Maharashtrians in the city of Bombay or blacks in the Southern United States, the group may be numerically strong—greater regional autonomy may threaten rather than enhance the group's position. Demands for regional autonomy may accompany claims to preferential treatment, as in the case of Telengana. But in situations where greater regional autonomy is not a viable

22. See Esman, *Ethnic Conflict in the Western World*, p. 14; and Nathan Glazer and Daniel Moynihan, *Ethnicity, Theory and Experience* (Cambridge: Harvard University Press, 1975), p. 25.

strategy, the demand for preferential treatment becomes a likely goal of ethnic agitation.

A second situation under which such demands are likely to arise occurs where an ethnic community is both a political majority *and* an "economic minority." Although Maharashtrians are economically disadvantaged in Bombay, they exercise predominant control over *state*-level government affairs. Similarly, the Assamese, Kannadigas in Karnataka, the Malays, the Sinhalese in Sri Lanka, have all found it possible to use their political preeminence to seek, through policies of preferential treatment, redress for their economic subordination. Political dominance is, however, a common but not necessary precondition of a group's claim to preferential treatment. Neither the tribal population in Chota Nagpur nor the Telengana "natives" in Andhra Pradesh dominate the governments of their states or even, in the case of the tribals, their region. But in both cases, historical factors (the *mulki* rules in Andhra and constitutionally sanctioned protective discrimination of tribals) have given a special legitimacy to their preferential claims.

A third condition under which the demand for preferential treatment is sometimes broached occurs where the group's perception of itself is one of extreme disadvantage—where, that is, it holds little hope of competing in the existing, allegedly meritocratic competition for jobs and university places. The demand for preferential treatment is in some sense, and is indeed often recognized to be, a plea of desperation. This is indicated by noting the groups that do *not* support preferential treatment. At the time of the Constituent Assembly debates in India, for example, when the possibility of separate electorates was under discussion, several of the stronger minorities expressed a disinclination to seek protection through such political measures. While the Parsees and Sikhs, for instance, did not pressure for special electorates, the Anglo-Indians were adamant in their demand for such assurances. The Anglo-Indian community recognized that its favored positions in the railways and bureaucracies would be quickly undermined if competition were increased. The Constituent Assembly, while rejecting separate electorates in most other cases, recognized that preferential treatment for Anglo-

Indians was justifiable on the grounds that the future of the Anglo-Indian community was especially vulnerable.²³

Elsewhere, too, it seems that a group must be persuaded of its inability to compete under existing conditions in order for support for preferential treatment to be forthcoming. In Scotland, for instance, despite the resentment of the large numbers of English thought to hold faculty positions in Scottish universities, the Scots never sought "preferential treatment." To do so would have been a gesture of self-admitted incompetence which the Scots did not feel. In the United States, too, the reluctance of Asian-Americans and the contrasting greater readiness of Hispanic-Americans to support programs of "affirmative action" can be traced to the greater confidence among the former of their ability to compete according to the prevailing "rules of the game."

Are sons-of-the-soil movements and the demand for preferential treatment now a permanent feature of contemporary India? In India as elsewhere, political mobilization around the perception of inequality—the core ingredient of ethnic conflict—has acquired a legitimacy which cannot be expunged. As Walker Connor has suggested, ethnic sentiment is a modern phenomenon; but although it is of relatively recent development, it has for several reasons taken a firm hold on contemporary society. Connor writes, "The person who is convinced that self-determination is a self-evident truth has trouble remembering that this truth was not at all evident to man prior to the late 18th and the early 19th centuries."²⁴ Yet, as Connor comments, two developments have made ethnic conflict a pervasive feature of contemporary society: (1) the growth of ethnic self-consciousness and (2) the growing ease of communication, which can

---

23. One of the arguments made by the Anglo-Indian representative at the Constituent Assembly meetings, Frank Anthony, was that the Anglo-Indian community was "completely dependent" on their position in the services and that without special reservations, the community would suffer severely. See Frank Anthony, *Britain's Betrayal in India* (Bombay: Allied Publishers, 1969), p. 209. Also see letter from Sardar Patel in B. Shiva Rao, *The Framing of India's Constitution* (Nasik: Government of India Press, 1968), vol. II, p. 421.

24. Walker Connor, "The Politics of Ethnonationalism," *Journal of International Affairs*, 27:1 (1973), 4–5.

make a given group aware not only of itself but of "alien" communities as well. A third development on which the politicization of ethnic conflict depends, one might add, has been the growing acceptance of the ideology of equality. In traditional societies, prevailing inequalities among classes and ethnic groups were not regarded as illegitimate but, in fact, buttressed political authority. With equality now a "right" to which at least theoretically all groups in India can lay claim, the potential for ethnic discontent and protest is significantly enhanced.

The translation of ethnic sentiment into organized demands for equality, however, presumes far more than the perception of disadvantage. It is the contention of this book that the politicization of sons-of-the-soil sentiment in India depends not simply on a sense of inequality but on the presence, in most cases, of ethnic heterogeneity joined with low out-migration, middle-class job competition, and the effective political mobilization of youth.

If this contention is correct, what can be said about the future of nativism in India? Again certain observations can be made: First, the possibility of Shiv Sena-like organizations proliferating is by no means boundless. Few of India's other large cities present the combination of middle-class job competition and ethnic heterogeneity so conducive to the growth of nativism. Calcutta has a large number of nonnative residents, but the in-migration of out-of-state migrants is mostly into working-class jobs. Similarly, in Madras, the local Tamil population dominates the middle-class occupations of the city. There are a few cities, mostly in tribal areas and along state borders, where large interethnic migration and middle-class job competition may indeed provide a seedbed for nativist sentiment. But it is in such smaller cities or towns, rather than in Calcutta, Delhi, Madras, or India's other large cities, that nativist organizations might be expected to emerge.

A second possibility exists which bears close watching: the development of within-state nativist movements modeled more along the lines of the Telengana movement than those of Shiv Sena. Many states contain culturally distinct regions: Vidharbha in Maharashtra, Saurashtra in Gujarat, the Maithili regions of Bihar, the tribal regions of Madhya Pradesh. Efforts to encourage both the industrial and the agricultural development of these mostly backward regions might, as in Telengana, encourage intrastate migration from nearby regions into these areas. The potential for protectionist demands developing in these areas is not to be discounted.

Finally, even where the conditions for the development of an organized nativist party are not present, nativist sentiment may now acquire sufficient visibility and legitimacy that claims for preferential treatment can achieve prominence even in the absence of an organized movement. The state of Tamil Nadu is an illustration of this possibility. Although there was on one occasion a vociferous nativist (anti-Malayalee) outburst, no effective nativist organization emerged. And yet, because of the increased currency given to protectionist policies in other states and the presence of at least some nativist anxiety in Tamil Nadu, it became virtually irresistible for the DMK, then the dominant party in the state, to adopt a similar nativist posture. With the issuance of protectionist guidelines in August 1974, that is exactly what the DMK did.

Government Response to Claims for Preferential Treatment

If the foregoing account of the conditions underlying ethnic claims to preferential treatment holds true, sons-of-the-soil demands are likely to be one of the enduring features of Indian politics. How the government responds to nativist claims then becomes the crucial concern.

The government (at both national and state levels, in the legislatures, bureaucracies, and the courts) has generally supported nativist claims. Not surprisingly, there has been greater ambivalence at the national than at the local level. On the one hand, central government officials have expressed concern that sons-of-the-soil movements threaten to compromise national objectives, particularly the achievement of interethnic unity and economic efficiency. On the other hand, prominent government leaders, such as former prime minister Indira Gandhi, called for a limited recognition of nativist claims. To ignore such claims, it was argued, would court political instability. Administrative directives of the central government accordingly set out a series of recommendations calling for preferential hiring of local persons in lower-level jobs.

Despite the unlikely constitutionality of residential requirements not endorsed by parliament, many of the state bureaucracies have instituted preferential policies for jobs and university admissions. The application of these preferential policies has not been limited to employment in the state services. In Maharashtra, the state government has endeavored to induce the private sector to conform to the strictures issued in the public sector; in Maharashtra, moreover, as in Bangalore, Chota Nagpur, and Assam, public-sector central government employment (which has traditionally recruited the best national talent) has also been the object of nativist governmental pressure. Further, if Maharashtra is representative of the more activist states, protectionist policies have not been merely symbolic. In Maharashtra, symbolic gestures aimed at soothing nativist discontent characterize the policies of the Bombay municipality. But the *state* government has threatened, and on occasion applied, sanctions which have come to be taken seriously by both private- and public-sector employers.

The courts have ranged from reticence to support of nativist policies. In the case of preferential policies in employment, a clear judicial doctrine has not yet developed. State directives on the preferential treatment of local persons in employment have so far gone mostly unchallenged. In the case of university admissions, however, the courts have generally upheld statewide residential requirements. Although within-state residential requirements have been struck down, the courts have upheld requirements giving preference in admission to students who have graduated from the local university. The courts have thus condoned policies which in practice, if not in theory, promote within-state restrictions.

Why should the state and central governments respond favorably to sons-of-the-soil claims, particularly given their questionable constitutionality and the inefficiency and disunity such preferences are thought to generate? The answer lies in a combination of ethnic, political, and ideological reasons. The supportive policies of the state governments derive in large part from the ethnic ties shared by those who govern in the state legislatures and bureaucracies and the nativist claimants. Often these ethnic ties are enriched both at the state and national levels by shared political interests. Reciprocal political interests are certainly one of the explanations underlying the Congress party's responsiveness to Shiv Sena. Finally, the pursuit of preferential policies can be attributed to various ideological factors—a conviction held by some that accession to sons-of-the-soil pressure is essential to the maintenance of political stability, and the view held by others that preferential policies in employment and university admissions represent an appropriate and important instrument for ameliorating the handicaps suffered by some ethnic groups.

The Impact of Preferential Policies

What has been the outcome of the preferential treatment of sons-of-the-soil? Although a satisfactory answer to this question is still remote, some definite observations can be made. The economic position of middle-class Maharashtrians has clearly improved. The numbers and relative proportion of Maharashtrians in clerical, supervisory, and managerial jobs in Bombay have grown. Maharashtrians are also more visible in certain non-office occupations. Their numbers have grown, for instance, among workers in Bombay's numerous small restaurants, jobs that have been traditionally the domain of non-Maharashtrians.

What role preferential policies have themselves played in bringing these gains about is more uncertain. The status of middle-class Maharashtrians began to improve even before the adoption of preferential policies in the late 1960s and early 1970s. It is thus clear that preferential policies alone did not effect an amelioration in Maharashtrian occupational status. At best it can be said that preferential policies strengthened existing trends. The rise in the numbers of educated Maharashtrians, a growth in the job market itself, and pressure exerted directly by Shiv Sena personnel on industrial employers all joined to stimulate the upward mobility of middle-class Maharashtrians.

The impact of preferential policies on interethnic relations in Bombay is also a matter on which only tentative conclusions can be drawn. Those who feared that preferential policies and Shiv Sena's activities would be destructive of interethnic harmony warned that migration into the city from outside would decline and that Bombay would lose its "cosmopolitan" nature. Indeed, there is evidence that in-migration into Bombay diminished in the decade 1961–71.[25] No published figures yet exist, however, indicating whether the decline occurred unevenly as between migrants from within or from outside the state. Nor is the explanation for the decline in in-migration unambiguous: it may reflect as much the slow rates of economic growth which characterized the Bombay economy of the second half of the 1960s as the social tensions accompanying policies of localism.

The difficulty in sorting out the actual impact of a particular set of policies besets many policy studies. An analysis of preferential policies in Assam, research on the consequences of protective discrimination and scheduled caste mobility, an inquiry into preferential policies in Malaysia, are but many of the studies which attest to the often intractable problem of assessing the outcomes of preferential policies.[26] This difficulty can be traced to one or more of three sources: an inadequate research design, the unavailability of relevant data, and co-varying or interdependent events that greatly encumber the possibility of isolating the independent effect of particular policies.

For practitioners or scholars intent on assessing the desirability of preferential treatment, the third problem is particularly vexing. The first two obstacles are superable: a research design can be altered; and the government can make decisions to ren-

25. Heather and Vijay Joshi, *Surplus Labour and the City: A Study of Bombay* (Bombay: Oxford University Press, 1976), p. 36.
26. See Myron Weiner, "Seeking Ethnic Equality: A Case Study of Migration and Employment Policies in an Indian State," Migration and Development Study Group #C/77-13, Center for International Studies, M.I.T.; Kusum K. Premi, "Educational Opportunities for the Scheduled Castes; Role of Protective Discrimination in Equalization," *Economic and Political Weekly*, Nov. 9, 1974, pp. 1902–1909; and Gordon P. Means, "'Special Rights' as a Strategy for Development: The Case of Malaysia," *Comparative Politics*, 5 (October 1972), 29–61.

der previously inaccessible data available (asking additional questions on a census; commissioning surveys or new studies). But often even the best research design or the most comprehensive data cannot help to identify policy outcomes when the situation is itself one of great complexity and interweaving social, economic, and political forces. Then decisions on preferential treatment will have to be based explicitly on particular conceptions of social justice rather than on considerations of economic or political efficacy.

Preferential Policies and Modernity

The core of Shiv Sena's ideology lies in the party's pursuit of preferential treatment for Maharashtrians. As an organizing tenet of many ethnic movements in India and elsewhere, this claim to preferential treatment marks an idea that has "come of age." Nineteenth-century liberal ideology in the West explicitly rejected the notion that opportunities (access to jobs or universities) should be based on ascriptive characteristics—race, ethnicity, religion, parentage, etc. In England, the repeal in 1828 of the Test and Corporation Acts barring non-Anglicans from employment was a critical event in the efflorescence of liberal society. Not that liberal society succeeded in eliminating all discriminatory laws or practices. Voting provisions that enfranchised men-only, whites-only statutes of the American South and laws that differentiated between Asian and white Americans reflected the existence of discriminatory policies of both a de facto and a de jure nature. Nevertheless, the idealized vision of nineteenth-century liberalism was to repudiate all ascriptive privileges in favor of a meritocratic social order.

In the United States, where Lockean liberalism had set down roots perhaps even more tenacious than in England, the meritocratic ideal of open competition has been subjected to increasing criticism during the last decade. The programs of the 1960s, Head Start and other early-education efforts, were intended, in liberal terminology, to level social and other differentials so that all could enter the "race of life" without unfair handicap. Increasingly, however, it has been argued that early handicaps can not be eliminated; that there can be no equal opportunity in the presence of continuing social and economic inequalities.[27] According to this view, attention must be directed not to securing equality of opportunity but to ensuring equality of results. The argument of former supreme court justice Douglas, that the Constitution must be racially neutral,[28] is now met by the assertion that race must be included as at least one factor in determining the allocation of privileges.

Although this position has only very recently won the support of the executive branch of the U.S. government,[29] it has long been appreciated in India. Preferential treatment of deprived sectors, scheduled castes, tribes, and other backward classes is embodied within the Indian constitution itself. The guarantee of equality of opportunity is modified by policies of "protective discrimination" which extend preferential treatment to those thought to be severely disadvantaged. The Indian constitution bars discrimination on grounds of religion, race, caste, sex, or place of birth (see Appendix VI). As an exception to this provision, however, the constitution also allows for special consideration to be extended to scheduled castes, tribes, and other backward classes. Defending the principle of protective discrimination, the sociologist M. N. Srinivas has argued that in India's deeply stratified society, "the principle of meritocracy would only sharpen existing inequalities." Referring to the apparent inconsistency between the proscription of discrimination

27. On Lockean liberalism in the United States, see Louis Hartz, *The Liberal Tradition in America* (New York: Harcourt, Brace and World, 1955). Two of the major contributions to this argument are Christopher Jencks, *Inequality; A Reassessment of the Effect of Family and Schooling in America* (New York: Harper & Row, 1973), and John Rawls, *A Theory of Justice* (Cambridge: Harvard University Press, 1971).
28. See n. 1, Chapter 9.
29. This recent shift is evidenced in the brief filed by the Department of Justice in the *Bakke* case. The position of President Carter and the Justice Department was to argue the constitutionality of taking race into account as one factor in making college admissions decisions. See *New York Times*, Sept. 20, 1977. Also see the summary of the Supreme Court decision (7–1, one justice absent) redistricting a section of Brooklyn with the explicitly racial purpose of enhancing black representation. Anthony Lewis, "Racial Quotas Will Come Again before High Court," *New York Times*, Mar. 13, 1977.

and the prescription of preferential treatment, Srinivas goes on to remark that "policies involving seemingly logical contradictions make sociological sense."[30]

This observation suggests, more generally, that political imperatives may overrule the prevailing view of what modernity is and ought to be. Much of the literature on economic modernization and political development posits a clear chain of historical evolution, progressing from a society organized by rules of ascription and group affinities to one based on meritocracy and individualism. A number of recent studies of ethnicity question this perspective. Observing that ethnic loyalties are not simply primordial sentiments of a preindustrial past, some argue that ethnic sentiments and the demands for preferential treatment are characteristic of societies in the *process* of rapid industrialization, while other studies view these sentiments and demands as features inherent in *post* industrial societies.[31]

This book agrees with those who question the view that ethnicity is a feature primarily of traditional societies. The resurgence of ethnic movements in the United States, in Western Europe, and in the modernizing sectors of less economically advanced nations speaks against the coupling of ethnic sentiment with the historical past.

The emergence of Shiv Sena in one of India's most industrialized localities points to the convergence of ethnicity not with

30. M. N. Srinivas, "Nation Building in Independent India," Zakir Hussein Memorial Lecture delivered at Northeastern Hill University, 1976, p. 13, mimeographed.

31. On ethnicity as a product of a transitional society, see Karl Deutsch, *Nationalism and Social Communication* (Cambridge: M.I.T. Press, 1966); Karl Deutsch and William J. Foltz, eds., *Nation-Building* (New York: Atherton, 1966); Cynthia Enloe, *Ethnic Conflict and Political Development* (Boston: Little, Brown, 1973), pp. 261–74; and Philip M. Rawkins, "Outsiders as Insiders," Minorities INTERNET, Working Paper No. 59, University Center for International Studies, University of Pittsburgh, April 1976. On ethnicity as a product of post-industrial society, see Michael Hechter, "The Political Economy of Ethnic Change," *American Journal of Sociology*, 79:5 (1974), 1151–78; Milton J. Esman, "Perspectives on Ethnic Conflict in Industrialized Societies," in Esman, *Ethnic Conflict in the Western World*, pp. 372–76; and Jeffrey A. Ross, "The Mobilization of Ethnicity in Post-Industrial Society," Minorities INTERNET, Working Paper No. 53, University Center for International Studies, University of Pittsburgh, April 1976, p. 5.

tradition but with modernity. The experience of Shiv Sena, moreover, exemplifies the gestation of a new form of ethnicity —one that caters not only to the individual's need to define an identity but also to the widespread demand for equality. The emergence of this new ethnicity sets alongside the values of individualism and meritocracy a competing set of principles. In their demand for preferential treatment, movements such as Shiv Sena seek to alter the rules by which the resources of modern societies are assigned. Whether persuasive or unacceptable, Shiv Sena's claims represent a quest that must be acknowledged.

Appendix I | *Indexes of Class Background, Voter Survey, 1971*

I. *Education.* Low (1, 2) refers to those who have been educated up to matriculation; (3, 4) or high, those who have matriculated, secured a diploma, or had any college or professional education. (Matriculation = completion of secondary education.

II. *Father-son educational mobility.* Low = none or negative change in educational status from father to son; high = change of more than 2 counts when scores are as follows:
   Education level:
   1. None
   2. Primary—incomplete
   3. Primary—complete
   4. Secondary—incomplete, diploma—incomplete
   5. Secondary—complete, diploma—complete
   6. College—incomplete
   7. College—complete or higher degree

III. *Property.* Computed according to following scores:
   2. Radio
   5. Icebox
   5. Cycle
   5. Gas stove
   10. Car
   10. Air conditioner
   10. Telephone

   Property score—low (1, 2) if respondent scores 2 or less
   Property score—medium-high (3) if respondent scores between 3 and 15
   Property score—high (4) if respondent scores 15 or greater

IV. *Occupation.* In the tables with occupation, only male respondents are tabulated. A scale from 1 to 4 is created, designating unskilled manual labor, skilled manual labor, clerical office, managerial or professional work.

Appendix II | Designation of Criteria for Sample Design

Previous party strength. Indicator chosen was election results of 1968 municipal contest. Shiv Sena strong areas defined as constituencies where Shiv Sena won over 35 percent of the vote. (In most of the areas chosen, designated as Shiv Sena strong, the party's vote had been considerably higher.) Shiv Sena weak was defined as constituting under 25 percent; in most areas chosen, it was a great deal less.

Ethnic character. The ethnic mixture of the constituency was calculated in advance by a sampling procedure involving the identification of ethnic background from the names of voters on the electoral rolls of the specified constituency. Maharashtrian-dominated constituencies refer to areas where Maharashtrians were estimated by the above sampling procedure to constitute over 70 percent of the population; ethnically-mixed areas refer to neighborhoods where South Indians were estimated to be over 20 percent of the population.

Class character. The class character of the neighborhoods was not quantitatively determined. The differences between slum, working-class, and middle-class neighborhoods are easily determined by observation of the areas themselves. The results of the survey—the reports of the class background of the respondents—entirely supported the classification.

Appendix III | *Purposive Sampling Scheme, Voter Survey, 1971**

	Slum	Working class	Middle class
Shiv Sena strong			
Maharashtrian dominant	Parel (1)	Parel (2)	Dadar (Shivaji Park) (3)
Ethnically mixed	(a) Parel (4)		
	(b) Dharavi		
Shiv Sena weak			
Maharashtrian dominant	(a) Cumballa Hill (5)	Wadala Springs (6)	
	(b) Wadala Springs		
Ethnically mixed	Dharavi (7)	Kamathipura (8)	Matunga (9)

*The survey was conducted jointly with Kartikeya Sarabhai, who supervised and analyzed the South Indian portion of the survey. Several sectors, as shown in Appendix IV, could not be filled in. This was, in itself, illustrative of the nature of Shiv Sena support. The slum areas of neighborhood types 4 and 5 were so small that a sample of 50 would have resulted in interview contamination. It was therefore decided to sample two slums areas (a) and (b) for each neighborhood type.

Appendix IV | *Ethnic Character and Shiv Sena Strength in Surveyed Neighborhoods*

	Slum	Working class	Middle class
Shiv Sena strong Maharashtrian dominant	Parel 65 S.S.: 47% Mah.: 74% S.I.: 2% I	Parel 65 S.S.: 47% Mah.: 72% S.I.: 3% II	Dadar 81 S.S.: 64% Mah.: 74% S.I.: 7% III
Ethnically mixed	Parel 65 S.S.: 47% Mah.: 41% S.I.: 37% IVA	Dharavi 92 S.S.: 35% Mah.: 30.5% S.I.: 44.1% IVB	
Shiv Sena weak Maharashtrian dominant	Wadala Springs 72 S.S.: 17% Mah.: 78% S.I.: 8% VA	Cumballa Hill 45 S.S.: 24.9% Mah.: 69.0% S.I.: 2.3% VB	Wadala Springs 72 S.S.: 17.0% Mah.: 53.0% S.I.: 7.5% VI
Ethnically mixed	Dharavi 91 S.I.: 8.8% Mah.: 26.0% S.I.: 22.0% VII	Kamathipura 35 S.S.: 22% Mah.: 32% S.I.: 37% VIII	Matunga 86 S.S. (did not contest) Mah.: 21% S.I.: 39% IX

S.S., % Shiv Sena vote in 1968 election; Mah. and S.I., Maharashtrian and South Indian populations in neighborhood according to 1971 survey.

Appendix V | Questionnaire, Voter Survey, 1971

(Questions from survey cited in tables or referred to in Chapters 4 and 5.)

A. Empirical assessment by respondent of non-Maharashtrian attitudes, identity, or role in Bombay.
   1. Do you think that most Gujaratis living in Bombay regard Maharashtra as their home state?
   2. How about South Indians? Do you feel they regard Maharashtra as their home state?
   3. Briefly, how would you describe the qualities of South Indians? What attributes would you say a South Indian has?
   4. Do you know approximately what percentage of Bombay's population is South Indian/Maharashtrian?
   5. Now, could you tell me what you think about the following statements? Do you agree or disagree with them?
       Some people say that: "Muslims living in this country do not really feel themselves to be citizens of India."

B. Normative assessment by respondent of interethnic and political issues.
   1. Could you tell me what you think about the following statements? Do you agree or disagree with them?
       Some people say that:
       a. "These days to counter the violence of certain groups, we must be prepared to use violence—you might say, 'sword for sword.'"
       b. "At least over the short run, what India needs is a dictatorship."
       c. "One way of solving the problems of Bombay would be to discourage people from other states from coming to live in the city."
   2. Do you feel that migrants living in Bombay should try to become like the local people, or do you feel that both the migrants and the local people should change or that neither should change at all?

Appendix VI | Constitution of India, Articles 14–16, 19 (as Amended up to November 1, 1969)

ARTICLE:
14. The State shall not deny to any person equality before the law or the equal protection of the laws within the territory of India.

15. (1) The State shall not discriminate against any citizen on grounds only of religion, race, caste, sex, place of birth or any of them.
    (2) No citizen shall, on grounds only of religion, race, caste, sex, place of birth or any of them, be subject to any disability, liability, restriction or condition with regard to—
        (a) access to shops, public restaurants, hotels and places of public entertainment; or
        (b) the use of wells, tanks, bathing ghats, roads and places of public resort maintained wholly or partly out of State funds or dedicated to the use of the general public.
    (3) Nothing in this article shall prevent the State from making any special provision for women and children.
    *[(4) Nothing in this article or in clause (2) of article 29 shall prevent the State from making any special provision for the advancement of any socially and educationally backward classes of citizens or for the Scheduled Castes and the Scheduled Tribes.]

*Added by the Constitution (First Amendment) Act, 1951, S.2 (18-6-1951).

16. (1) There shall be equality of opportunity for all citizens in matters relating to employment or appointment to any office under the State.
    (2) No citizen shall, on grounds only of religion, race, caste, sex, descent, place of birth, residence or any of them, be ineligible for or discriminated against in respect of, any employment or office under the State.
    (3) Nothing in this article shall prevent Parliament from making any law prescribing in regard to a class or classes of employment

or appointment to an office *[under the Government of, or any local or other authority within, a State or Union territory, any requirement as to residence within that State or Union territory] prior to such employment or appointment.

(4) Nothing in this article shall prevent the State from making any provision for the reservation or appointments or posts in favour of any backward class of citizens which, in the opinion of the State, is not adequately represented in the services under the State.

(5) Nothing in this article shall affect the operation of any law which provides that the incumbent of an office in connection with the affairs of any religious or denominational institution or any member of the governing body thereof shall be a person professing a particular religion or belonging to a particular denomination.

*Substituted for "under any State specified in the First Schedule or any local or other authority within its territory, any requirement as to residence within that State" by the Constitution (Seventh Amendment) Act, 1956, S.29 and Sch. (1-11-1956).

19. (1) All citizens shall have the right—
    (a) to freedom of speech and expression;
    (b) to assemble peaceably and without arms;
    (c) to form associations or unions;
    (d) to move freely throughout the territory of India;
    (e) to reside and settle in any part of the territory of India;
    (f) to acquire, hold and dispose of property; and
    (g) to practise any profession, or to carry on any occupation, trade or business.

Source: D. V. Chitaley and S. Appu Rao, *The Constitution of India; A.I.R. Commentaries* (Bombay: The All-India Reporter, 1970).

Appendix VII | Summary of Replies Received from State Governments regarding Admission of Students from Other States

(Rajya Sabha Debates, May 1, 1968, pp. 524–26)

122. Shri Ram Sahai: Will the Minister of Education be pleased to state:
(a) whether the suggestion of the All India Council of Technical Education that in each of the engineering colleges in the States a certain percentage of students should be admitted from outside that State, is likely to be implemented this year at the time of admission; and
(b) if so, in which States; and
(c) which of the States are not likely to implement it and the reasons therefor in each case?

The Minister of Education (Dr. Triguna Sen): (a) to (c) The State Governments who are the implementing agencies have reacted varyingly to the suggestion of the Council. A summary of the replies received from the State Governments is attached.

STATEMENT
Summary of replies received from State Governments regarding admission of students from other States

1. *Andhra Pradesh*—The State Government have agreed to admit some students from other States on reciprocal basis and this arrangement continued since 1966–67.

2. *Mysore*—Only 10 per cent seats will be filled by students from other States apart from seats arranged on reciprocal basis.

3. *Madhya Pradesh*—There is no domicile restriction but students should have qualified from institutions situated in M.P., or should have spent three years of study in such institutions.

4. *Assam*—Reservation of seats in engineering institutes exist only for Union Territories and J. & K.

5. *Punjab*—No domicile restrictions for admission to engineering courses.

6. *Madras*—10 per cent reservation on reciprocal basis.

7. *Kerala*—Reservation only on reciprocal basis and that not more than 5 per cent.

8. *Uttar Pradesh*—Admissions to technical institutions are made

purely on merit and no domicile restrictions exist except in the Regional School of Printing, Allahabad.

9. *Gujarat*—5 seats in each college can be reserved on reciprocal basis.

10. *Maharashtra*—63 seats are reserved in various institutions for students from other States and Union Territories. The Government considers this adequate reservation for ex-State students.

11. *Orissa*—7 per cent seats in the University college are reserved for students from other States.

12. *West Bengal*—No candidate of Indian nationality is denied admission on grounds of domicile.

13. *Bihar*—15 per cent seats in engineering colleges will be open for admission of students from other States.

14. *Rajasthan*—The Jodhpur University admits 50 per cent students from outside the State. The Birla Institute is an all-India Institute. The third one is a Regional Engineering College where 50 per cent students are admitted from outside the State.

15. *Jammu & Kashmir*—There is only one Regional Engineering College.

16. *Haryana*—There is only one Regional Engineering College.

(In Regional Engineering Colleges reservation of ex-State students already exists.)

Appendix VIII | Implementation of National Integration Committee Recommendations

Response to Unstarred Question No. 618 (a) to (c) Answered on the 26th November, 1969:

Action Taken on the Implementation of the Recommendation of the Srinigar Session of the National Integration Committee

(Rajya Sabha, Appendix LXX to Debates)

Haryana. (1) 50% seats in Regional Engineering College reserved for persons belonging to the State as approved by Government of India. (2) Admission to Government Polytechnic at Nilokheri, Ambala City, Jhajar and Sirsa open to all Indian nationals. Reservation of seats only for Scheduled Castes, Scheduled Tribes and backward classes. (3) No restrictions for admissions in the Teachers Training institutions. However, for admission to J.B.T. classes preference is given to local students specially from rural areas. (4) No restrictions for admissions in ITIs and other training centres run by Industries and Industrial Training Departments. (5) State Government has no objection to removing the domiciliary restrictions on admission of students from other States in the Northern Zone on reciprocal basis to the Medical College at Rohtak.

Jammu and Kashmir. (1) As education is free up to the highest level in the State and there are several scholarships/paid schemes for residents of the State, it is necessary to ascertain the domicile at the time of admission. (2) There is only one Regional Engineering College. 50% of the seats are reserved for students from outside the State. (3) There is one Medical College. Admissions are made on the basis of academic merit of eligible students of the State. Every year a fair proportion of students from other States are admitted to the first year of M.B.B.S. Course.

Mysore. (1) Restrictions apply to those Engineering, Medical Arts, Science and Commerce Colleges which are in the common general pool; private colleges not included in the general pool are not subject to domiciliary restrictions. (2) Seats reserved in general pool for candidates who passed pre-university examinations of a particular university. (3) Special provision made for children of Central Government servants and Defence personnel; 10% seats in engineering pool reserved for candidates who had not passed pre-university examination of the university. (4) National Integration can be promoted in a positive way by reserving seats on a reciprocal basis for bright students from different States for engineering and medical courses. (5) Seats for Engineering courses are now freely available. Similar position may be reached in the field of Medicine. Hence, no change in the existing rules appears necessary.

Rajasthan. (1) The matter is under active consideration of the State Government. (2) No domicile restrictions as far as admission to general colleges are concerned. (3) In technical institutions like Engineering Colleges 50% seats reserved for meritorious students from other States. In Pilani admissions entirely on All India basis.

West Bengal. (1) No domicile restrictions for admission to educational and technical institutions concerned with Engineering, Veterinary Science and Agriculture. (2) For admission to dental and medical colleges the candidates or their parents should be residents of the West Bengal for at least one year preceding the date of submission of applications for admission.

Tripura. No such restrictions imposed by Government for admissions to any institutions.

Madhya Pradesh. The restriction for admissions to technical institutions in the State has been imposed mainly because Madhya Pradesh is still a backward State and the students of this State do not get admissions elsewhere. As soon as the position improves and the students of Madhya Pradesh get admissions into other State Institutions the State Government will also by and by remove these restrictions.

Gujarat. (1) No domiciliary restrictions for admission in arts or science colleges or in secondary or primary schools in the State. (2) In Government Engineering Colleges, the only condition is that student should pass the qualifying examination from any of the universities in the State. At the Regional Engineering College, Surat, 50 per cent seats are open to students from any part of the country. At Baroda and Vallabh Vidya Nagar Universities unreserved seats are being filled by open competitive examinations of qualifying students from outside. (3) In Government Medical College students from any part are eligible for admission if they pass the qualifying examination from the universities in the State. (4) Gujarat Government is agreeable on reciprocal basis to the reservation of 25 per cent seats for outside students in technical institutions in the State from an agreed date for a period of 5 year in the first instance.

Himachal Pradesh. (1) If the recommendations of NIC have to be enforced on all-India basis then they have no argument except to agree in principle, as desired. (2) Punjab University caters to the needs of Himachal Pradesh and Delhi Board of Education has its jurisdiction over the Central School in Simla. The recommendation regarding preference to be given in admission to students passing the School Board, University or college examinations of that State would hardly work at par with the States that have their own Universities and School Boards. (3) Because of its backwardness in educational facilities reservation for lower services had to be ensured through an enactment of Parliament.

Uttar Pradesh. Domiciliary restrictions can be removed on reciprocal basis. However, the State Government is initiating action with the concerned Departments.

Goa, Daman and Diu. (1) In all institutions in the Territory no student is required to produce a domiciliary certificate for admission. (2) In engineering college 75% seats reserved for students passing out of institutions in the Territory and 25% filled by students passing the qualifying examination from other colleges outside the Territory. (3) In Medical College and College of Pharmacy 75% seats reserved for students passing I.Sc. from institutions in the Territory and 25% for students passing I.Sc. from outside colleges. A student from any other State passing I.Sc. from any of the colleges in the Territory is eligible for admission against the reserved seats.

Nagaland. No University or any professional colleges exist in the State. There are schools and colleges.

Bihar. State Government feel that in the present situation it would not be advisable to abolish restrictions on domicile in regard to admissions to Technical Institutions and Professional colleges. The State Government is considering a proposal to reserve 15% of seats in Engineering and Medical Colleges for students belonging to other States.

Appendix IX | *Education and Employment in Bombay*

Table A1. Organized sector employment, Greater Bombay, 1951–71 (in thousands)

	1951	1961	1966	1971
Private sector				
Factories	358	458	523	531
Other	n.a.[a]	94	116	97[d]
Total	445[b]	552	639	638
Public sector				
Union government	55	67	88	90
State government	28	41	57	61
Municipal government	52	70	89	94
Banks	3	6	10	30
Railways	51	91	96	105
Port	18	25	27	
Life insurance	n.a.	6	8	10
Other quasi-government	n.a.	24	38	
Total	215[b]	330	413	473
All organized sector establishments	660[b]	882	1052	1111
All workers (Census)[c]	1304	1687	n.a.	2198

[a] Figures for shops and establishments given in the source are not used here as they appeared to cover many small establishments and family workers.

[b] Based upon a very rough estimate of missing categories of organized workers.

[c] Note changes in Census definition of workers. The 1951 figure should be roughly comparable with 1961. It includes secondary earners and all major earners except those with unproductive sources of income. The 1971 definition is more restrictive. The Census in any case only covers workers resident in the city. Organized sector employees include some non-residents. The difference between the last two lines therefore understates the number of workers outside the organized sector.

[d] Note the effect of bank nationalization in 1969.

Sources: 1951—D. T. Lakdawala et al., *Economic Survey of Bombay City* (Bombay 1963), ch. 8; 1961, 1966, and 1971—Directorate of Employment, Bombay, Quarterly Returns, 1961, 1966, and 1971. Heather and Vijay Joshi, *Surplus Labour and the City: A Study of Bombay* (Bombay: Oxford University Press, 1976), Table III-1, p. 48, reprinted with permission of Oxford University Press.

Table A2. Applicants on the live register of employment exchanges, Delhi, Madras, Bombay, and Calcutta, 1956–1966

	Below matric.	Matric. and above but below graduate	Graduate and above	Total
Bombay				
1956	26,457	11,150	1,848	39,455
1961	25,825	15,826	2,586	44,237
1966	29,568	18,294	2,386	50,248
Calcutta				
1956	21,352	21,357	3,918	46,627
1961	106,138	39,613	7,958	153,709
1966	92,153	59,865	11,261	163,279

Source: Unpublished material from the Directorate General of Employment and Training, Ministry of Labour and Employment, Government of India, cited in Mark Blaug, Richard Layard, Maureen Woodhall, *The Causes of Graduate Unemployment in India* (London: Allen Lane The Penguin Press, 1969), p. 255. © London School of Economics and Political Science, 1969. Reprinted by permission of Penguin Books Ltd.

Table A3. Educational enrollment in Greater Bombay in Marathi-medium schools

	1967—all standards	1970—all standards
City	63.2%	63.8%
Suburbs	58.1%	57.4%
Extended suburbs	49.4%	52.1%

	1970 Standard I	1970 Standard II	1970 Standard V	1970 Standard VII
City	59.0%	61.8%	67.4%	70.1%
Suburbs	52.4%	55.9%	63.2%	62.5%
Extended suburbs	49.6%	52.1%	54.2%	50.5%

Sources: Calculated from Appendix 1; *Administrative Report of the Municipal Commission for Greater Bombay*, 1967, mimeographed; Statement of Education Officer, P. Desai, Apr. 1, 1970, mimeographed.

Figure A1. Employment growth in Bombay's organized sector

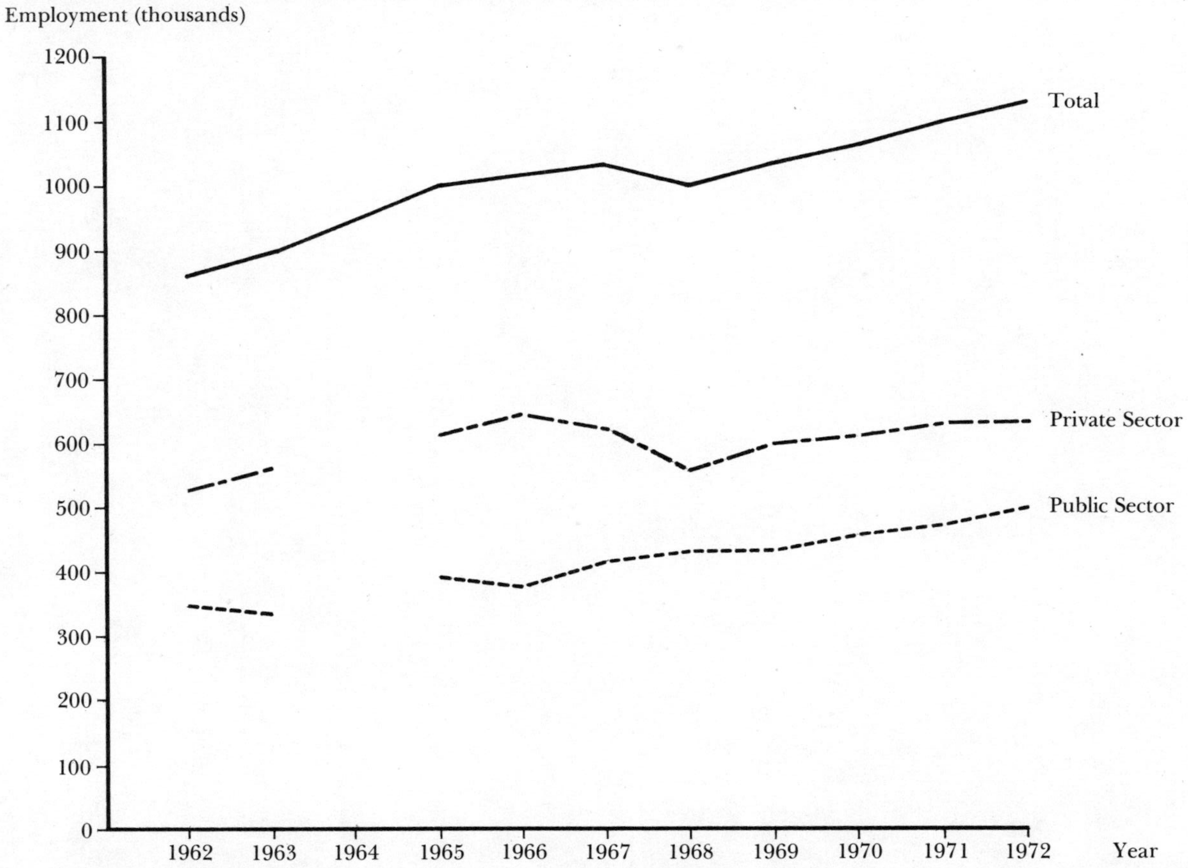

Source: City and Industrial Development Corporation of Maharashtra, Ltd., *New Bombay Draft Development Plan*, October 1973, Appendix S, Diagram S.22.

Index

Ambedkar, B. R., 164, 165
"Army of Shivaji," see Shiv Sena

Barnett, Marguerite, 20
Basu, Jyoti, 22
Bell, Daniel, 27
Bengalis, 25, 40; employment for, 28–29
Bharatiya Kamgar Sena, see Trade union
Bombay
  businesses in, 17, 18, 30, 34, 44–45, 141, 142; see also Industry
  as capital of Maharashtra, 18, 40, 46
  economy of, 75–76
  ethnic diversity of, 31–32, 40, 42–43
  history of, 41–45
  migration to, 57–58, 60, 62, 196
  nativist setting, 30–33
  politics in, 116–26, 131, 134, 136, 140, 154–55, 158–59, 207
  population of, 42–43, 48, 57–58, 62, 66–67
  See also Bombay Municipal Corporation, Bombay university system, Elections, and Voter survey
Bombay Municipal Corporation, 82, 117–18, 148–51
  politicians in, 118–26
  rules, 108n
Bombay university system
  colleges in, 77n
  entrance restrictions, 149
  increased enrollment in, 156, 181
  Ruia College, 116, 116n
  use of English in, 148–49
Brass, Paul, 36–37
Burger, Angela, 119

CIDCO (City and Industrial Development Corporation), 134
CPI (Communist Party of India), see Political organizations
Calcutta, 40, 61, 80n; education in, 227–28
Cariappa, 136
Caste system, 20, 23, 25, 94–95, 122
  and group disparity, 28
  Maharashtrians in, 44–45, 46, 64
  preferential treatment for, 161
  and Shiv Sena activists, 100n
Chandrashekhar, Justice, 178
Connor, Walker, 204
Constituent Assembly
  debate over residential requirements, 162–65
  and preferential treatment for Anglo-Indians, 203–4
Curran, J. A., 104–5

DMK (Dravida Munnetra Kazhagam), see Political organizations
Das Gupta, Jyotirinda, 21, 28–29
Demographic pressure, 53–54
  in Bombay, 57–58
  in other Indian cities, 58–60
  in states of India, 196–97
Desai, Krishna, 111, 129
Dobbins, Christine, 44, 45
Douglas, Justice William, 211
Dua, Justice, 178

Ebb, Lawrence, 177
Education
  in English, 122, 139
  growth in Bombay, 77, 227–28
  growth in Calcutta, 227–28
  growth in Maharashtra, 156

231

Education (*cont.*)
 for non-Maharashtrians, 134–35
 regional language in, 24
 rise in enrollments, 77–78, 156, 181
 varying levels of, 27
 See also Bombay university system *and* Maharashtrians
Elections
 Bombay municipal: (1873), 46; (1961), 35; (1968), 34, 35, 69, 82, 98, 123; (1973), 36, 69, 82; (1978), 191
 Bombay parliamentary: (1967), 34; (1971), 36
 Parel bye-election (1970), 103–4, 107, 111–12
Embree, Ainslie, 21n
Emergency (June 1975), 23, 50n, 129, 151, 187, 192
Employment, 27
 in Bombay, 76, 78, 227
 competition for, 63, 65–66, 67n, 79–81, 85, 195, 197–200
 pressure for, 25–26, 142–43, 146–51, 189
 private-sector, 30
 problems of, 18
 public-sector, 30, 143–55, 207
 See also Maharashtrians, Preferential treatment, Quotas, *and* Reservations
Equality, 19
 acceptance of, 204–5
 ethnic, 20, 39
 governmental support of, 193
 liberal concept of, 20, 210
 new view of, 20, 27, 27n, 39, 160
 right to, in constitution, 29, 160–61
 See also Preferential treatment
Esman, Milton, 199
Ethnicity
 conflicts of, 22, 24, 25–27, 37, 54, 127, 135, 194, 197–200
 ethnic distinctions, 32, 92
 mixtures, 31, 38
 "new," 18; history of, 19; as modern phenomena, 19, 193, 204, 212–13; and national integration, 21–25; objectives of, 18, 19, 20, 25–29, 192–93

"old": in India, 20–21; objectives of, 19
 See also Interethnic group relations *and* Nativist movements

Freeman, Gary, 197
Free Press Journal, 33

Gandhi, Indira, 50, 50n, 129, 131n, 165, 192; and preferential policies, 166–67, 189–90, 206
Gandhi, Mahatma, 23; philosophy of, 130
Gujaratis, 31, 32, 33, 45, 56, 79, 80, 100n
 education of, 77, 77n
 sentiment against, 80n, 137

Hansen, Marcus Lee, 54n
Harrison, Selig, 20–21
Hegde, Justice K. S., 183
Hindus, 23, 44, 64, 89, 113, 163
Hitler, Adolf, 127, 127n, 128
Horowitz, Donald L., 198

India
 British in, 28, 41, 44, 45, 162, 163
 ethnic diversity of, 20
 Independence, 162, 163, 171
 linguistic states movement in, 19, 22–25
 nation-building, 21, 22–25
 North, 24
 partition, 20
 politics in, 20–21, 23
 reforms, 23
 secessionist movements in, 22
 South, 24
 See also Indian government, Indian states, *and* Population
Indian government
 economic policy, 23, 23n
 employment in, 25, 78
 National Employment Service, 166
 and preferential treatment, 29, 160–61, 171–74, 179, 211, 220–21
 pressure on industry, 144–45
 See also Constituent Assembly, Elections, Emergency, *and* Judiciary

Indian states
  admission policies, 222–23
  out-migration from, 59
  reorganization of, 24, 40, 46, 47, 157
  Andhra Pradesh, 22, 124, 171–73, 175, 179, 180, 186–87, 203, 222
  Assam, 25, 30, 198, 222
  Bangalore, 25, 30, 198
  Bihar, 28–29, 37, 60, 60n, 223, 226
  Gujarat, 40, 42, 157, 223, 225
  Karnataka, 27, 133
  Madhya Pradesh, 222, 225
  Madras, 24, 132, 162, 205, 222
  Meghalaya, 170
  Tamil Nadu, 22, 24, 25, 167, 170, 206
  Telegana, 24, 25–26, 30, 37, 171, 197, 202, 203, 205, 206
  Uttar Pradesh, 222–23, 226
  Vidharbha, 37
  West Bengal, 167, 169, 172, 223, 225
Industry in Bombay, 68, 87
  ethnic specialization in, 84–85
  job differentiation in, 84
  Shiv Sena pressure on, 141–43
  state government pressure on, 146–48
Interethnic group relations, 37
  Shiv Sena impact on, 127, 133, 135, 136
  Shiv Sena sensitivity to, 136–38
  views of, 73, 74, 92
  See also Preferential policies

Jobs, *see* Employment
Joshi, Manohar, 69n, 89, 116–17, 154;
  political views of, 117
Judiciary
  court cases: *Arun Narayan v. State of Karnataka*, 178–79; *Balaji v. Mysore*, 189; *D. N. Chanchala v. State of Mysore*, 180, 183; *D. P. Joshi v. State of Madhya Bharat* (1955), 177, 183; *Dorairajan*, 188; *Kumar v. Uttar Pradesh*, 186; *Periakaruppan v. State of Tamil Nadu*, 183; *Sidappa v. State of Mysore*, 180; *State of Uttar*

Pradesh v. *P. Tandon*, 182, 184, 185; *Subhash Chandra* v. *State of Uttar Pradesh*, 181, 182
  court decisions (on preferential policies): employment, 174–75; and future action, 188–90; recruitment, 172–74; residential requirements (for university admissions), 171, 175–89
  high courts: Andhra Pradesh, 186–87; Karnataka, 178, 179, 197; Madhya Pradesh, 186, 187; Madras, 188; Orissa, 175; Uttar Pradesh, 181, 182, 184, 185, 186
  supreme court, 172, 178, 182, 183, 188

Kapoor, Jaspat Roy, 163–64
Khadi, 24; definition of, 17

Lakdawala, D. T., 66
Language
  associations, study of, 21
  conflicts in India over, 22–25
  English: education, 122; need for, 24; speaking of, 32, 65, 123, 126, 139; teaching of, 24–25, 109, 148
  Hindi, 132, 148; speakers, 56; use of, 24, 25, 32
  legislation on, 148
  Marathi, 49; education in, 134–35; and *Marmik*, 49–52; speaking of, 17, 18, 26, 55–57, 66, 123, 124, 138; use of, 138–39, 149n, 157, 169
  regional, use of, 24, 25
  Three Language Formula, 24
Leftist politics
  criticism of Shiv Sena, 80
  parties, 90–91
  See also Political organizations
"Local" people, 17, 18, 26, 37, 59, 60, 95n, 160, 168
  definition of, 169
  policies of localism, 170n, 173, 187, 188
  See also Maharashtrians *and* Preferential treatment

Mahadik, W., 112, 139n, 149n
Maharashtra, 18, 110, 122
  creation of, 46–47, 63, 78, 134, 194
  government of, 143–48
  growing education in, 156
  history of, 41, 46, 47
  preferential policies in, 167, 168n, 169, 175, 207
  See also Bombay *and* Maharashtrians
Maharashtrians, 18, 31, 113
  in Bombay, 40, 44, 46–47, 55, 57–58, 194, 203
  definition of, 26, 26n
  discrimination against, 18, 33, 48, 67, 69
  economic status of, 43–45, 66–69, 78, 81, 151–55, 208
  education of, 73, 77, 156
  employment for, 17–18, 26, 33, 63, 65, 76, 142–43, 155–58
  as ethnic group, 32, 135
  in government, 30, 40, 143–51
  as laborers, 44, 91, 94
  literacy among, 47–48
  political position of, 45–47, 71, 73, 78, 123–26, 194, 203
  in RSS, 105
  in Shiv Sena, 26, 30, 34, 70–75, 82–96, 100, 110, 113–14, 123, 124
  See also Preferential policies *and* Voter survey
Marmik (Marathi weekly newspaper), 33, 48, 78, 81, 89, 95n, 127, 136
  content of, 49–51, 137, 137n, 138
  exposure of business discrimination, 34, 48, 49, 141–42
  popularity of, 49–51
  and Shiv Sena, 48–52, 105n
Mathur, Justice D. S., 182
Mehta, Arun, 26n, 100n, 111
Menon, V. K. Krishna, 34, 49, 131n, 151n
Meritocracy, 39
  in hiring and recruitment, 27–28
  policies to protect, 165
  principle of, 20, 193, 210, 211
  versus state interest, 184–85, 186
  See also Equality

Migration, 37–38
  to Indian cities, 53
  in-migration, 56–62, 209
  out-migration, 56–62
  rate of, 54–56
  studies of, 54n, 134, 196–97
Montagu-Chelmsford reforms, 28
Morley-Minto reforms (1909), 28
mulkis, 172, 175; definition of, 171
Muslim community, 28, 136, 163
  attacks on, 96n
  as Shiv Sena targets, 131
  special treatment for, 162

Nag, G. D., 169
Naipaul, V. S., 87–89, 97
National integration, 22–25
National Integration Committee, 143, 165, 224; formula of, 166, 172–73
National Socialists (Nazis)
  and Shiv Sena, 137
  youth groups, 115
Nativism
  demographic causes of, 54–62
  emergence of: in Bombay, 63; in India, 61
  in the United States, 60n
Nativist movements, 18, 61, 187
  in Bombay, 30–33, 37, 52, 63, 80–81, 198
  consequences of, 29, 38–39
  demands of, 25–29, 202–3
  future of, 204–6
  governmental interest in, 144–45, 193, 206–8
  objectives of, 25
  origins, 36–38, 193–95
  studies of, 196
  within states, 205–6
Nehru, Jawaharlal, 131n; government, 24
Non-Maharashtrians
  economic preeminence in Bombay, 30, 43–45
  education of, 134–35
  job competition with Maharashtrians, 65, 81, 198–200
  Shiv Sena campaigns against, 136
  support for Shiv Sena, 136

Index | 235

"Outsiders," 18, 26, 37, 59, 95n
 in Bombay, 59, 60, 62, 63
 changing policy toward, 136–38
 competition from, 66, 84
 Shiv Sena campaigns against, 136

Pathare Prabhus, 43–45, 64
Political organizations in India: leadership study, 117–31
 Communist party (CPI), 35, 49n, 50, 105, 112–13, 117, 118n, 154; Shiv Sena attacks on, 49, 50, 95n, 111, 129
 Congress party, 34, 35, 70, 82, 90, 91, 119; Congress (O), 36, 101, 112, 113, 118, 120, 126; Congress (R), 36, 112, 113, 118, 120, 126; cooperation with Shiv Sena, 150–51; leadership of, 101, 117–31; and Shiv Sena, 50n, 150–51, 208; supporters and Shiv Sena supporters, 71–75, 82–83, 90–96
 Dravida Munnetra Kazhagam (DMK), 22, 200, 206; description of, 22n; youth in, 201
 Janata party, 191
 Janatha Vimukhti Peramuna (People's Liberation Front), 201
 Peasants and Workers Party, 35, 49
 Praja Socialist Party (PSP), 35, 36; leadership study, 117–31
 Rashtriya Swayamasevak Sangh (RSS), 104–5, 106, 113, 114, 202; Maharashtrians in, 105, 106n
 See also National Socialists and Shiv Sena
Population
 of Bombay, 42–43, 48
 urban, 53, 58, 59
 See also Bengalis, Demographic pressure, Gujaratis, Hindus, Maharashtrians, Migration, Muslim community, and Non-Maharashtrians
Pradhan, 106n
Preferential policies
 and constitutional issues, 174–88

effect on Maharashtrians, 141–59, 208
 governmental, 165–74, 186–87, 193, 206–8
 history of, 28–29, 162–65
 judicial response to, 160–90, 207
 residential rights, 161–65, 176–77
 and university admissions, 171, 175–89, 222–23
 See also Judiciary, Quotas, and Reservations
Preferential treatment
 constitutional provisions for, 29, 160–61, 179, 211, 220–21
 demands for, 18, 19, 27, 72, 202–6, 210
 in education, 167–68
 in employment, 25–26, 141, 161, 168–74
 impact of, 155–59
 and Maharashtra government policy, 143–48
 and municipal policy, 148–51
 origins, 19, 39

Quotas
 government establishment of, 144–45, 167
 history of, 28
 as objective of "new" ethnicity, 19, 27
 state establishment of, 224–26
 See also Reservations

RSS, see Political organizations
Ray, Chief Justice A. N., 161, 182
Ray, Sidhartha Sankar, 169–70
Reservations
 of jobs (80% for Maharashtrians), 18
 for special groups: history of, 162–65; in university admissions, 176, 189
Rudolph, Lloyd and Susanne, 21

Sarabhai, Kartikeya, 164n
Schermerhorn, R. A., 54n
Shelat, Justice M., 180–81, 183
Shivaji Maharaj, 41, 105, 112, 113

Shivaji Park rallies, 50n, 103; 1966
  rally, 34, 40
Shiv Sainiks, 97, 98, 110–11, 154
  profile of, 99–100
  See also Shiv Sena, activists
Shiv Sena
  activists, 97–115
  activities of, 106–10, 191
  and Bombay, 41, 52, 99, 99n, 100, 117
  demands of, 26, 30, 72, 142–43, 210–13
  emergence of, 33, 38, 54, 63, 75, 80–81, 126, 135, 194–96, 202, 212
  formation, 18, 34, 63, 76, 117
  history of, 33–36, 40
  ideology, 34–35, 83, 127–33, 137, 195, 210
  leadership, 47, 47n, 101–2, 105, 117–26, 128–29
  middle-class support for, 69–75, 75n, 218
  and migration, 54, 55
  militarism of, 105, 113, 132
  municipal councilors of, 17, 118–27
  organization, 87, 97–106, 109, 114–15
  and other parties, 71–75, 82–83, 90–96, 104–5, 106, 113, 114, 116–26, 192
  party meetings, 102–4
  party office, 17, 112
  party structure: *shakha pramukhs* (branch leaders), 98, 98n, 99–102, 106, 109, 115, 143, 195–96; *upshakha pramukhs* (assistant branch leaders), 98, 98n; *vibhag pramukhs* (division leaders), 98, 99, 100n, 101, 105
  party worker, 63–65
  rightist image of, 83, 89–92, 95, 137
  services of, 87–89, 109, 196
  social reforms of, 64–65
  and state government, 30, 141
  success of, 65, 69–70, 78, 90–92
  targets, 33, 50, 55, 79–81, 131, 142, 194
  and use of English, 139

and violence, 89, 90, 105, 127, 129, 130, 131, 133, 140
  working-class support for, 82–96, 195, 218
  and youth, 72, 94, 97, 98, 106, 107–9, 110–14, 126, 154, 195, 200, 201
  See also *Marmik*, Political organizations, *and* Voter survey
Singh, G. S., 46
Social workers, 64, 121, 121n; definition of, 64n
"Sons-of-the-soil" movements, *see* Nativist movements
South Indians, 32, 56
  attacks on, 105, 105n, 133
  attitudes toward, 75n, 92, 93, 135, 136, 137–38
  in job market, 65
  migration of, 55, 134
  as Shiv Sena targets, 33, 50, 55, 79–81, 131, 194
  survey of, 83
Sri Lanka, 199; uprisings in, 200, 201
Srinivas, M. N., 211
Sriramulu, Potti, 22
Stern, Robert, 80n

Thackeray, Bal, 33, 48, 49n, 50, 50n, 65, 89, 95n, 105, 106n, 114, 142, 149n
  commitment to nationalism, 131, 132, 133
  praise of Hitler, 127, 127n, 128
  as Senapati (or party father), 97–98, 100–101, 112
  support for the Emergency, 50n, 129, 192
  views on dictatorship and violence, 102, 127, 128, 131n, 132
Thackeray, Keshav Sitaram, 33
Times of India, 116, 144
Trade union movement (Shiv Sena), 86n, 89, 111, 191
Tyagi, Mahavir, 164

Vidyarthi Sena, 132
Voter survey (1971), 70–75, 83, 85–96, 108–10, 135

Voter survey (*cont.*)
   sampling scheme, 216–17
   voter profile, 215n

Wanchoo Committee, 172
Weiner, Myron, 23, 53n, 196
Welfare state, modern, 19, 19n, 20;
   consequences of, 39
Williams, Robin M., Jr., 54n

ETHNICITY *and* EQUALITY

Designed by Richard E. Rosenbaum.
Composed by G&S Typesetters, Inc.
in 10 point VIP Baskerville, 2 points leaded,
with display lines in Baskerville.
Printed offset by Thomson/Shore, Inc.
on Warren's Number 66 Antique Offset, 50 pound basis.
Bound by John H. Dekker & Sons, Inc.
in Holliston book cloth.

Library of Congress Cataloging in Publication Data

Katzenstein, Mary Fainsod, 1945–
   Ethnicity and equality.

   Includes index.
   1. Bombay—Politics and government. 2. Shiv Sena. I. Title.
JS7032.K37   320.9′54′792   79-4163
ISBN 0-8014-1205-6